EVERYD

RITUALS AND
CEREMONIES

To Le Plan,
Diane and Trish

EVERYDAY

RITUALS AND CEREMONIES

Special ways to mark important events in your life

Lorna St Aubyn

PIATKUS

'He' and 'man' are used
throughout this book in the
interests of fluent English, not as a
slight to womankind.

First published in 1994 as
Rituals for Everyday Living by
Judy Piatkus (Publishers) Ltd of
5 Windmill Street, London W1P 1HF

This edition published in 1998

The moral right of the author has been asserted

*A catalogue record for this book is
available from the British Library*

ISBN 0–7499–1927–2

Set in Baskerville by
Action Typesetting Limited, Gloucester
Printed and bound in Great Britain by
Butler & Tanner Ltd, Frome and London

CONTENTS

THE NEED
FOR
RITUAL

Everything in the universe moves in rhythms and cycles; the changing seasons, the birth and death of galaxies, even our own sense of who we really are. For thousands of years our ancestors were aware of life and death as a continuous flow. They understood that it was important to mark the cycles of renewal – those of the solstices and equinoxes, for example. They believed that by doing so they helped the cosmos grow and change. They did not take life for granted; they honoured it.

Ritual, then, stems from pagan times when the Earth Mother Goddess was worshipped as the symbol of birth, growth, death and regeneration, and life was seen to be inter-related on all levels. The Earth was linked to the universe as part of one living organism. What affected one affected all, and ritual was regarded as a way of enlisting other parts of that whole to strengthen and bring about change in the community.

In the Western world the tradition of an Earth Mother eventually gave way to religions based on a Father God. From this time our sense of being part of the cosmos and of participating in its evolution was lost. A feeling of separation set in. Our knowledge of magic and mystery declined. Our respect for the Earth as a part of ourselves was left behind, and we came to exploit and abuse it.

Today, ritual has almost disappeared from Western society. In this country, for example, the Church still observes its calendar of ceremonies such as Harvest Festival or Rogation Sunday, but as its influence decreases fewer people participate in these rituals. In many people's lives, the only important milestone or rite to be observed is their funeral. Other major events of all kinds remain unacknowledged; no cycles are defined. Instead of celebrating beginnings and endings and transition points, we drift through the years, dragging behind us tatters of the past which should have been unequivocally buried. This in turn prevents us from stepping into the future wholeheartedly.

Yet at this time of apparent crisis we need rituals as never before. They are as important to us today as they were to our ancestors. The basic cycles of our lives have not changed, nor have the fears and ills which beset us. On the contrary – we have considerably added to them.

The return to performing rituals is one way to reinstate a belief in the connectedness of all life. In today's society many people feel a sense of separation and isolation. For many there is a nagging sense that there must be something more to life. Rituals can help us to see we are part of something larger, a part of a living, breathing earth. They can give us a feeling of unity and a sense of security and support in an increasingly difficult world. We can again begin to sense the sacredness in the ordinary which can add the depth and meaning so often missing from our lives.

To practise rituals requires courage, vision, humour and creativity and a belief that we have the ability to transform ourselves and our values. But it can be most rewarding. It helps us to look to something bigger than ourselves, whether we call this God or a universal force concerned with our wellbeing, and links us to it. We can re-connect with the mystery of life. By helping us sense and understand the unseen forces working on subtle levels and filtering into our world, we will become at one again with our Earth and the cosmos. We will restore a sense of balance within ourselves and our world.

What are rituals needed for today?

For what events are rituals needed today? Who should perform them? And how can we prevent them losing their significance and effect by becoming too stylized and impersonal?

All major life stages need to be clearly marked: puberty, marriage, the menopause, death and so on. In addition, many situations such as retirement, which did not exist in simpler societies, now need to be acknowledged. Events particular to our own life story now also need to be externalized. Completing therapy, or dealing with an abortion, could fit into this category.

Another area which has not traditionally been dealt with by ritual but which could be considerably clarified by it are events such as leaving a job or being burgled. Emotions of joy, achievement, and empowerment can all stem from observing the significant events in our lives with a suitable ritual. It can also give us valuable time for contemplation which is so often missing in our busy lives.

Who should perform a ritual?

The question of who should perform a ritual marks one of the great divides between the past and the present. In tribal society only the shaman – the medicine man – could mediate for his people; in the Christian tradition this role has been given to the priest. The rest of the people provided the audience, the crowd scene, and were never the initiators. It was also simply assumed that everyone in the community had the same needs. But as the energies of the Age of Aquarius, which we are now entering, make themselves felt, individuals' needs are no longer perceived as identical and self-expression can no longer be suppressed. This will be the age of harmony, but harmony through diversity rather than egality.

This tendency, so inherent to the next two thousand years, plus the fact that we live in a more complex society, requires a far more flexible form of ritual. The leader role once held by the shaman or the priest is gradually being taken over by the layman or groups of them. Although the established rituals of baptism, marriage and funerals still generate great force and comfort, many people are finding it increasingly difficult to accept the old forms that are performed within the framework of a particular religion. Events such as marriages and funerals are becoming personalized in a way which would have been unthinkable even a short while ago. More and more people are opting to create their own ceremonies.

Making rituals personal

By enacting, even at times creating, our own rituals we can prevent them becoming overly stylized and impersonal and thereby losing their significance. With this in mind, the ceremonies described in this book are to be regarded as suggestions rather than as having inflexible form. They can be adapted to comply with each person's own symbolism, language and tastes. Only the basic philosophy and intent behind each ritual should be conserved.

You can, for instance, perform a ritual alone if the presence of others would make you shy, or you can do it with friends. You can also enact it physically, or just work it out in your imagination. Equal latitude applies to the props which are used. If music, for example, is a familiar accompaniment to your life, it can greatly enhance a ritual; but if its presence feels forced, it is better omitted.

Why do rituals work?

This question is increasingly easy to answer as we grow more familiar with the concept of the unconscious and its language. Both rituals and symbols speak this language and therefore communicate with us at a far deeper level than we could achieve – or even imagine – with our conscious minds. However heartfelt it may be, a statement made in everyday life has very little punch compared to one made during a successful ritual when our subconscious, our conscious mind and our will are all working in unison. Through ritual we create a special and sacred atmosphere. We invoke help from our guardian angel, our spirit guides and helpers (see p. 17) which empowers us to bring about results beyond anything we would normally expect. We are able to tap into the enormous strength and energy of the universe.

At a wedding, for instance, when the two families have assembled, special traditions been adhered to and a familiar, well-loved ceremony used, the vows exchanged have infinitely more power than would a simple statement of intent made during a conversation. It goes without saying that any ritual undertaken for the wrong reasons can cause considerable damage and may well backfire on those performing it. But with the right intention, and an attitude of love and gratitude, we can see beyond the rational and change ourselves profoundly. Everything becomes possible.

PERFORMING
THE
RITUALS

When to hold your ritual

As this chapter contains instructions common to all the rituals in the book, please make sure you read it before embarking on any of the ceremonies.

With some rituals it is obvious when they should be performed. Others should simply be held when you feel ready for them – that is to say, when you are able to release or take on whatever is necessary for change and moving on. This could be quite a long time after an event of significance. A woman could, for instance, reach her late sixties before feeling ready to perform a ritual concerning an abortion she experienced in her thirties. It could well take her that long – and even then possibly only with the help of a therapist – to recognize its influence on her life and allow her to create the ritual needed for her peace of mind.

The actual day and time for a ritual again vary greatly. Some of them can be totally spontaneous – the right people will just suddenly be there to support your need. In other circumstances you might want to spend the whole day meditating and performing the ritual and even celebrating its completion. Yet others may need to be done in two or three parts over a period of time. Some careful organization with your helpers will be needed here. In a ritual for a miscarriage, for instance, the parents might wish to carry in their minds a symbol representing the baby for a week or two before the ritual. This could be a soft toy or a small cushion, possibly one specially bought for the purpose. During that period there would be a deep honouring of the child's memory. Only when the parent was really ready to name the child and release it would the ritual take place.

Preparation

Sound preparation for a ritual is as important as its actual enactment. Before starting, make certain that you have allowed yourself enough time and that you will not be disturbed. Any form of anxiety will lead to lack of concentration and reduce the efficacy of what you do. Relax yourself thoroughly first.

It is also very important to be completely familiar with the working of the ritual before it starts. Any hesitations or whispered consultations during the course of it will seriously detract from its power. A list of instructions is given with each ritual; either memorize it or copy it on to a small piece of paper which you can then hold in the palm of your hand. For some of the more complicated rituals there is a layout to show the positions of the participants.

Where you have to make quite a long and complex statement in summary of the past or as an intention for the future, it is very helpful to carry around with you for two or three days before the ceremony a piece of paper on which you can jot down your ideas. This monologue will enter your subconscious, evoking responses of which you yourself were hardly aware. It will put you very effectively into a state of mind conducive to a successful ritual. This will usually be done as preparation for your own ceremony, but in some cases you may be taking responsibility for someone younger or less familiar with ritual.

Forming a square or circle

All rituals need a circle or a square, to safely contain the energy required for the work. A circle is the more usual shape, but when using symbols to represent the four elements (see below) a square is often quite naturally formed.

When creating this square or circle, many different moods or intentions can be expressed. If you want a fresh, pretty impression, for instance, mark out the shape with flowers. Where a more masculine feeling is appropriate, dried grasses, seeds or branches can be used. Stones of different colours are another possibility. A more mystical atmosphere can be created by candles of a colour which express for you the feeling you wish to create. You can also, of course, use a combination of any of the above.

Symbols

You will find symbols referred to frequently throughout this book. Unfortunately it is difficult to give precise guidelines about this because symbols are by their very nature both universal and personal. They form a link with something greater than oneself, and reveal aspects of reality which escape other forms of expression. A candle can, for instance, represent either the entire element of fire or some particular aspect of it connected with a specific memory or type of behaviour. On the other hand you may feel a candle inadequate for your purposes, and prefer to use another symbol which is far more evocative for you. Your drawing of a forest fire or a photograph of a building collapsing in flames could well express, far better than any traditional symbol, your terror of being overcome by emotion or fear. Don't be shy of using anything that is really meaningful to you, even though it may have no significance for others. If you want to make an in-depth study of this subject, books such as Jung's *Man and His Symbols* are very helpful (see the reading list on p. 218).

The four elements

Frequently, reference is also made to the four elements of earth, air, fire and water. These do not need to be present at every ritual, but are usually required in those of a more spiritual nature. They can be represented either by simple symbols such as a stone, a feather, a candle and a bowl of water, or you can use more personal symbols. You can also dispense with symbols altogether and simply acknowledge their presence and ask for their help at the time of your invocation.

Each element has specific qualities. Earth helps to ground ideas and intentions, whereas air brings clarity. Where unwanted dross has to be burned away, fire is your greatest ally. When purification is required, water in some form should be prominent. Conversely, where an experience is already very emotional and watery, the other elements can be used to temper the situation.

Making changes in the rituals

Throughout this book creative licence over symbols and wording is encouraged. Specific guidelines are once again difficult to give because these things are so personal. So don't hesitate to invent your own words, as long as they are clear and sincere all will be well.

What is important is not to deviate from the ritual's basic aims and procedures, which could weaken or even destroy it. Should you find yourself making a lot of changes, you should consider devising an entirely new ritual whose aims and form are better suited to your needs.

Psychodrama and ritual

The fundamental difference between ritual and psychodrama is a point to bear in mind at all times. In a psychodrama you are re-enacting a particularly distressing circumstance in order to work out your emotions and relationships with the other people involved. But in a ritual this psychological work should already have been done. You are now anchoring the results. By stating what has happened and your intentions for the future, you are drawing together everything visible and invisible connected with the event and affirming that the desired result will occur – in accordance with the stage at which all those involved now find themselves.

So don't perform a ritual too soon. If anger, resentment, envy, hate or jealousy are still bubbling so near the surface that they cannot be contained, wait and work them out with a therapist or friend before embarking on a ritual.

Make your intention clear

It is through the intention that a ritual becomes real and alive for all concerned. This can either be stated out loud, or expressed silently through the use of a symbol. If you choose the latter, make certain that all the participants are clear about what the symbols mean in this context.

Rituals are powerful. They call on the help of unseen realities empowered to act with us and on our behalf. This is not fantasy. By deciding to do a ritual you are engaging yourself at a deep level, and bringing your intention into material form. Rituals work; they are not to be trifled with.

Closing a ritual

The importance of closing or thoroughly undoing a ritual is based on the fact that its sacred quality must last *only* for the duration of the ceremony. Once it is over, thanks for their contributions should be given both to the energies and to the sacred space used. Those energies then need to be consciously released. If you fail to do this, the room may well feel uncomfortable later on. A powerful meditative atmosphere is inappropriate to a room in which everyday life is being conducted.

Be sure to remove all the props you have used, starting with the circle or square. Stones, flowers, seeds, feathers and shells can be ceremonially thanked and restored to the garden. Other objects should be returned to their normal position in the household or be disposed of.

The question of 'de-roling' at the end of a ritual is also important. The objects you have used will have taken on special significance: a cushion may have become a frontier, a broom handle a tree. Be sure that you disassociate them in your mind from the part they have temporarily assumed. The same applies to the people who have taken part in the ritual. Once it is over they must consciously drop the role they played. When you have finished, the environment should be entirely neutral.

Opening and closing the chakras for a ritual

We do not consist only of our physical body; we have several other bodies, amongst them an etheric one, which we cannot normally see. These other bodies are simply different manifestations of energy from the seemingly solid one which we experience in everything around us. The etheric body is a direct counterpart of the physical body with all its weaknesses and strengths. In it are rotating movements of energy which, where these interweave more closely, produce a flow of colour. Quite a few of these energy centres, known as chakras, exist in the etheric body. Clairvoyants have until now generally agreed that it is the seven major chakras which constitute

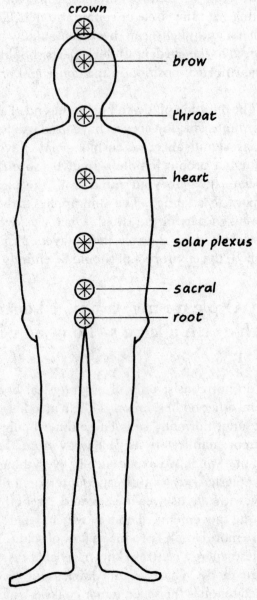

The seven major chakras

our main energy system (see opposite). However, recent exploration suggests that as new energies enter the planet, a more extensive energy system will be required and a further five major chakras will soon be generally recognized.

These force centres are the focal points through which energies are received to vitalize the physical body.

When you are working in a ritualistic, symbolic way, it is essential that the chakras be open and receptive to receiving energy. It is equally important that they should be closed down at the end of the ritual so that you do not return to the everyday world in an over-sensitive and vulnerable state. If you are unfamiliar with this psychic process, read the section entitled 'Opening and Closing the Chakras' on p. 184.

The subtle bodies

It is through what are known as our subtle bodies that unseen energies and beings interact with us. There are seven bodies in all, each one vibrating at an increasingly finer rate. The physical body is surrounded and protected by the etheric body which in turn is surrounded by the astral, through which we register our emotions. Beyond that and pervading the physical, etheric and astral bodies is the mental body. The two finest bodies are rarely perceived or worked with. It is thanks to these subtle bodies that our soul is eventually linked to the highest spiritual dimensions of the universe (see p. 16).

See the ritual for undergoing surgery on pp. 127 – 130 for a practical use of the subtle bodies in ritual.

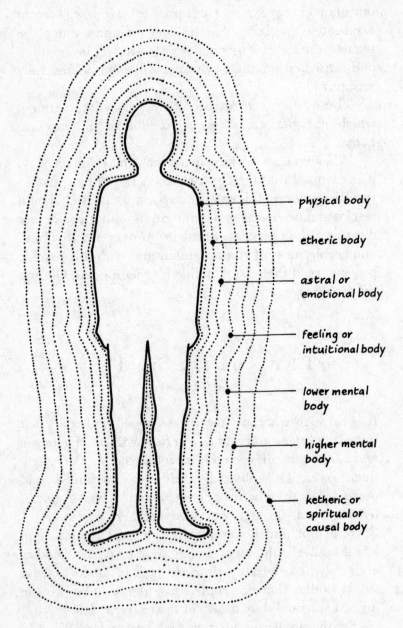

physical body

etheric body

astral or
emotional body

feeling or
intuitional body

lower mental
body

higher mental
body

ketheric or
spiritual or
causal body

The seven subtle bodies

Our guides and helpers

We are constantly assured by a wide range of spiritual teachers that, if we only ask, we can wholeheartedly count on help from the higher realms. Our guardian angel, whom each of us is given at birth, helps us through our various experiences in life and is always available to a soul desiring strength and guidance. Prayer, meditation and ritual are ways by which we can most easily reach these guides and helpers. For committed Christians they will often appear as Jesus and Mary; for those of other religions they will have different names. Further guidance can come to us from human beings who are discarnate (beings who are between incarnations). Many of us are quite unconsciously inspired by these.

Visualization

Some of the rituals in this book are more 'imaginary' than others. These require the ability to visualize, a technique often used in therapy because the unconscious works in images, and the symbols or pictures arising in the mind's eye speak the language of the unconscious. These are therefore extremely helpful in all work that benefits from the participation of the unconscious.

Not everyone finds it easy to picture something in his mind, but practice works wonders. As a start, close your eyes and try to imagine a simple object such as a lighted candle or a place you know well. You may need to spend some time on this, gradually mastering more abstract and complicated visualizations.

Repeating a ritual

There are no hard-and-fast rules for the frequency with which any ritual can or needs to be performed, but here are a few general guidelines. Some of the rituals in new beginnings will probably only need to be performed once, although others such as those for birthdays and New Year may be repeated annually. Rituals for life stages will need doing again only if an event such as marriage or divorce recurs. But some of the rituals in the other three sections may well need several attempts before achieving their goal. In the rituals for your spiritual journey, each ceremony will deepen as you yourself advance; conversely, your next step forward will be helped by each of the rituals. For the various traumatic events, you may want to repeat a ritual when you find that your increased detachment or sense of forgiveness has taken a strong step forward. If you find the rituals for healing the chakras helpful you will be repeating them often: the health and balance of your chakric system are essential and will need constant attention.

Tie-cutting

This is an exercise used for severing connections between two people or between a person and a situation. This practice is based on the teaching of the Hunas, the sect who were said to have instructed Jesus and whose few survivors are the Hawaiian Shamans (see Reading List for books by Max Freedom Long). Their premise was that whenever we experience an emotion, we emit 'aka threads' through our solar plexus. These are tiny psychic threads which link us to a person, place or thought-form. As our love or hate-filled feelings accrue, the threads become ever more binding cords. On the same principle, 'thought-clusters', said by clairvoyants to look like bunches of grapes, are formed by constantly repeated thought patterns. It is when a relationship, a situation or a way of thinking have become intolerably destructive or stifling that these ties should be cut or the thought-clusters broken up.

Here is a good exercise for achieving this.

Imagine yourself on the bank of a fast-running river. Place on the opposite bank the person or situation from which you wish to be freed. Visualize the cords linking whatever chakra or chakras are involved. See them pulsating with life, causing an energy exchange between you. State clearly why you want these cords dissolved, and ask them to wither away. When you feel certain that they no longer have any power over you, cut them with imaginary scissors at both your chakra and that of the other person or situation. Watch them being carried away by the swiftly moving water. Visualize a cross within a circle of light and place it over each chakra that has been affected – both yours and those of the person or situation on the opposite bank. If it is a thought-cluster with which you are working, use the same basic method, simply pulling it to pieces gently so that its constituents are carried away by the river.

After a ritual

The deep release allowed by the ritual may well help you to make decisions about your life and unleash in you a new sense of purpose. This may in turn create the need to talk to someone. In the absence of a counsellor or therapist, a trusted friend – possibly someone who assisted in the ritual – could help you to evaluate and integrate the experience into your everyday life.

Keeping a detailed journal of the rituals you have performed can be extremely useful. Not only will you gain helpful general insights, but you will also build up invaluable knowledge of yourself.

RITUALS
FOR
LIFE
STAGES

INTRODUCTION
TO THE
RITUALS

Ritual is about moving on. It is about including something new into our lives or letting go of something that no longer serves us. It marks important transitions, witnessed if possible by others. It gives us the opportunity to offer up something for ourselves or others. It helps us to feel seen and heard in a world that is often too busy to listen. It gives us a sense of security in plotting our path through life. It defines a period of time, making conscious what is happening to us and helping us to recognize where we are in life.

The rituals in this chapter are designed to help us through various rites of passage – those stages in life when we move from one cycle to another. These cycles are determined by a change in our civil or family status (marriage, a naming ceremony, a son or daughter leaving home, divorce, becoming a parent-in-law, death), or by physical changes (the onset of puberty, a girl's first period, the menopause), or the termination of a cycle (retirement from one's working life). Rituals for other occasions which fall into one of these categories can be adapted from the ones described here.

Success in changing civil or family status means ending one cycle properly before starting another. If you cease to be a wife through divorce, or to be the mother of an unmarried child because your son or daughter gets married, you are actually changing roles. You need to disengage yourself from the previous role in order to avoid any blurring of the two. In this way you will also prevent yourself becoming chronically nostalgic for what no longer exists. You will be able to move completely into the new situation, even if it is a less pleasant one than its predecessor.

On those few occasions for which a life stage is still celebrated by nearly all religions (a naming ceremony, marriage and death), it is hoped that these new rituals will perform one of two roles. They can either replace a religious rite which no longer holds meaning for the individual, or they can be used in addition to the traditional ceremony. Where no rite of passage is performed in our society (when a son or daughter leaves home, when we get divorced, or when we become a parent-in-law), these rituals will draw attention to the issues at stake. In either case, the most important thing to establish beforehand is exactly what you want the ritual to accomplish.

Sexual matters are now discussed more openly in our society, and greater account is taken of them as significant components in our psychological health. Nevertheless it could be argued that we are in a greater state of confusion about the true nature of sexuality and its role in our overall soul journey than we have ever been. By acknowledging through ritual the basic biological stages of our lives, we can work more consciously with them. We can start and finish each one more tidily, extracting its lessons and its enjoyments but not confusing them with those of an earlier or later cycle. From an apparently simple ritual there can emerge a deeper understanding of how our sexual natures in childhood, adolescence, adulthood and the post-menopausal years influence our whole selves and need to be understand as part of the overall process of our self-development.

In the ritual for retirement, both a role change and an age progression are involved. Becoming a 'pensioner' brings to the fore many interesting questions on values, self-worth and the use of time. Performing this ritual will, it is hoped, provide an opportunity to consider these questions creatively.

REACHING PUBERTY

In most societies, the shift from childhood to adolescence is recognized as one of our most important life events. Although the form of the rituals differs from one civilization to the next, the need to celebrate the physical and psychological changes occurring at puberty remains. Western society's neglect to acknowledge this shift formally can be quite unnecessarily traumatic to adolescents. Worst of all, we have become so accustomed to the problems associated with adolescence that most of us now think of them as 'normal'. But do young people need to be subjected to so much unhappiness, rebellion and self-doubt? Do we wrongly accept as inevitable many of their reactions – reactions which have in fact been brought about by our society, our educational system and our frequent lack of parental guidelines?

One of the main difficulties in choosing the right moment for performing a ritual for puberty is that children nowadays grow up so much earlier on one level, yet are still bound by the developmental ages of their chakras. The root chakra, for instance, develops during the first three years of life, the sacral chakra between the ages of three and eight and the solar plexus between the ages of eight and twelve (for a full explanation of these stages see pp. 183 – 4). Childhood and adolescence are no longer well defined and separated from each other, and so no definite age can then be prescribed for this ritual because it might prove too juvenile for some and too advanced for others. The ceremony must also be sensitively adapted to the individual, so that it seems neither embarrassingly overt nor so understated that the participant feels that nothing has really occurred.

Another important fact to consider is that most

Western societies now encompass many religions and races, beliefs and traditions. Finding the right approach is therefore not always easy. So in devising this particular ceremony, be alert and sensitive to the individual needs of the young person at the centre of it. Be prepared to make adjustments in the wording and the symbols until both generations involved feel completely at ease.

The principal objective of this ceremony is to declare that the participant, having progressed from childhood into adolescence, is now ready to embark on a new phase of his development: that of his emotional self. This is a very important moment in his life. If he is not to drown in the potentially treacherous sea of his emotions and his sexuality, he needs to start out from a secure place. To make this crossing safe yet expanding to his heart chakra he must take with him all the best things from his childhood while leaving behind the now inappropriate behaviour of a child. He must be given a sense of excitement at knowing himself to be in the ante-room of adulthood. If this transition can be presented as one of the many natural progressions already made in his life, the physical and emotional changes he goes through will seem less alarming. If he can take firm responsibility for both his own body and his place in society, he will be spared a great deal of anxiety. Instead of experiencing the feelings of shame and confusion so often connected with adolescence, he can be given a sense of self-worth and dignity, not only in his own eyes but also in those of his family.

The Ritual

The ideal layout for this ritual is two interconnecting rooms, one of which leads into a garden. If this arrangement is not available, use a single room divided into three sections with a 'doorway' between each section. Childhood is in section 1. The present is in section 2. Adolescence is in section 3.

The ritual starts with the boy going to his chair in section 1. On one side of it is a symbol representing the childhood he has outgrown and which is to be left behind during the course of the ritual. Until now, the needs and behaviour of that childish self have been right and acceptable, but if carried forward into the next phase of his life they would be totally inappropriate. On the other side of him is an object which symbolizes for him the positive, happy aspect of his early years. This secure, open, imaginative part of himself will be taken forward into adolescence.

Considerable thought should be given to the choosing of these two symbols, either by the young person alone or by him in conjunction with a trusted adult. Through the first symbol he is acknowledging that that child is still part of himself – in no way rejected – but that its voice is no longer the dominant one. A teddy bear or some much-loved toy could represent those years. His second symbol would probably be more personal and abstract, denoting a quality and his ambitions rather than a period of time. It could, for instance, be the pencil with which he draws or a piece of sports equipment, or a certificate from school. All these exteriorize his new awareness of cycles and the different behaviour needed for each of them. If the new one is well prepared for by the previous one, fear and confusion will not dominate it.

In section 2 those relations and friends whom the young person would like to have present now assemble in a semi-circle in front of the chair which he will later occupy. The group of people can range from one friend to his entire family. Even if his omissions and inclusions cause difficulties, he should be allowed total freedom of choice. This is *his* day, and it is particularly important for him to be surrounded by those people whom he feels are best able to help him. The only restriction on his choice is that no one be younger than he.

As this ceremony is declaring not only a change in the boy's relationship with himself, but also a shift in his status within the family, it should preferably be a family affair. But if circumstances make this impossible, other adults can be substituted.

One of the elders from the semi-circle now goes to the doorway between sections 1 and 2 and invites the boy or girl to move from childhood into adolescence. He rises, bearing his two symbols, walks towards the door, bows to the grown-up and lays on the threshold the symbol of his childhood self. The grown-up returns to his place in the semi-circle.

The young person then goes to sit in the central chair of section 2, still carrying with him his second symbol. One by one the grown-ups come up to him and greet him with a kiss, a bow, a handshake or whatever seems appropriate. The important thing is that they make clear both to themselves and the boy that they now recognize him as an adolescent. He has made his statement that he will no longer act childishly; they in turn will no longer treat him as a child.

If any of them wants to say something to him or give him something such as a family ring, a Bible or a watch, this is a good moment to do so. In return the young person might like to thank his family for his childhood or make some statement about his new status. A few words at this point will help to ground the changes which are occurring, but too much talking will be counter-productive. The ritual's power lies in its simplicity.

From section 2 the boy now moves into section 3, still carrying his symbol and also any gifts that have been given to him. The grown-ups remain quietly in their semi-circle. After sitting in the adolescent section for a few minutes to adjust to his new status, the youth leaves through a door that does not take him back to the family. He now has their entire support, but he is also a person on his own.

The guests leave by another door. The officiating elder gathers up the symbol for the young person's childhood and disposes of it in whatever way was agreed with him beforehand.

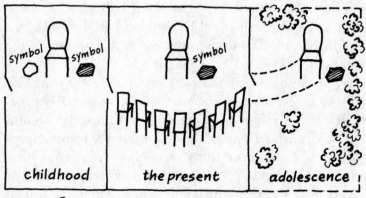

Setting for reaching puberty ritual

Preparation

This is to be done by the young person with an adult of his choice. Find a symbol for what is to be left behind and another for what is to be carried forward.

Divide the available space into three sections, leaving a 'doorway' between each of them.

Put one central chair in each section.

In section 2, form in front of the central chair a semi-circle of chairs for the guests.

Place on each side of the chair in section 1 the young person's two symbols.

Decorate the three sections in any way you feel to be appropriate; carefully mark the differences between them.

Checklist

The young person goes to section 1 and sits down.

The guests sit in their semi-circle in section 2, holding their gifts, if any.

After a few minutes of silence, an appointed elder, standing in the doorway of sections 1 and 2, invites the youth to step out of his childhood.

The youth leaves his childhood symbol at the doorway and, carrying with him his second symbol, goes to his chair in section 2.

Each of the guests greets him and gives him a gift, if appropriate.

The youth expresses his thanks and anything else he wants to say.

He moves into section 3.

A few minutes later he leaves, preferably not passing again through section 2.

The guests leave section 2, except for one elder who clears the three sections and disposes of the childhood symbol as previously agreed with the youth.

FIRST MENSTRUATION

Rituals were first enacted thousands of years ago when the Earth Mother was worshipped at full moon as the triple goddess of birth, love and death. Womanhood was then celebrated as the holder of power over the awesome mystery of fertility and regeneration. But, as the new male pantheon of Greek gods took over and led to the patriarchal religions of today, women's power became denigrated and their physical bodies often despised.

So until quite recently sexual matters, including menstruation, were seldom openly discussed in our society. As a result, a girl's first bleeding was often a fearful occasion, one of shame and disgust from which she retained – sometimes for her whole life – a deep distaste not only of her menstrual cycle but of her entire sexuality. Such disastrous lack of preparation is now luckily rare, and young girls usually know the 'facts of life' long before puberty.

Yet the stark facts as presented in a biology class are not the answer either. What of the psychological changes that are taking place in the girl? What of her new relationship with her body, and of her body with the young boys she knows? What mention is ever made of those ancient sacred feminine rites connected to the moon and its cycle, or of the spiritual nature of blood? There is still a long way to go before we succeed in integrating our sexuality so that we can pass on our knowledge effectively to the next generation.

Too often the modern emancipated girl is dramatically split. On the one hand she knows all the facts about contraception, AIDS and abortion, while on the other hand she feels herself a bewildered child who longs to ask questions and receive reassurance about all the possible consequences arising from her alarming new sexuality. So disconnected has Western woman become from her womanhood that we urgently need a ceremony which can help a young girl pass from childhood into adolescence with pride, seeing her first menstruation as part of the excitement of growing up rather than as a miserable event that may cause her pre-menstrual tension for the rest of her child-bearing life.

Any difficulty or embarrassment which the older generation may initially envisage about the following ritual will, it is hoped, be dissolved by the very ritualization of what is being taught.

If tensions exist between the girl and her mother, it is best if the mother is not at the ritual. Her presence could so inhibit the daughter that little good would come of it. The fact that the girl has experienced the ceremony may, however, in time so improve the mother – daughter relationship that many things will be released and discussed. The mother's difficulty – conscious or unconscious – in acknowledging her daughter's new adolescent state might well form part of this discussion.

If, on the other hand, the girl wishes to invite a friend to participate in the ceremony, this is quite in order and can be very helpful. But the friend must already have had her first period.

Older women, too, can benefit greatly from performing this ceremony. By getting back into their teenage selves they can undo much of the harm they experienced when they first became aware of their own womanhood without any preparation for it.

The Ritual

As this is a very special occasion, all the participants should dress up. The circle of flowers or foliage or candles to contain the ritual should also be especially pretty and feminine.

At the start of the ceremony an older woman – representing the concept of the Wise Old Woman (an honoured title used by the Native American Indians for those women who had attained spiritual maturity) – will already be standing in the circle. The girl is outside it, waiting to be invited in. Any other participants are behind her but within the circle. In her hand she holds whatever symbol she has chosen to represent the moon: perhaps a moonstone, a painting of the moon, or something crescent-shaped. From now on the girl will come under the particular care and protection of the moon.

The girl then places at the entrance to the circle whatever object she has chosen to represent her childhood. This she should do with care and love and respect for her life until this moment. She then moves into the circle and offers you the object she has chosen to represent her as a maiden. This symbol should carry the quality of purity and a new beginning. It could be a flower or something white. You, in turn, hand her the symbol you have chosen for the moon. During the rest of the ritual you are entrusted with her maidenhood, while she has been united with womanhood through this symbol.

She then states to you that the physical change in her is not a matter for alarm, and affirms that she regards her body as a precious vessel.

As you stand opposite each other, convey to her silently that she has all the time she needs, that the space is entirely hers and that she can discuss with you anything that is worrying her. In the sacred atmosphere of this circle you will have taken on for her a different dimension, almost that of a priestess; both of you will be able to speak freely of anything that is required, including such difficult subjects as the sacredness of sexuality, the joy of being a woman and the respect she owes to herself and her body.

When the dialogue is over, place both your symbols in the centre of the circle and leave it together. Afterwards, return to clear the circle.

Preparation

The girl, either alone or with a trusted adult, chooses the two symbols needed for the ritual.

The older woman creates a very feminine, pretty circle.

Before the ceremony starts, the older woman sits in the circle, holding her symbol for the moon. The other participants form a semi-circle behind her.

Checklist

The girl comes to the entrance of the circle holding her symbols.

The woman and the girl converse, if they wish.

The girl leaves her childhood symbol at the entrance to the circle.

She enters the circle

Symbols are exchanged.

The girl asks the woman any questions she has.

Both symbols are placed in the centre.

The woman and girl leave the circle together.

The woman returns to clear the circle.

MARRIAGE

An increasing number of people today reject the idea of a church wedding, yet a civil marriage also feels unsatisfactory to them. Although fulfilling the legal requirements, it bypasses that commitment which is so vital to a marriage. For such people this ritual is offered either as an alternative or as an additional ceremony.

An essential ingredient of any marriage rite is the sense that the two people are joining together at a level beyond the romantic heart. The marriage service itself calls for the union to be made 'in the eyes of God'. This could also be expressed as a joining of the bride and bridegroom through their higher selves – that part of them which is connected to the divine. In this way their marriage is committed to a sacred purpose, and help for it is invoked beyond the mundane. Without having something beyond themselves towards which they can strive, their marriage would lose a vital dimension.

This ideal, this sacred purpose is one of the most important issues for the couple to discuss. Any common concept which transcends worldly differences and considerations is a uniting factor. The more both parties can bring into everyday life the love and wisdom gathered at this higher point, the greater their chance of a successful marriage. This ritual aims to strengthen the pathways by which an ideal can be reached.

This ceremony can be performed by the two of you alone or else with a group of people to whom you feel a strong heart link. As this is a spiritual rather than a social event, make sure that all its participants will be backing you wholeheartedly. Any show of scepticism, even embarrassment, emanating from any of them will partly negate the ritual.

The Ritual

If this ceremony can take place out of doors, you will receive the additional help of the nature spirits, trees and plants. If this is impracticable, bring into your room as much greenery as possible.

Put a large flat stone in the centre of your space. Set on it two vases with a flower in each of them to represent your higher selves. If you have two crystals with which you feel at ease, place one next to each flower, seeing them as the earth energy available to you. Place two candles on this central stone as symbols of light. Between these two groups of objects leave a well-defined gap; never forget that you are two individuals, however much joined through love.

Depending on whether or not you have chosen to include two witnesses in your ritual, form a circle of candles around the stone that is large enough to accommodate either two or four people comfortably. Leave an entrance to this circle, which represents the life space you have agreed to share. If you would like accompanying music, the musician or musicians should remain outside the circle.

When everything is in place, both of you light the candles. Each starts with one of those on the central stone, lights their half of the circle, and ends with the candle nearest the entrance. You both then enter this space which has been made sacred by the beauty and love invested in it. Stand one at each end of the stone. If there are witnesses, they now enter the circle and take up their positions behind and slightly to the side of you.

The commitment to which they are bearing witness is two-fold. The first is made in silence, then each of you invokes their higher self to help manifest the love and joy created by this union. You then speak your vows, affirming that this love will not only be directed inwards towards each other but also outwards into the world. If either of you wants to add to this some form of undertaking to the Creator or any being beyond the human, further power will be added to your vows. Anyone who doesn't yet feel ready to do this can always do so later on.

Having pledged yourselves to the common good of yourselves as a couple, it is now time to affirm that you also remain two separate individuals who must be complete in yourselves in order to achieve a successful marriage. In a beautiful poem (see opposite) from his book *The Prophet*, Kahlil Gibran speaks of how to avoid those arch-destroyers of love: possessiveness, jealousy and envy. Reading this poem aloud could be a good ending to the ritual.

When this is done, the witnesses should leave the circle. Then each of you blows out your own central candle, and your own half of the circle, starting at the entrance.

Leave the circle together.

Dismantle the ritual site.

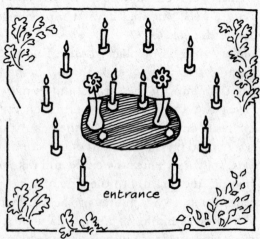

Setting for marriage ritual

Kahlil Gibran's poem

Love one another, but make not a bond of love:

Let it rather be a moving sea between the shores
of your souls.

Fill each other's cups but drink not from one cup.

Give one another of your bread but eat not from
the same loaf.

Sing and dance together and be joyous, but let
each one of you be alone,

Even as the strings of a lute are alone though they
quiver with the same music.

Give your hearts, but not into each other's keeping,

For only the hand of Life can contain your hearts.

And stand together yet not too near together:

For the pillars of the temple stand apart,

And the oak tree and the cypress grow not
in each other's shadow.

Preparation

If the ritual is taking place indoors, decorate the room
with greenery.

Make a circle of candles.

On a large central stone place a group of objects
(flower, crystal and candle) chosen to represent each
person.

If you are having musicians ask them to take their
place outside the circle.

Checklist

Light candles as directed.

Re-enter the circle and stand at your end of the stone with your witness behind you and slightly to one side.

Each of you invokes his higher self.

Each speaks his vows, adding a commitment to the Creator if desired.

Read Kahlil Gibran's words or any other poem of your choice.

The witnesses leave the circle.

Each blows out his half of the candles.

Leave the circle together.

NAMING CEREMONY

Our name carries a particular sound and vibration which links us to a particular type of experience for the rest of our lives or until we change our names! The importance of choosing an individual's name cannot therefore be over-emphasized. It will deeply affect his relationship with everything and everyone he meets.

The formal, ritualistic declaration of this name affirms him as a member of the human race. To deny him this important first rite of passage is particularly distressing at a time when every human being needs the best possible integration between his body and spirit and the closest possible connection to the Earth, a process which can take a significant step forward at the time of his naming.

This ceremony is, however, so closely associated with structured religion that many parents today are reluctant to have it performed. They do not want their child formally committed to one specific form of worship.

In any naming ceremony it is important to acknowledge the crown chakra (see p. 208), through which we touch into our higher self, that link to the divine. Through ceremony we offer to the baby or adult the highest to which he can reach in this lifetime. The conscious uniting of his body and spirit and the recognition of him as a person in his own right constitute a very important moment.

If it is a baby for whom a name is being sought, attune to him closely to find the name best suited to his soul in this particular lifetime. Do not let family tradition or pleasant associations with a name allow you to impose something inappropriate.

If the person performing the ritual is an adult, and until now there has been a lack of harmony between himself and his name, this is the perfect moment for selecting a new one. Where someone has made radical spiritual advances, the name with which he was once in tune may now need changing.

As the only assumption made by this ritual is that we all derive from a common source, it can be used either in conjunction with a formal religious ceremony or on its own. It can also be performed indoors or outdoors, but it benefits enormously from taking place outside, as you are specifically seeking to connect the person with both Heaven and Earth. If, however, this is not practicable, do not worry; provided the ceremony is performed with love and good intent, all possible help will be given to you.

The Ritual

The sponsors form a square into which all those who are to be present will be summoned in turn. Place at its four corners a symbol for each of the four elements: earth, air, fire and water. These could be simply a stone, a feather, a candle and a bowl of water, or something more elaborate. As those elements form both our planet and the person being named, they will initiate the first stages of resonance between the two.

Next, invoke the assistance of this soul's higher self and guardian angel. Their presence will raise the vibrational level within the square and call into it the guides and helpers (see p. 17) of all those attending the ritual.

Once this preparation has been completed, the person being named enters the square with his parents and his two sponsors – a man and a woman – who should stand one on each side of him. They are followed by any friends and members of the family who wish to attend the ceremony, either in person or symbolically represented by a photograph or an object which evokes them. This family group should include those members who have died but whose love is still felt as a very positive asset to the family. Their symbolic presence will also introduce a desirable sense of continuity. This group forms a semi-circle facing the person being named.

For the sake of simplicity, the person being named will from now on be referred to as 'you' and directions will be given as though he were able to move and speak freely. If that person is in fact a baby, obviously the appropriate adult will carry him and speak for him.

When everyone is in place, one of your sponsors steps forward to greet you and formally assume the duty of familiarizing you with whatever spiritual concepts are built into this ritual. He also agrees to assist in the important process of grounding or earthing you. If it is a child being named, he also commits himself, on behalf of both sponsors, to fulfil the roles complementary to those undertaken by the parents.

He next explains to you the role of the four elements in the ceremony. Fire is there to activate your intuition; air will bring clarity of mind; earth offers you stability, and water adaptability.

He then greets your guardian angel, explaining that this being's sole function is to guide and protect the soul entrusted to its care.

Your higher self is then acknowledged as your direct means of contacting the higher worlds and receiving guidance from them.

It is next recognized, in whatever terms seem appropriate to the occasion, that you are a droplet of the divine, still trailing clouds of glory from your sojourn in Heaven. As such you are the giver and receiver of great gifts.

When the sponsor has finished speaking, you respond with whatever thanks, commitment or contribution you wish to make. Any questions you have can also be put at this point.

After a moment of silence, you will be asked whether you are ready to receive your name. When you assent, your parent or sponsor says: 'I name you   , the name by which you shall henceforth be known to mankind and also to the plant and animal and crystal kingdoms. Be proud of your name and make it proud of you.'

A gift of welcome and celebration can now be offered to you.

You should be the first to leave the square, followed by everyone except the person who invoked the four elements, your guardian angel and your higher self. These he must thank, and bid them return whence they came.

In order to close down the energies generated by the ceremony and leave the place in tranquillity, he can either make the sign of the cross encircled with light, or, if this symbol is not meaningful to him, just quietly give thanks.

This closing-down ceremony can either be attended by the family and friends from outside the square, or be done alone.

Preparation

The sponsors form a square with the four elements.

Checklist

If a candle has been used for the element of fire, the sponsor lights it, invoking the four elements and the higher self and guardian angel of the person being named, plus those of his parents and sponsors.

You enter the square.

The sponsors stand one on each side of you.

Your family and friends stand in a semi-circle in front of you.

One of the sponsors holds a dialogue with you.

The sponsor asks if you are ready for your naming.

You assent.

He names you.

Gifts may be offered.

Leave the square with you leading. Only the sponsor who has invoked the four elements etc. remains to thank and dismiss them. He clears the space while the others either observe him or not.

A SON OR DAUGHTER
LEAVING HOME

Sadly, in modern urban society we have lost the traditions
and guidelines which once helped to ease the important step
of a young person leaving home. These days, girls are
rarely expected to remain at home until they get married.
They not only leave their parents for higher education, or
a job, or to share a flat with another girl, but they also leave
to set up home with a boyfriend. Even very traditional
families have had to come to terms with this development
if they want to remain on good terms with their daughters.
To the emotive elements already inherent in this rite of
passage have been added a whole gamut of moral and social
questions. For boys, the changes in custom have been less
dramatic but this century has seen a blurring of boundaries
which has created new scope for family squabbles.

Timing is important here. If the parents are not
properly prepared for the event, they may feel
abandoned or fearful. If the young adult leaves hastily,
he may well feel alarmed by the sudden responsibility for
his own life. On the other hand, if the departure is over-
delayed there may be irritation on either side followed by
a distressing sense of relief.

The rising incidence of divorce has also complicated
the issue. A stepmother or stepfather may now be the
cause of early departure, whether or not this is openly
stated. As far as the ritual is concerned, a step-parent can
be included or not. Even if his relationship with the step-
child is not ideal, it is preferable for the step-parent to be
present as long as his presence does not defeat the object
of the ritual. Where there is only one parent at home,
space should be visibly kept for the second one as he will
influence the situation – if only by his absence.

Whatever their experience of the parental home, the young can derive nothing but benefit from leaving it cleanly and tidily. Whatever their feelings, these should not be left hanging around the house like ghosts but should be removed from a place where they no longer belong. The departure of a son, daughter, stepson or stepdaughter, however loved, feared or disliked, will leave a large gap in the life of the household. A reshaping of the remaining family will have to take place. The person who is leaving has a responsibility to make this reshaping as painless as possible.

Leaving home should be an exciting time for young people, but it can be very traumatic if there is tension which cannot be expressed. A ritual can help considerably.

The Ritual

The room should be laid out in three sections representing the parental home, a neutral territory and the new home. Place three chairs in a triangle in the first section. This figure acknowledges the fact that, although two of the people involved in the ritual form a block as parents to the third person, those parents are also individuals whose feelings on this matter do not necessarily correspond. This present situation may in fact have split them in some very fundamental way.

Before the ritual begins, the young person should place behind his chair in the parental home a symbol for his life until now; he will leave this behind when he moves out. In his new home he should put another symbol for himself as a householder next to the place where his chair will later form part of the same triangle that is now being made in his parents' home. (Taking the three chairs with you as the ritual moves from one section to the next will underline the physical and psychological changes taking place.) No symbol is needed for the neutral territory.

As the three people take their places in the triangle representing the parental home, they are at first mainly concerned with establishing the new status of the young person, not only with regard to himself but also in relation to his parents. Each of the three needs to define what he is prepared to offer and what he hopes to receive in the new situation. If the young person's departure is part of the same progression that took him from childhood into adolescence, the advantages and freedom he is gaining will be counterbalanced by his new responsibilities (see the ritual for puberty on p. 26). If both sides recognize this, the ties based on a child's dependence can be painlessly dropped; without any lack of love or interest being implied, the parents' protective role will also be released. Those ties still appropriate to the new status can be lovingly cemented.

If either parent has something they want to voice, this is an ideal opportunity to right any existing frictions between the generations. Do they, for instance, feel that there has not been enough preparation for this major step? Are they fearful for the future? What do they still hope to contribute to their offspring's welfare, either materially or otherwise? Are they upset by the reaction of family or neighbours if an unmarried relationship is being entered into?

The son or daughter should respond equally openly, but if possible not in anger. None of these rituals should turn into psychodrama. He or she can also raise issues that have been difficult to express before. They could centre around something he has done of which his parents disapproved, or his failure to do something they expected of him. These could be issues concerning work or marriage which would benefit from a friendly airing.

When this dialogue has drawn to a close, whatever symbol is representing the years lived under the parents' roof should be ceremonially left behind. This is particularly important for those girls who are leaving home with some sense of trepidation. If they are to make a success of their new life, they should pay special attention to the symbol they are abandoning. They must make a clean break with it; otherwise they will become one of those women who never really grow up because the little girl in them is forever fearful that no happiness or care could ever equal what she was given at home.

The second part of the ritual provides the necessary pause in which everyone can accustom themselves to the changed situation. Here no role has been ascribed to anyone, so the chairs need not be placed in a triangle. Nor is anyone in his own house, so any unresolved subjects can surface and be dealt with on more equal terms.

When there is no more to be said for the present, move into the new home section. The young person enters first in order to receive his parents from beside his chair, which he should set well into the home. The symbol behind him clearly proclaims his new status. When his parents enter and form the new triangle with their chairs, they are visibly the visitors. Little need be said at this stage. Even if things here are not exactly as his parents would like, they must now comply with his rules and tastes as he formerly complied with theirs. Should any new issues arise as they sit here, any one of the three can ask to return to the netural territory for further discussion.

The ritual should end with the son or daughter sitting in his or her new home and the parents in theirs. Remember that the neutral territory between the two homes is at all times available at either household's request.

Leave the room.

Undo the ritual.

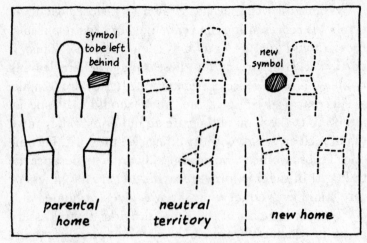

symbol
to be left
behind

new
symbol

parental
home

neutral
territory

new home

Setting for leaving home ritual

Preparation

Separate the room into three sections: the parental home, a neutral territory and the new home.

Put a triangle of chairs in the first section.

Place beside the young person's chair a symbol for his life until now.

Beside where his chair will be when the triangle is formed in the new house, place his symbol for a householder.

Checklist

The two parents and the son or daughter sit in a triangle in the parental home.

They hold a dialogue.

The young person ceremonially leaves his symbol there.

They move into neutral territory with their chairs, placing them wherever they feel comfortable.

They hold a dialogue.

They move with their chairs into the new home, the son or daughter leading.

They hold a dialogue.

The parents return to the parental home while the young person remains in his new home.

Everyone leaves the room.

The ritual is undone.

DIVORCE

In this ritual the word 'divorce' is used to include not only the termination of a marriage but also the definitive ending of a well-established affair. The finishing of any deep relationship necessarily involves pain and often regrets. One's mistakes and inadequacies taunt one; the moments of greatest joy together rise up overwhelmingly.

In order to come to terms with this shutting down of a whole section of one's life, a ritual can be very helpful. It should include asking to be released from the vows once made, assessing the relationship's successes and failures, giving thanks for all that was good in it, forgiving the ex-partner if necessary and then – possibly the most important of all – moving on. If circumstances make it possible for both partners to be present at the ritual, its potential benefits will be enormously enhanced.

Because few of us are as honest alone as when faced with someone whose opinion we respect, it is preferable to have present at this ritual someone who is both open-minded and well acquainted with the circumstances. This is also a ritual which is more effective if spoken aloud. The anger, the compassion and the tone of the forgiveness actually need to sound in the room. So try to overcome any shyness or reserve you may feel and say what is needed – though bearing in mind that this is a ritual, not a psychodrama. However painful reality may prove to be, the more scrupulously truthful and objective you are, the more healing you will receive. Vindictiveness, self-pity and blaming yourself will have the opposite effect.

If an observer is to be present, his role is that of a sounding board against which any lie or prevarication rings untrue. He should speak only if asked a direct question, or if the purpose of the ritual is being destroyed through acrimony or uncontrolled emotions.

Before starting the ritual, there are four assessments which need to be made: (1) the positive and creative contributions made by you to the relationship, (2) those made by your partner, (3) the destructive, unkind elements you brought to it, and (4) those contributed by your partner.

The Ritual

If possible, let this ritual take place on neutral territory – neither in your home nor your partner's.

Form a circle with stones. Sweep the area clean.

Put two chairs side by side in the circle, touching each other. If an observer has been invited, set his chair slightly apart but well within the circle.

If one of the partners is absent, place on his chair a photograph, a symbol or a card bearing his name.

When everyone has taken their place, the two main protagonists turn to each other and make eye contact at as deep a level as possible.

If marriage vows were formerly undertaken they are now spoken again by each of you – however hollow they may sound in the light of subsequent events. (If one person is absent, the other partner moves to his chair and speaks for him.) Reminding yourselves of the expectations once put on the relationship will help you to assess realistically whether those expectations were over-idealistic, whether one or both partners failed to honour them and why, or whether your incompatibility was so deep-seated that the relationship could never have worked.

Once the vows have been reiterated, place the chairs

opposite each other to indicate that a measure of object-ivity has entered your dialogue.

You and your ex-partner now speak in turn, neither one interrupting or cutting short the other one's time.

Start with the positive contributions you made to the relationship. Avoid all false modesty and self-deprecia-tion, and don't let your ex-partner's view of you colour your words. However much your self-confidence has been shaken, you undoubtedly did contribute good and helpful elements to the partnership. They may have been grossly under-valued but they were there, and it is essential both for this exercise and for any future relationships you have that you appreciate these contributions.

If it is you rather than your ex-partner who is to enumerate his positive contributions to the relationship, try to be as stringently just and unbiased as possible, speaking from his point of view rather than your own.

Evaluating your negative contributions will probably be yet another painful process. In what ways did you sabotage the relationship, either consciously or uncon-sciously? When and how did you hurt him, not back him up, undermine his work, complicate his relationships with other people and so on? If any of these memories seem to need acting out, acknowledge them and do so at some other time.

Your ex-partner's assessment of his negative contributions will probably be the most difficult part of the ritual, especially if you are speaking for him. It will be only too easy to attribute to him for the millionth time every fault in the book, but try to remain detached enough for the voice of clarity to have its say. Much may well have been promised and not fulfilled. But *why* was it not? Was there really total lack of goodwill? Did he never intend to keep the promises, or were they way beyond anything that he, or anyone else, could hope to achieve?

When we want something badly enough, it is only human to promise anything in order to obtain the desired object.

If you can be fair and clear-sighted now, whether talking or listening, much destructive resentment can be dropped. Few people act all the time out of 100 per cent vindictiveness and the desire to destroy. By entering the other person's skin and knowing the fears and inadequacies which have bedevilled his behaviour as much as your own have bedevilled yours, you will start to disarm that self-protective mechanism which builds up such a multitude of fantasies and half-truths.

The next part of the ritual, a thanksgiving, can be tearfully poignant but it is vital to the balance you are trying to achieve. Even if the relationship ended acrimoniously, the time and love you invested in it were not wasted. By thanking each other for what the association brought you, that gift of yourselves is validated. Where the relationship ended by mutual consent because its life force had been expended, the giving of thanks is also helpful because it acknowledges the need to seal off a completed cycle. Through understanding how it has enriched you, you can make full use of it and carry into the next cycle only what will be helpful.

For some people this thanksgiving can be expressed in a few words – even silent ones. Others may prefer to exteriorize it through, for instance, a dance or by building an imaginary bonfire in the centre of their circle.

The section of the ritual dealing with forgiveness is of great significance because feelings of resentment and hatred are as binding and powerful as those of love, and self-forgiveness is as important as the forgiving of others. This is particularly true in the area of relationships, where self-blame can do untold damage for many years – especially if it is unjustified. So even if you don't yet feel ready to start forgiving your ex-partner, use this section of the ritual for the self-forgiveness which can be so deeply releasing and healing.

In either case, if he is not present, use his photograph for your dialogue. However difficult it may be to look into his eyes, doing so will help make the experience significant.

To complete the ritual, prepare now to move away from the old situation as definitively as is possible at present. Turn your two chairs back to back as far apart from each other as feels comfortable. Sit on them in silence for a few minutes.

Then stand for a moment facing each other. Say, either aloud or to yourself some words of farewell which explicitly recognize that this part of your life is over.

If the chakras are a reality to you, at this point you could go through a short ceremony to cut the ties which still join you at the solar plexus and possibly also the sacral (see p. 19 for a description of this ritual). End the ceremony by sealing your own chakras and those of the other person with a cross within a circle of light. If a good and unpossessive heart connection still exists between you, spend a moment or two strengthening it.

Move a few steps further towards the exit of the circle and, again facing each other, say aloud the words: 'You are now my EX-husband/wife/partner.'

Turn your backs on each other and leave the room, preferably by different doors, or at least at different times.

Clear the circle.

Should you want to repeat this ritual in a year or two when you have had time to step back, to grow and to meet new people, more will almost certainly emerge. The divorce can become more complete. But do not force anything. Just remain receptive to what happens in your life.

Preparation 🖊️

Make a circle of stones.

Sweep the area.

Place two chairs side by side, touching each other.

Place another chair to the side if an observer is to be present.

Checklist 🖊️

If you are alone, carry in with you a photograph, symbol or card bearing your ex-partner's name and place it on the second chair.

Each of you in turn speaks the vows undertaken at the time of marriage (if any).

Place your chairs opposite each other.

State what positive contributions you made to the partnership.

He (or you on his behalf) states what positive contributions he made.

You state what negative contributions you made to the partnership.

He (or you on his behalf), states what negative contributions he made.

Give thanks.

Forgive him and yourself.

Turn your chairs back to back and move them apart.

Sit down in silence for a few minutes.

Stand facing each other and say farewell.

If so desired, perform the ceremony for cutting the ties (see p. 19).

Declare that you are now an EX-husband/wife/partner.

Turn your backs on each other and leave the room separately.

MENOPAUSE

Many women dread the menopause because they see it primarily as a time of loss. But there are many positive aspects to this phase of a woman's life which can emerge if she will only highlight them.

As a fundamental difference exists for the purposes of this ritual between those women who have borne children and those who haven't (either voluntarily or involuntarily) and again between those who have been a natural mother or an adoptive or foster mother, adaptations for each category will be suggested. The basic format, however, remains the same for all the groups.

The Ritual

First, divide the room in two and place a single chair on the dividing line.

Starting with those women who have raised a child of their own, take three symbols or photographs to represent the three phases of their life: the young girl, the mother and the older woman. Place them in a row on the floor. From your secure position on your chair in the here and now, reach out mentally to yourself as a girl, ascribing to her a colour, a texture, an energy or anything that will bring her to life for you. Take as long as you need. Really try to define this phase of your life so that you know in every fibre of your being what it was like to be a young girl. Recall both your shyness and your excitement about life. Remember your relationship with your body. Did you feel it was clumsy and gawky, or were you at peace with yourself? Did you express your femininity, or were you a tomboy? Really re-experience your first period and your first love affair. Don't be shy with yourself, and don't spare yourself the unpleasant memories from that time of your life. It is particularly important at this time of transition that the past should not be idealized. This could be detrimental to the future.

As you move on to your mother symbol, try to draw up all your memories connected with motherhood: your pregnancies, the births, the feeding of the babies, the raising of the children, their education, their marriages. These will include pain as well as joy, but this is no time to envelop the facts in a rosy haze. Only by looking them fearlessly in the eye can you cope creatively with this shift from the past into the future.

Moving into the unknown territory of the older woman you will, it is hoped, experience a gentler, less red-coloured atmosphere, a new freedom, a sense that you can now take more time for yourself and be less used up by others. With your children probably by now independent, the hurly-burly of a full house need no longer be yours unless you yourself choose it. Your commitments to social functions and committees can now also be a question of choice rather than of 'oughts' and 'shoulds'. If you have been a working mother, you will most likely be reaching the moment when you can afford not to work unless you want to. You can begin to do all those things for which you never had time. As your emphasis shifts from doing to being, it will be on harmony that you focus.

When you have explored your three phases as deeply as you can for the moment, pick up your symbol for the older woman and sit with it on your lap. Try to make friends with her, even grow to love her. This is you from now on. When you feel ready, get up and place the symbol in the second part of the room. If you would like to light a candle to the years ahead, do so. Then leave the room.

Dismantle the ritual.

The above format can be used by all groups of women; they need only make small adaptations in order to fulfil their specific needs.

Those women who have adopted or fostered a child need to substitute for memories of early babyhood their satisfaction in having given a home to someone who would otherwise have known only institutional life.

For women who have chosen not to have a child, the menopause can sometimes elicit a sense of regret. Although their marriages or their careers, or both, have amply compensated for not having children, they may nevertheless experience a slight nostalgia as they reach the end of their child-bearing years. Let this nostalgia become part of the clear assessment you now make of your middle years as wife, businesswoman, professional woman, creative woman or whatever label applies to you at this time. You want to know exactly what it is that you are bringing forward into your older woman phase.

For women who have yearned for children but been unable to have them, the menopause can be a time of great sadness, even bitterness. As hope is finally relinquished, it is very difficult for them not to feel left to one side and not to be jealous of other women's joy in their children. They may even bear the added burden of considering their life a failure because of their inability to bear children. It is essential for these women to produce in the ritual symbols for *everything* they have achieved in their mid-years, thus giving them maximum importance both in their own eyes and in those of others.

Spinsters for whom the dividing line between their maidenhood and womanhood is less well defined should identify the moment when the second phase of their life started. Putting aside any regrets or sense of failure is probably one of their most important tasks at this point. If such feelings are dragged behind them into the third phase of their life, little satisfaction or joy can be expected from it.

Preparation

Divide the room into two parts.

Place a chair on the dividing line.

Prepare three symbols for maidenhood, motherhood and wise older woman, or for maidenhood, wife/career woman and wise older woman.

Have a candle ready if desired.

Checklist

Sit on the chair with the three symbols in front of you.

Consider all aspects of your girlhood.

Consider all aspects of your motherhood or yourself as a wife or career woman.

Consider all aspects of the wise older woman.

Pick up symbol no. 3 and sit with it on your lap.

Place it in the second part of the room.

Light a candle beside it if you like.

Leave the room.

Undo the ritual.

BECOMING A
PARENT-IN-LAW

Many adjustments and compromises need to be made when you become a parent-in-law. The following ritual is designed to help you assess what the role entails. It has been planned to be done by either one or both prospective parents-in-law.

The Ritual

Whether the ritual is for a son or a daughter, the layout of the room is the same. The differences lie in the symbols and the points stressed.

Place one chair (two if both in-laws are participating) in the centre of the room with four other chairs standing in line in front of it. During the first part of the ritual you sit alone on this single chair, as a separate individual, needing your own space and existing in your own right. In front of you is a symbol which is very personally yours. It attaches you to no relationship, certainly not to parenthood.

The first part of the ritual is introspective and consists of subtly shifting your relationship towards your son or daughter so that you can gladly accept the fact that 'your child' is now to become a separate householder with his or her central focus away from your home. Even if he or she has been living alone during the past years or is marrying a well-established live-in partner, this delicate but significant shift is necessary. It does not consist of self-abnegation, which leads to deep resentment; nor does it entail pretending that everything is perfect. A

realistic acceptance of this new member of the family and
of your offspring's new circumstances is all that is
required of you. If successful, it can lead to an even richer
relationship between you.

This definition and acceptance of a new set of
boundaries which should ideally be made by both
generations, is not a simple process. Much that would
have been taken for granted a few years ago cannot be so
any longer. Individual attitudes have to be tested. Family
behaviour has also become less regimented, so that more
radical adjustments now have to be made to the
expectations of the two families.

Another way in which you can recognize the young
couple's uniqueness is by not making comparisons
between your circumstances and theirs. Your expectations and personal experience of marriage will have been
very different from their reality. Give them all the room
they need to develop as a couple without making them
carry your relived joys and sorrows as well.

When you are ready, move on to the next part of the
ritual, remembering that a creative inner process will
have been set in motion by your having become conscious of what you want to achieve through this ritual.
Further work can be done later.

Starting with the marriage of a son, turn your chair
towards his, which is the first one on the left. On it stands
a photograph of him. Try to see him first as your son, and
then as though he were not your son. Honour what he has
achieved at school, in his job, in his relationships.
Consider his ambitions and ideals.

Now draw a circle around your chair and his, using a
piece of string. That circle encapsulates those portions of
your lives which have until now overlapped. When you
feel certain of the modifications now necessary, remove
the string and form a new circle to represent the future
area of exchange between you. As the generation gap

narrows with marriage, parent and son can meet on an adult basis.

Remove the string.

Now turn towards your daughter-in-law's chair, which is the fourth one in the line. There too you have placed a photograph. Express to it how you feel about her as an individual quite separate from your son. Try to see her as a whole person, emphasizing to yourself all that you most like and respect about her as an individual. It is important to establish this image so that neither you nor she ever feels that she is a mere appendage to your son.

Now draw the string in a circle around your two chairs. Consider yourself in your new relationship. How can you make your daughter-in-law feel really welcome into your family? How can you help her transition into married life? What have you to give each other as individuals?

Remove the string.

Take away the two chairs you have used so far.

On the two remaining central chairs place the white flowers or whatever symbol you have chosen for their marriage. Repeat with the couple, as you did with the two individuals, the process of seeing them dispassionately but lovingly. Try to get a real sense of their weaknesses and strengths, their relationship to one another, and their soul attachment. While doing this, set aside the anxieties of a parent. Don't let any jealousy or envy tinge your views.

Draw a circle around your chair and theirs. Explore this new triangle which has been formed; acknowledge the new dynamic which has been created. How well this triangle works will depend largely on you, particularly if you are a mother-in-law. This power held by the mother-in-law is one of the reasons why she is so feared, at times shunned. As you consider this new shape within the family, think carefully about your relationship to possessiveness, interference and domination. Do you want or need to be the most important person in a triangle? Do you understand creative compromise?

Remove the string and sit quietly for a while. If you wish, end the ritual with a thanksgiving.

A daughter's marriage tends to evoke in a parent a different set of fears and needs for adjustment. Will the new husband look after her properly? Will his ideas and way of life predominate so entirely that the girl becomes alienated from her own family? Such fears can easily lead to the rapid and effective destruction of what the parents most desire: a happy relationship with their son-in-law.

As you enact the ritual for a daughter and her new husband, following the above pattern, try to intuit what would be acceptable or unacceptable to your son-in-law and his family. Although families vary radically in their interpretations of interference or support, especially where cross-cultural marriages are concerned, this issue is probably the most devastating bone of contention for all in-laws, especially those with daughters.

As a parent-in-law you have no rights. You can only work hard to establish a relationship which will make you a welcome guest in the couple's home.

When you have gone as far as you can for the moment, leave the room.

Undo the ritual.

Preparation

Put out one chair (two if both in-laws are taking part) with four other chairs in front of it.

Choose a symbol for you as an individual.

Place on the first of the four chairs a photograph of your son or daughter and on the fourth chair a photograph of your daughter-in-law or son-in-law.

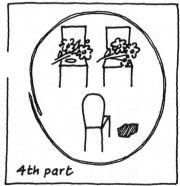

Settings for parent-in-law ritual

Have ready your symbol for the marriage and a length of string.

Checklist 🖋️

Sit on the single chair with your personal symbol beside you.

Consider the shifts and new boundaries needed in your relationship with your son or daughter.

Form a circle with the string around your son (or daughter) and yourself. Consider how your lives have until now interconnected.

Remove the circle of string.

Form another one to contain your subtly new relationship with your son or daughter.

Remove the circle.

Consider your prospective daughter-in-law or son-in-law as a separate person.

Form a circle around you and the fourth chair.

Contemplate your relationship with her or him once she or he has become your daughter (or son)-in-law.

Remove the circle.

Take away chairs numbers one and four and place on the two remaining chairs your symbol for their marriage.

Consider the couple as dispassionately as you can.

Draw a circle around the three chairs.

Explore this new territory.

Remove the circle.

Give thanks.

Leave the room.

Undo the ritual.

RETIREMENT

In a society where work and careers are given excessive importance, retirement is often viewed as the end of a person's significant life. It is felt to herald a period of gradual disintegration during which that person becomes an increasing anxiety to others. Few people, especially men, take seriously the plans they make for their retirement years – or expect anyone else to do so. Western society has so little regard for older people that they are made to feel that their activities are of no more significance than the games of children. Only money-producing work is truly valued in most of our civilization, to such an extent that many of us define ourselves by our job. 'I am a doctor . . . a writer . . . a farmer,' we say. Not, 'I am a person who loves sailing and reading and being with my family.' No wonder that retirement is officially rated as one of the stress factors most conducive to serious illness.

How can we help to defuse this potentially dangerous, at best dreary, situation? How can we make ourselves look forward to retirement as the beginning of an exciting and satisfactory phase of our life when we are entitled – often for the first time – to consider our own needs rather than those of others.

It is a question of adjustment. There is nothing wrong in shifting one's emphasis from doing to being, or in becoming more inward-looking. To relate differently to all questions of power and responsibility, to find new interests and to value a sense of tranquillity are all activities appropriate to that time of life, and should be enjoyed. This may well be the only period of our life which we can actively shape – something we were never able to do as young people or when bound to the wheel of job/advancement/pension-earning.

Strong fear factors can emerge during this time and be very hard to eradicate. Our economic situation, for instance, could make the future feel uncertain. Our health could worry us. The desire not to be an increasing burden on our family or neighbours could also be dominant. But whatever these difficulties, if our fundamental attitude towards our post-retirement years is one of curiosity and optimism, even these fears will have less power.

The Ritual

Arrange the room so that the left half of it represents your working life and the right half your future life. Between them stand a chair. In each section place the appropriate symbols. Those you choose for your retirement need particularly careful thought as they will define your view of yourself during the coming years. There could, for instance, be a notebook ready for the committees on which you will serve; a gardening tool or golf clubs or a chess set could remind you of the more leisurely pace you will now be able to enjoy. Photographs of family and friends would assure you of the extra time now available for people. Any creative talent you wish to encourage could be represented by a paintbrush or musical instrument.

Friends who are helping you with this ritual can start on whichever side of the room they want to be. If someone was part of your working life and will now continue to see you as a friend, he may prefer to start out on the left-hand side and later move with you to the right in order to indicate the new, less formal way in which you will now relate to each other.

Go to the left-hand section of the room and address

your working life symbols. If you were happy in your job, thank them for all the knowledge and pleasure they have given you. If it was unsatisfactory, acknowledge whatever advantages it brought and try to dismiss its disadvantages so that they cannot become a kernel of bitterness. If your working life has been so grim that you are 100 per cent delighted to be free of it, admit to that fact but don't get stuck on it. It's gone, and better things are coming.

When you have finished this part of the ritual, pack these symbols into a suitable container and put them to one side for storing or destroying later. While you are doing this, register deeply in your being that you are no longer trapped into your job, nor are you primarily defined by it. You are the sum total of all you have done and been, which includes far more than you as a money-earner.

Move now to the central chair, in which you are in a state of transition. From it, look carefully at your symbols for the coming years. Imbue them with all the hope you feel.

Walk into the retirement area and invite into it – whether they are present or not – all those with whom you want to share your new cycle. If you wish, address them individually.

Now take a moment to consider this major step of detaching yourself from a certain aspect of Earth life. Far from being frightening, it can be seen as a step of great importance. If you have successfully shed old behaviour and outdated thought patterns, future detachments – and eventually the final one – will be not only easier but more positive.

Leave the room, followed by the other participants.
Undo the ritual.

Preparation ✐

Divide the room into a working life area and a retirement area, with a single chair as the dividing line.

Place in them the symbols and photographs representing each phase of your life.

Provide a container into which to pack your working life symbols.

Checklist ✐

Your family and friends go to whichever section they want to start in.

You go to the working life area and address its symbols.

Pack the latter into the container.

Consider your new position.

Sit down on the central chair and contemplate your retirement symbols.

Move into the retirement area and address those who will participate in it with you.

Consider the element of detachment which there has been in this ritual, and the further detachment for which it has prepared you.

Leave the room, followed by your friends.

Undo the ritual.

DEATH 1

Funerals, like christenings and weddings in our Western society, are nearly always conducted according to the precepts of a formal religion. But for many people the finality of a Christian or Jewish burial is unsatisfactory because it contradicts their belief that we return many times to Earth: that this life is only one bead on the necklace of our total life. If this is so, then death is not only a temporary condition, it is one we have experienced many times. We are certain, therefore, at a level far beyond our conscious thinking, that the place to which we go between lives is where we find the harmony and love constantly sought on Earth. It is the restriction and pain of Earth life which are the difficult things to support.

For those who are convinced of this, the whole tone of a ritual for death can be shifted. While mourning the loss of a beloved companion we can at the same time be celebrating his release into a period of reunion with the Source and with his many soul companions.

In this ritual, then, you are saying only a temporary goodbye; the emphasis is on celebrating what that soul has accomplished on all levels during his earthly sojourn. You are also affirming the presence at your ritual of all those souls, incarnate and discarnate, who have been closely linked with the dead person in this and other lifetimes. They will be helping you in every way and will be preparing his welcome on the other side, where they will share with him their Earth experience.

In order to assist the deceased in passing from Earth consciousness into wider consciousness, you and all those participating in the ritual must first reach a point of stability within yourselves from which this help can be given. In preparation, each of you needs to express your grief, preferably alone, and if possible out of doors. The cycles of life and death are more easily contacted in the presence of trees and plants, the earth and sky. The closer you were to the person who has died, especially if the death was unexpected, the more time you will need. Any attempt to hasten or cut short this, or any other stage of your mourning, will only result in it requiring even more time and attention later on. It is a process which needs to seep through your whole body and psyche.

If you feel the need to formalize this preparation time, mark out a small circle with stones. Place within it whatever objects you associate with the dead person. A photograph or a present he has given you could also be helpful. Then step into the circle, leaving all other considerations behind you. You two are alone and perfectly safe here: anything can be said or acted out, any regrets or failures expressed, any unspoken thanks given. If, on the other hand, you simply want to sit quietly thinking of the person, that too is perfectly acceptable. The important thing is that your thoughts reach a degree of serenity from which you can help your relative or friend during the ritual.

Remember always that someone's death does not end your shared journey. The giving or receiving of forgiveness can, for instance, continue. With this in mind, do not confine yourself to carrying out this ritual only for people you have loved. Those with whom you have had the most difficult relationships are sometimes the ones for whom it would be most beneficial – both for yourself and for them.

The main ceremony should take place at some time within three days of the death, its object being to help the process by which the spirit returns to its true home. This process takes three days and consists of relinquishing all earthly attachments and disintegrating the various 'bodies' with which it was clothed for its earthly visit.

The Ritual

Create a circle of stones and flowers and step into it, either alone or with friends.

Go into a meditative state with your eyes shut. Imagine a spiral circling ever upwards, bearing on it the physical, etheric, astral and mental bodies which are now no longer needed (see diagram on p.16). Visualize the air elementals joining with you to help transmute these bodies so that they return to a state of pure energy. As the spiral moves ever upwards, the soul is finally released to soar towards the Source.

When you feel that you have done as much as you can, put a cross within a circle of light on to the spiral and let it gently fade away. Open your eyes. When all of you have ended your visualization, join hands and chant the Buddhist Om three times. (To do this, sound the word Om on whatever note you prefer and allow it to last as long as is comfortable for you.) This will harmonize all that you have done, and carry it out into the world.

Leave the circle.

Dismantle it.

Preparation

Reach as great a degree of serenity as you can.

Create a circle of stones and flowers.

Checklist

Stand in a circle within the circle of stones.

Visualize a spiral taking away the various bodies of the
deceased.

Visualize the air elementals helping you.

Chant three Oms.

Leave the circle.

Dismantle it.

DEATH 2

Church funerals can be highly unsatisfactory and even anger-provoking to those who cannot wholeheartedly endorse the teachings of the Christian or other Churches. At a time of grief, this is a great pity. We need to say our goodbyes in peace and in a way that feels complete for both parties involved.

The ritual proposed here is very adaptable and could be carried out either in addition to a traditional funeral or on a separate occasion. It can be performed alone or with friends.

One of the most distressing features of a church funeral is the feeling of finality created by the whole concept of 'ashes to ashes and dust to dust'. The immense peace and joy of being at one with the Godhead is barely mentioned. The promise of a future reunion with loved ones is not emphasized enough. We are also so fervently bidden to identify the dead person with his body ('man who is born of woman', etc.) that it is generally forgotten that we are *not* our bodies. We are an immortal droplet of the divine which, in descending to the dense atmosphere of Earth, was forced to take on for a while a mortal body. The fact that this has ceased to exist is very sad for those who are left behind, but it is not sad for the soul, which has returned to that state of bliss spoken of by mystics throughout all times.

We are not, then, at a funeral to mourn the dissolution of a physical person. We are there to help his soul pass safely and peacefully into another realm of consciousness where he will continue, in a different mode, on his path. For this our encouragement and strength can be a great help.

The Ritual

This ceremony should take place no sooner than three days after the death. This is the period of time needed for the soul to free itself of its physical body.

If at all possible, choose for your ritual the place at which you feel the deceased would most like to bid his farewell to the world.

For this ceremony you need two symbols. The one for his body should be something that will burn easily, such as a paper flower in his favourite colour. The one used for his soul must on the contrary be indestructible, such as a stone or crystal. If you feel that something is still lacking, you could use the additional symbol of a star or a sun to serve as a reminder that our souls belong for all eternity to the whole infinite universe.

Place four candles in a square, at the centre of which you put his symbols and anything which represents for you his gifts to the world. In addition to these, you could also make a short list of his qualities and personality traits.

Light the candles.

Standing in a circle within the square, pass the symbol for his body slowly around the circle. Say good-bye to him, one by one, aloud or in silence. When you have finished, set fire to the symbol, letting it burn away completely.

Then, in silence, pass around the symbol for his soul. It is this which is left amongst you, as alive and vital as ever. After a moment, take a step backwards in acknowledgement of the soul's need to be released from all earthly concerns.

Blow out the candles and leave the square, taking the candles with you.

The symbol(s) should be left for a few minutes alone.

Then one person picks them up and you go together to consign them with great reverence into whatever place you feel he would be most at home.

Singing a song or a hymn or chanting the Om at the end of this ceremony can bring great release and even joy.

Preparation

Have ready a container in which to burn the symbol for the deceased's body.

Form a square with four candles.

Place the symbols in the centre of the square.

Decorate the square with flowers.

Checklist

Light the candles.

Form a circle within the square.

Pass around the symbol for his body, each of you bidding him farewell.

Burn that symbol in a container.

Pass around the symbol for his soul and then put it back in the centre.

Take a step backwards.

Blow out the candles.

Leave the space for a few minutes, taking the candles with you.

One person picks up the symbol(s) for his soul and together you consign it (them) to a chosen place.

Sing a hymn or song, or sound the Om.

RITUALS FOR YOUR SPIRITUAL JOURNEY

INTRODUCTION
TO THE
RITUALS

This group of rituals is concerned with the individual's spiritual development. In all the situations envisaged here, it is assumed that something, possibly not consciously defined, is preventing the person from attaining his potential. This chapter is for people who have already made a partial spiritual commitment and are now ready to dissolve their particular obstacle in order to come into their full strength.

None of these rituals should be embarked on lightly. They will considerably alter your relationship with yourself and everything around you.

It is assumed that if you are ready for them you will already have met suitable people with whom to perform them. By asking for this help, you will in turn be helping your friends towards their own next stage of development.

INCARNATION 1

An astonishing number of people are walking our planet almost despite themselves. The reasons behind their reluctance to be here are varied, but its consequences are always disastrous. Feeling that they do not really belong on Earth, they cannot fully commit themselves to any situation or relationship. Their discontent goes far beyond any normal state of restlessness; they are, in fact, never whole. Either consciously or subconsciously recognizing themselves as unable to cope with the demands and pain of everyday life, they protect themselves by leaving their lower chakras under-developed. In other words, they are not 'grounded'. Skimming lightly over reality, with their higher chakras hyper-active and their heads in the clouds, they are constantly drawn towards those realms for which they so yearn.

For anyone who wants to alter this unsatisfactory sitution, it is important first of all to understand why you cannot slot wholeheartedly into life. Before descending to Earth you were without doubt aware of this incarnation's general pattern. If sufficiently evolved, you will even have helped your guides choose what you were prepared to handle during this lifetime. So you have not been taken by surprise. When actually faced with the difficulties, fears and sadnesses of this life, however, you may quite understandably have been so appalled that you decided to remain as remote as possible from your body and life. Another possibility is that, as you re-entered Earth's vibrations and reconnected with the memory of excessive suffering in a past life or lives, this proved so distressing that you folded in on yourself.

Whether our reluctance to incarnate fully stems from anticipated or remembered fears and sadness, the message offered through a ritual must, in order to have any practical effect, be both reassuring and encouraging. For this we need to listen to the repeated messages from the Higher Worlds. Over and over again they have pledged their word: however daunting, nothing will be required of us that is beyond our strength. This knowledge is not easy to rekindle in people who have the best reasons for blocking it off. Those who need this ritual will inevitably be both sensitive and wounded. Only great compassion and patience will finally coax them fully on to Earth.

The following ritual has a strong North American Indian quality, and should be undertaken only if you feel an affinity with the native American cultures. It is particularly designed for people who feel that loneliness and detachment are preferable to the possible pain and sadness of commitment. Although it may seem difficult to involve others in such a ritual, they do need to be there; their presence asserts that the person has taken the first step in accepting people as part of his world, as possible instruments of his learning.

The Ritual

The layout consists of a circle of twelve pebbles, each one representing a sign of the Zodiac. The full circle they form symbolizes the world into which you are at last choosing to incarnate. These pebbles should be laid out clockwise in the correct astrological order starting at the south-west of the circle with your own Sun sign. (In the diagram on p. 86 Cancer has been used.) The only break in this pattern is that the stone representing your Ascendant should be placed at the south-east of the circle, and the one which would normally be there replaces the Ascendant. (The Ascendant is also known as the 'rising sign' and can be established for you by an astrologer who is given your date, place and time of birth. In the diagram, Sagittarius is used as the Ascendant.) Because you entered the world at a certain time of the year, manifesting certain patterns connected with that Sun sign, your pathway of entrance into the circle should be to the left of your birthstone. Equally personal to you is your Ascendant sign, whose characteristics will colour your approach to the world. Your exit pathway from the circle will therefore be to the left of your Ascendant stone. In order to emphasize your special contact with these two energies, touch these two stones lightly as you enter and leave the circle.

In the centre of the circle build a small mound of earth

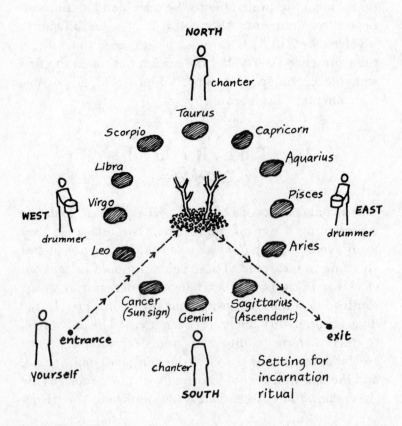

Setting for incarnation ritual

and plant in it two sticks or branches representing your two favourite trees. Together they symbolize the beauty and stability of the natural world.

At each of the circle's cardinal points place one of your four helpers, the chanters at the north and south, the drummers in the east and west. The choice of position should be made with care, because in all North Amercian Indian ritual the points of the compass have deep significance. The energies of each helper should coincide as closely as possible with the traditional energies and gifts of the four directions.

From the north come the winds that bring discipline and order; from the south flow the tenderness and ful-filment of summer. The east brings us new beginnings and the freshness of youth; while in the west lies the wisdom which feeds our constant rebirth. Working as a team with movement and sound, your four helpers are there to call you into the safety of the circle and welcome you to your special place on planet Earth.

The ritual opens with you standing, barefoot, to the south-west of the circle. Since it is from the east that new beginnings come, it is that drummer who makes the first movement – a very slow rocking from one foot to another. His counterpart in the west responds with the same movement. By this definition of the sun's daily passage from east to west, its presence as a spiritual being has been evoked for the ritual. The rhythmic foot-shuffling can now be accompanied by a very gentle drumming from the east. Movement has drawn out sound, which is that of the heartbeat of the universe. It is lightly picked up by the drummer in the west. As the two gain strength, their feet stamp more persistently.

As soon as the chanters intuit that the time is right, the northern one begins calling. Although his song is demanding, his symbol of the Eagle is also the bearer of far vision and courage, so that as that section of the circle joins with the ritual you feel your backbone strengthen. The world may be hard, but it is where you belong and where you will shortly go – of your own free will. As the gentler sound of the south responds, the Being of the Moon is evoked. Back and forth the chanting goes, the drumming now softened.

'It is safe,' the first voice murmurs to you.

'This is home,' another affirms.

'You are secure,' calls the other.

'We welcome you,' comes the reply.

As simply as possible, expressing complete reassurance and acceptance, the message is given over and over again.

When you know in the deepest part of yourself that the world is truly an acceptable place for you to enter, go forward at your own pace. Do not be bound by the rhythm of the drums or the chanting; simply be aware of their sound which calls, even coaxes, but never intrudes. The sorrow and loneliness in which you have spent so much of your life cannot be dispelled in a few moments.

Move unhurriedly into the circle, remembering to make contact with your birthstone as you pass it. When you reach the mound of earth, wriggle your feet deeply into it facing south. Touch your two trees. You are now really and truly on Earth. Gradually the drums and chanting die down.

When you are ready, leave the circle in silence, touching your Ascendant stone as you go to affirm your acceptance of whatever pattern of behaviour you have chosen for this lifetime.

The helpers follow you out of the circle in the following order: eastern drummer, southern chanter, western drummer, northern chanter.

Leave the room.

Undo the ritual.

Preparation 🖋🍃

Obtain two drums, or improvise with other suitable objects.

Form a circle with twelve stones representing the signs of the Zodiac; follow the order given above.

Place their name cards beside them.

Build a small mound of earth in the centre of the circle.

Plant two sticks or branches in the mound and give them the names of your two favourite trees.

Checklist 🖋🍃

Two chanters stand at the north and south.

Two drummers stand at the east and west.

You stand barefoot with your Sun sign on your right.

The eastern drummer rocks gently from one foot to another.

The western drummer responds with the same movement.

The eastern drummer beats his drum gently.

The western drummer responds and both of them start stamping.

The northern chanter starts calling.

The southern chanter responds.

Enter the circle, touching your birthstone as you pass it.

Dig your feet well into the earth mound.

Touch each tree.

When you are firmly rooted, the drums increase their volume.

The drumming and chanting die down.

Leave the circle with your Ascendant stone on your right, touching it as you pass.

The eastern drummer, the southern chanter, the western drummer and the northern chanter follow you out of the circle.

Leave the room.

Undo the ritual.

INCARNATION 2

In this second ritual you will also be given a lot of time in which to overcome your reluctance at being on Earth. By participating in each of the animal kingdoms before becoming a human being, it is hoped that you will lose some of your fear of incarnation.

The Ritual

Imagine your room as a beautiful island. Separate it into three sections with cushions. The right-hand area, which you cover with a blue cloth or blanket, represents the sea. Warm and clear, it is an intermediate realm between the heavens from which you have descended and the world to which you now want to belong. The central section of the room is the beach; to the left of it stands a small temple.

This temple can be reached only by imaginary steps winding up a steep cliff; in it can be perceived all your spiritual goals for this lifetime. If going there today seems premature, do not worry. Simply knowing that it exists will add a further dimension to the ceremony and, as with all these rituals, it can be taken a step further later on.

For the same reasons as were given in the first incarnation ritual, it is best to enact your incarnation as part of a group. They may stand together or separately, wherever they feel to be appropriate. Their positions can change for each part of the ritual.

During the first stage of this ceremony you are a seagull, hovering and swooping above this lovely little island. You are still in many ways free: no demands are put on you; very little threatens your comfort and safety.

It is your dependence on the sea for sustenance which gives you your first physical contact with this planet. Explore the air and the sea thoroughly, feeling their inter-relationship. When you are really at ease with them both, pause for a moment.

Now transform yourself into a sea serpent and swim unfettered through the clear water. Everything you need is at hand, feeding you. Enjoy that. When you feel really happy and safe, rest for a little to take stock of your progress.

Next you are to become the reptile of your choice and start experimenting with the element of earth by exploring the beach, knowing that you can retire immediately into the familiar sea should any danger, real or imagined, threaten you. Pause again when this stage is complete.

When you feel certain that you are prepared for a further commitment, turn into whatever four-legged creature you feel closest to and walk about the beach as that animal. Explore the trees and rocks and caves of the cliff face. If at any moment you feel vulnerable, these places will offer you shelter. No demands are being made upon you beyond that of self-preservation. No human fears or sadnesses can touch you. Move about freely, confidently – joyfully.

Pause again, a little longer this time because you are now to take the step into human incarnation. You are to stand upright and become Man. When you feel ready to do so, say aloud and with conviction: 'I am here at last.'

If you can do so comfortably, add to this the statement: 'I am glad to be here. This is where I belong for the coming years.'

If you feel that this is as far as you can go for the moment, leave the room, followed by your helpers.

Undo the ritual.

If, however, you feel able to enact the last stage of the ritual now, move slowly and alone into the temple section of the room, leaving your helpers to give you their support from the beach.

Imagine yourself climbing up the steps cut into the cliff. On reaching the beautiful little white building above the sea, hold up your arms and proclaim your enviable and unique position as that creature who is part of both Heaven and Earth.

Return to the beach.

Leave the room, followed by your helpers.

Undo the ritual.

Should you feel that your life until the present moment has been painfully incomplete because of your half-hearted participation in it, a postscript to this ritual can be added either now or later. Act out, however briefly, the highlights of your life's journey. Doing so in this setting will really anchor your past into the new reality you have created.

Preparation

Separate the room with cushions into three sections:
the temple, the beach and the sea.

Cover the sea section with a blue cloth or blanket.

Ask the helpers to take up whatever positions they find comfortable.

Checklist

Be a seagull, occasionally dipping into the sea.

Pause.

Be a sea serpent.

Pause.

Be a reptile.

Pause.

Be a four-legged creature of your choice.

Pause.

Be yourself as a human.

Express your joy at being incarnated.

Leave the room.

Undo the ritual.

If you want to continue: climb the steps to the temple, leaving your helpers on the beach. Declare yourself a spiritual man.

If you feel the need, enact the highlights of your life's journey in order to anchor it in to your new reality.

TAKING YOUR POWER

Many people who are now ready to stand in their own power are still operating at half-steam. Some of them are unaware of this but others, to whom it is a source of grave frustration, are still unable to make the breakthrough. Why is this? What is holding them back?

Our present period of transition into the Aquarian Age is a time of great crisis when each of us needs our maximum spiritual power. But that power must be sound and be rigorously tested. The Higher Worlds cannot at this point risk us treating it lightly, let alone deliberately abusing it – as we may well have done in the past. If this has been the case, our present lives will almost inevitably include knowledge of what it is like to be at the mercy of others, manipulated for their own ends. We may have been brought up by a stepfather who hated us, or been married to a tyrannical partner. Perhaps we were born crippled or were so poor that our creative talent had to be abandoned in order to earn a living wage at a menial job. It is only after learning, in the deepest part of our being, that power and responsibility equal each other that we will be allowed to assume our true power.

The psychologically undermining effects of these present-life conditions combined with more or less conscious memories from the past – often terrifying ones – may well have sapped our self-confidence. If we know first-hand the consequences of the abuse of power, we will greatly fear a repeat of patterns from the past. Instinct will warn us that a failure this time would be disastrous. As urgently as the Higher Worlds, we ourselves need to know for certain that we are ready to serve unequivocally.

The Ritual

If you do feel ready to step into your power, the following ritual is suggested. It contains certain safeguards so that you can retreat at any moment if you want to.

The design for the ritual is a circle of stones, at the centre of which is placed the symbol for your power. This could be a crystal, a crown, a flame, a quill pen or even a blank space. The important thing is that is should have no limiting quality. It represents the maximum amount of power to which you now have access, but it can always grow if you yourself are willing to grow.

Around the outside of this circle place a scarf for each of the fears or needs or hesitations which are trying to prevent you from accessing your power. As you place each scarf on the floor name it clearly, and define how it is affecting you. Then walk slowly around the entire circle, once more committing yourself to this on-going process.

Your scarves form a magic circle which can be crossed only when you have disposed of the hindrances they represent. After holding a dialogue with each one, drop it into a waste paper basket which you have placed at the entrance of the circle. Hide nothing from yourself which stands between you and your power. If you have any doubts at this point, it is better to stop the ritual rather than to go ahead in a state of fear or confusion.

As you move around the circle keep in strong contact with your power symbol in the centre. Is it calling to you? Do you feel comfortable with it? Do you fully understand to what you are committing yourself? Have you reckoned the cost of everything you must renounce? Are you strong enough physically and psychologically? Keep moving around the circle until these questions are satisfactorily answered.

Now, asking for all the strength and protection available to you, and remembering that you are making a move with long-lasting consequences, step into the circle. Holding your symbol in your hands, dedicate yourself and your life to using your power for the good of mankind.

After a few minutes, walk out of the circle carrying the symbol.

Undo the ritual.

If you repeat this ceremony, each time reassess thoroughly the qualities and force held by each of your remaining scarves and by your symbol for power. Take nothing for granted. Every time you re-enter the circle you will undergo a deep change, not only within yourself but also in your relationship to the world.

Preparation

Form a circle of stones.

Place in the centre the symbol for your power.

Have ready as many scarves as you will need.

Place a waste paper basket at the entrance to the circle.

Checklist

Place the scarves around the outside of the circle, naming each one as you lay it on the floor.

Dialogue with each of the scarves, while keeping contact with the power symbol in the centre.

As you finish each dialogue, place that scarf in the waste paper basket.

Walk slowly around the circle, concentrating hard on your power symbol.

When you feel ready, move into the circle.

Holding your symbol, dedicate your power to service and to the highest good you can attain.

Stand for a few minutes in the centre of the circle.

Leave the circle, holding your symbol.

Undo the ritual site.

RE-ATTACHING YOURSELF TO THE SOURCE

Many people today feel themselves cut off from the Source where they originated; many others do not even believe that such a Source is accessible to us – or even exists. This leaves both groups vulnerable and lonely, a prey to every fear. A ceremony for contacting this being, whatever form it takes for you, can be a very potent instrument in dispelling these fears and restoring the sense of oneness with which you came into the world.

The Ritual

The symbol suggested for the Source in this ritual is that of a united Sun and Moon, a very ancient way of depicting completion. If, for any reason, this is unacceptable to you, find a more abstract symbol. Place it on a table in that part of the circle which faces you as you enter. Lay in front of it a series of wooden or fabric strips to represent the steps you must climb in order to reach the Source. Tie on to your symbol a cotton thread which you will hold in your hand throughout the ceremony.

If there are other participants, they should stand along the left-hand side of the steps. Theirs is a non-active role but their faith and support can contribute enormously.

At the beginning of the ceremony you are standing on the 'lowest' step. The thread attaching you to the Source is now slack, symbolizing your present isolation from it. Explore this thread to see when that natural link was first broken. Or did it atrophy slowly? Test for any flaws that have been created by fear and mistrust. Try to unravel any scepticism which has destroyed your belief in the Source and your link to it. If there seem to be no actual flaws in your thread, but rather a musty feeling as though lack of use had disempowered it, breathe into it all the force you can summon, assuring it that neglect is now a thing of the past.

With the thread between you and the Source taut, move slowly 'up' the steps, pausing whenever you need to. You may well feel that your thread has expanded to the consistency of a rope. Your original assumption has now been confirmed for you: the Source is always fully available unless you yourself break the connection.

After dedicating yourself to it in whatever measure feels right for you now, you and your friends may wish to chant some simple affirmation such as: 'Our link with the Source is real. Our link with the Source is good.'

Walk slowly backwards, keeping your thread constantly taut. It provides the most direct route between you and the Source and must not be allowed to go slack again. When you reach the foot of the 'steps', stand for a moment absorbing the great gift you have been given: an eternal and infinite spring responding to all your needs long before you even know them.

Lay your thread on the floor; you no longer need a physical witness to your oneness with the Source.

Leave the circle.

Disband it.

Preparation

Make a circle.

Place your symbol for the Source on a table in the circle.

Tie to it a thread which is long enough to be held loosely from the foot of the steps.

Place four wooden or fabric strips below the symbol to represent steps. They should be far enough apart so that you can stand comfortably on each of them.

Checklist

Stand at the foot of the steps, holding the thread slackly in your hand.

The other participants stand on the left of the steps.

Sense into your thread.

Breathe force into it. Reassure it.

Climb the steps slowly with your thread taut.

When standing by your symbol, chant if you wish to.

Dedicate yourself to the Source.

Walk slowly backwards with your thread taut.

Stand for a few moments at the foot of the steps, appreciating the gift you have been given.

Lay your thread on the floor.

Leave the circle.

Disband it.

FINDING YOUR
SOUL GROUP

The tales of changelings which run so consistently through folklore and fairy tales seem particularly meaningful to people who have felt, since childhood, that they were born into a completely alien atmosphere. What other explanation could account for the deep malaise they endured until such time as they were able to create their own lifestyle and choose their own companions?

Luckily, there is an alternative to the changeling theory which transforms the loneliness of those early years into a wonderful learning time. It asserts that the circumstances into which we were born are in fact the ideal ones for strengthening our particular weaknesses and helping us to recognize what we really want from our lives. Had we landed at birth into a deliciously congenial atmosphere, this assessment might never have been made and the missing elements never sought.

This ritual assumes that each of us belongs to what is called a soul group. Within this group are all those with whom we have worked most closely since first incarnating on Earth. Because all its members are, generally speaking, following the same ideal, we can at the same time help each other individually and also progress the work of the group. Some of us may still need to pass through an intermediate phase after leaving behind the uncongenial circumstances of our birth, but when we finally set our feet on the path that is common to the group our joy will be boundless – we will finally feel at home.

Few of us have been brought up to believe in the existence of soul companions – those with whom we can become friends at such a deep level that backgrounds, age, tastes and common interests no longer matter. But once we come into contact with these people, and know that being of one mind over the few really important issues is all that counts, our path grows clearer. As this happens, we start meeting more members of our group – it is with them that we start sharing the unfolding of our purpose on Earth.

The Ritual

This ritual is usually best done alone. Form a semi-circle of cushions to represent the group members with whom your soul resonates. Sit in this semi-circle and go in your imagination to whatever place in the world is most sacred to you – preferably a very secluded one such as a clifftop or a mountain meadow. Visualize it in the greatest detail, feeling yourself there, thoroughly centred.

Affirm that the time has come for you to make contact with members of your soul group. Define as closely as you can the purpose of that group, which is almost certainly at some level totally familiar to you, as you will have been working with it for many thousands of years. The more vividly you can feel the common thread between you and those you wish to join, the better will your call go out to them. Try to imagine the already deep ties existing between you and them: the close family relationships you have known; the work done in religious brotherhoods throughout the ages; the joys shared in working together at all kinds of professions and trades. You are one another as closely as human beings can be.

As you send out this call, either in silence or by sounding the note you feel to be that of the group, or by chanting your readiness to join your companions, remember that the spiritual law of attraction is very powerful. If the time is right, your wish will be fulfilled.

When you feel that your call has been thoroughly registered, make your semi-circle into a full circle. Stand in its centre and state the purpose of the group as you now understand it. Stay there for a few minutes in tune with it and the group. The process has now been set in motion.

Leave the circle.

Undo the ritual.

Preparation 🌿

Make a semi-circle of cushions.

Checklist 🌿

Sit within the semi-circle.

Go in your imagination to a sacred and secluded place.

Imagine it in detail.

Call to your soul group.

Intuit the purpose of the group.

Imagine your ties with the group.

Turn the semi-circle into a full circle.

Stand in its centre and state the purpose of the group.

Leave the circle.

Disband the ritual.

RE-MEMBERING
YOURSELF

It is possible to give yourself away to others, or to allow them to draw on you – almost dismember you – to such an extent that virtually nothing remains. This is an extremely unhealthy state of affairs, and the following ritual will help you to reclaim those parts of yourself of which you have been dispossessed, either through excessive self-sacrifice or through deliberate vandalism.

These symbolically missing parts could be either an organ, a sense, or even a psychological function such as discrimination. By someone else claiming one of these as his own, he is compelling you to see life or digest ideas through his eyes and mind rather than through your own – which in a sense no longer exist. You could also have allowed your life force to be taken from you, the most dangerous theft of all.

The Ritual

Place yourself in the centre of a circle of empty chairs. Have on your lap a pencil and a stack of blank cards. Sit there quietly asking to be shown who now controls some vital part of yourself. You may already know some of the answers; others may surprise you. It is highly likely that one of them may be a member of your close family; your boss or a particularly forceful friend could also appear. As you recognize them, write their names on cards and place each one on a chair. For the moment do not try to identify the organ or psychological function that has been taken from you – just identify the people concerned.

By the time they are all present, you may have seen certain patterns emerge which you wish to emphasize by grouping the chairs in a particular way. This can be very helpful.

Now imagine yourself divided into sections as though you were a medical diagram (you may want to have an actual drawing on your lap which would include the chakras and their functions). Starting with your feet, work upwards, ascertaining whether each part of you is intact and well attached to your body. Are your feet making the journey *you* wish to make? Is your liver performing its filtering function as you would choose it to do, or is someone else deciding what should or should not be part of you? Is your heart present, or has someone else taken it over? If so, is it one of your parents or the person with whom you are in love? Are your emotions now so coloured by someone else that you no longer know what you really feel? What about your hearing? Is everything you are told interpreted for you by another person? If so, by whom? A teacher? A relative? And what about your life substance? Has someone simply commandeered it because they need it themselves, or have you given it away in a misguided excess of generosity?

Make a card for each part of your body which seems to be missing and place it on the appropriate chair. Start a dialogue with whichever person you feel has most seriously vandalized you. Explain to him how distressing it is for you to be so incomplete, and how unsuitable it is for him to be interpreting your life or to be drawing on your strength.

He should then be given the chance to explain how this situation has arisen. Listen carefully to this explanation, because it will help you prevent the circumstances recurring. Allow him also to describe what it has been like for him to live so intimately with something which was basically foreign to him. You may be surprised to find how disastrous and muddling it has been for him as well as for you.

Do a small ceremony together in which you retrieve what is rightfully yours. When it is finished, take from his chair the card bearing his name and that of the organ or sense. As his claim on you is renounced, turn his chair to face outwards from the circle.

Repeat this dialogue and ceremony with each of the people concerned.

When this is finished, go and sit in the centre of the circle with the cards in your lap. Welcome back the missing pieces. Affirm that you are now complete and will never again allow yourself to become scattered amongst other people.

Leave the room.

Undo the ritual.

This ritual is one that may well have to be repeated before all the desired results are achieved.

Preparation

Place a chair at the centre of a circle of chairs.

Put on the central chair a pencil, a stack of blank cards and, if you like, a rough drawing or diagram of the human body.

Checklist

Sit in the central chair and sense who is holding some aspect of yourself which needs returning.

Write their names on cards and place one on each chair.

If helpful, rearrange them in groups.

Starting at your feet, sense through your body and find out which parts of it are missing.

As you discover these, write them down on cards and match them up with the names already placed on the chairs.

Dialogue with each person in turn.

Retrieve his card and turn his chair outwards.

When this process is complete, sit in the centre of the circle and welcome back each missing part.

Affirm that this situation will not arise again.

Leave the room.

Undo the ritual.

RITUALS
FOR
TRAUMATIC
EVENTS

INTRODUCTION
TO THE
RITUALS

The rituals in this chapter are for events of either violence or loss of some sort. The immediate and obvious benefit to be derived from rituals such as the ones for rape and abuse is the liberation of one's body through cutting all ties with the violator. The more long-term healing will come through forgiveness, a very important quality. It is the mechanism for freeing our souls from situations which, if left unattended, can fester in us not only for the whole of this lifetime but for many lives to come. Our soul's ultimate goal – however tough this may be – is to reach a state of unconditional loving. Nothing will obstruct this purpose more than the hatred and fear left by violence.

The other theme underlying most of these rituals is our urgent need to reunite ourselves with our bodies, to become more aware of them, to work with them rather than neglecting them or abusing them with alcohol, drugs, overwork, tobacco etc. The alienation of modern Western people from their physical selves, despite all the fuss and bother they expend on them, is disastrous. We tend to regard our bodies as objects of beauty, athletic machines, workhouses, damned nuisances or deteriorating hulks, but hardly ever as the temples of our soul which they rightfully are.

Sadly and wastefully, a traumatic event is often needed in order to focus our attention on this matter. Because a rape, an operation, an abortion or the consequences of child abuse provide this shock, such events can become the opportunities for growth. Slowly a wonderful new mutually beneficial relationship with our body can be formed. By giving it the love and tenderness it needs, we can coax it into becoming a faithful ally and working partner.

All the rituals in this section can help us come to terms with painful events and with grief and loss. They play a valuable part in the healing process.

RAPE

It is not only the fear generated by a rape which is so difficult to dispel, it is also the feelings of violation and dirtiness. The destruction of your trust is another severe problem with which to contend. A lot of time and work are needed before all these can be safely housed in the psyche.

A ritual can be helpful, but only if done at a pace acceptable to you. Deliberately to remember the event will almost certainly be acutely painful; to confront in your imagination the man who has perpetrated it could be a cause of further trauma unless you are properly prepared and well surrounded by whatever help you need. So if you do decide that a ritual could be liberating, assure yourself that you will go only as far as you comfortably can at present. You can always repeat the process later.

With support from friends, you could probably go further than on your own. However, when choosing them remember that a high degree of sensitivity and patience will be required of them. Should you feel them in any way intrusive during the ritual, you would defeat its purpose. They must be people who would not make the slightest gesture to make you feel that you should be advancing more quickly or more confidently; they must also be individuals in front of whom you can express, without embarassment, all your fear and distress.

If you can include amongst the participants a man or men on whose understanding you can rely utterly, this will be enormously healing. If, however, you want only other women present, that is fine. The situation will be confrontational enough without introducing additional difficulties.

This ritual is based on two premises: first, that a man who resorts to rape is to some degree ill and disturbed; second, that the only deep and permanent means of obtaining release is through forgiving the rapist. This idea may appear ridiculously idealistic, but it is nevertheless true that the only infallible means by which to cut all ties with someone is through forgiveness. Hatred binds as effectively as love. Forgiveness does not, however, in any way constitute the condoning of his actions.

Because of the immense resistance which will understandably be set up in you by these almost unreasonable demands on your imagination and heart, a good deal of preparation will be needed before this ritual can be performed. But don't be discouraged. Even if you achieve only part of what you had hoped for, you can repeat the ritual as many times as necessary. This is a major issue and you can only expect to shift out of your pain slowly. The speed at which you do so will depend on many factors. What pain and fear, for instance, were you already carrying in your body at the time of the rape? What earlier patterns were evoked by the event? Did you already think of yourself as a victim, someone to whom dreadful things inevitably happen? What had been your experience of sex before this violence?

Engage, then, with this ritual in an atmosphere of great gentleness towards yourself, remembering always that it is *you* who are setting both its pace and its limits.

This ritual works equally well for a man who has suffered homosexual rape.

The Ritual

This is a ritual which benefits greatly from being enacted outdoors, preferably in a secluded place in the country.

The earth, the trees and running water can help enormously in absorbing your unwanted feelings. If, however, your ritual has to take place indoors, be sure to invite in the four elements. Have the windows open, place a large bowl of water somewhere in the room, bring in as many plants as you can, and place candles in the four corners of the room.

Whether done indoors or outdoors, the layout for this ceremony is very simple. Draw two circles of equal size, each one composed of whatever materials you feel are appropriate.

Only you are allowed inside the first circle; within it you are entirely safe. Place there an object symbolizing the rape itself. This should be made of wood, sand or paper so that it can be easily disposed of in either water or fire.

In the second circle place a symbol for the man. This object may at first reflect the aggression you feel towards him and emanating from him. But as time progresses, or even during the course of the initial ritual, you may want to replace the original symbol with something more gentle. In this circle, the man is safe. Here neither the law, nor you, nor the public can attack him.

If you would like, in addition, a symbol for release through transformation, a stale loaf of bread which can be crumbled out of a window and ultimately eaten by the birds would be suitable.

If you have friends assisting at the ritual, they should form a semi-circle behind the man's circle. If you are alone, replace them with objects representing non-vindictive human beings. These should be made of something soft and natural. It is important that the man should not be isolated.

After lighting the candles, go and stand in your circle with your back to him. Centre yourself. Quieten the whirling sensations in your solar plexus. Declaring that you now want to disempower this event so that it does not overshadow the rest of your life, pick up the object symbolizing the rape and step with it outside your circle. If you are outdoors, bury it under a tree or allow it to be taken away by running water. If you are indoors, burn it in a container or dispose of it in the bowl of water or out of the window. Ask that its enormous destructive energy should be dispersed and transmuted into neutral energy of help to someone else.

If the elementals are realities to you, they could be asked to help in this important task.

Return to your circle, always keeping your back towards the man. If you feel music or some other sound would help, play a tape or beat a drum or sound an Om. Be sure to remain as relaxed and well-centred as possible. Feel yourself held in total safety between the Earth and the heavens.

When you are ready, remembering that both of you are entirely safe within your respective circles, turn and face the man. Imagine him as vividly as you dare and say aloud: 'I am doing my best to forgive you. I know that there were pressures and needs on you which led you to behave as you did. I am doing my best to forgive you.'

Concentrate all your strength on the certainty that forgiveness will lead to your psychic release from him.

This may well be as far as you can go the first time you perform the ritual.

If so, dispose of the man's symbol, undo both circles, blow out the candles and pour away the bowlful of water, consciously releasing all the fear and dirtiness it has absorbed.

If, however, you feel absolutely confident over releasing the man from his circle, continue with the ritual by taking his symbol and placing it on the floor in another part of the room. Stand opposite it, imagining a wide river between you, its fast-flowing water both reassuring and distancing. Call on whatever help you depend on at difficult moments, including that of your guides and higher self. Ask to have the links severed between you and this man. Although these will feel immensely strong because of the intensity of the emotions generated at the time when they were formed, remember that they arose out of a very brief contact. They haven't, therefore, the staying power of long-standing bonds. If not entirely dissolved on this occasion, they should be at a later date. Remain assured that they will not in the meantime regain any of their strength.

As you face each other across the river, imagine yourselves linked at your solar plexus and sacral chakras. These bonds will probably appear as violent red and orange and be very unpleasant in both texture and energy. As you stand looking at them, ask that they shrivel up, losing their life force. Using symbolic scissors, snip the cords where they join to your chakras and his. Make the sign of the cross within a circle of light on each chakra. To the bonds floating away down the river, make whatever gesture of farewell you feel is appropriate.

This exercise can be repeated as often as needed.

Return to your two circles, which now represent your entirely separate lives. Stand there for a moment appreciating this fact.

If you would like to, wash your feet in a second bowl of water, allowing them to represent your entire body.

Undo both the circles, starting with his. Blow out the candles and dispose of the water from the bowl.

Preparation

Put a candle in each corner of the room.

Place a large bowl of water containing sweet-smelling oil somewhere in the room.

Place lots of plants or flowers around the room.

Make available any sources of music that are wanted.

Have available a container in which to burn the symbols.

Form two circles of equal size but made of different materials.

Put the symbol for the rape in one circle.

Put the symbol for the man in the other.

Checklist

Light candles.

If there are helpers, they stand in a semi-circle around his circle.

Go to your circle and stand there with your back to the man.

State your intentions.

Step out of the circle and dispose of your symbol.

Ask for whatever help you feel to be available to you.

Return to your circle, always keeping your back towards the man.

If you like, chant the Om or play some music.

Turn towards the man and speak to him.

If this is the end of your ritual for the moment, dispose of his symbol, blow out the candles, dispose of the water, undo the square and leave the room.

If you continue the ritual:

Do the exercise for cutting the ties that bind.

Wash your feet in a second bowl of water.

Return to your circle, and give thanks.

Dispose of his symbol, blow out the candles, dispose of the water, undo the square and leave the room.

INCEST AND
CHILD ABUSE

The devastating misery, fear and shame provoked by incest and child abuse often come to light only years later, sometimes never. If they do, the physical violation that has been suffered usually seems to take second place to the intense despair of having one's trust shattered. If the child is abused by someone very close to him, as usually happens, he will not only have been physically hurt and betrayed but also deprived of anyone to whom he can turn for help. Either the other adult members of his family will be too afraid to help him, or else for some reason they will be colluding with the abuser. To seek help from a teacher or some other grown-up outside the family would also usually be very difficult, as it would set up all sorts of anxieties and questions of loyalty.

To his feelings of violation and betrayal will have been added the pain of loneliness. Isolated from other children by the secrecy imposed on him and the 'dirtiness' he feels, he will be withdrawn. Living in constant nervous fear, he will fumble his way through childhood, waiting for the moment when he can escape the adult's tyranny.

The wounds left by such experiences are some of the most difficult of all to heal. Yet much can be done, especially if a spiritual ingredient is allowed for. With this in mind, the ritual breaks down into four sections: (1) an acceptance of the situation as it is; (2) as great a forgiveness of the violator as possible – without in any way condoning his actions; (3) a disassociation from the abuse; and (4) a moving beyond it so that all life is no longer dominated by the experience.

For those who are still bound by secrecy about the

past, this ceremony can be performed alone. By exteriorizing their experience within the safe demarcations of a ritual, they may at last be able to share the past. For those who have moved beyond secrecy, doing this ritual with a trusted friend could affirm their tremendous need to deal with the abuse at a very deep level.

Whether you perform this ritual alone or with someone, you should *never* take it further than the point at which you feel entirely safe. If your memories become intolerable, stop. You can perfectly well deal with them slowly, at later stages.

If the ritual is cut short, be sure to finish it off according to the instructions for the ending. Otherwise you will be left tied to the past even more compulsively than before.

This ritual works equally well whether the abuser was a man or a woman.

The Ritual

Form a square with four candles and place in it two chairs, one for yourself and one opposite you for the absent adult. In front of the latter stand a photograph or symbol of him. Beside the third candle put a bowl of water. Outside the square place the chairs needed by your witnesses, if you want any. They should already be seated when the ritual starts.

Stand for a few moments outside the room, making certain that you are well centred and not overcome by anger or resentment, which would nullify anything you could achieve. Allow all the compassion you can summon to enter your heart, making sure you include the adult in question as well as the child of former years. Breathe deeply and regularly to help calm any anxiety you feel.

As you enter the ritual room say to yourself, preferably aloud, 'I am now a grown-up who cannot be harmed in this way. I am now safe. I come here to put to rest these events from the past, but as I am no longer a child, I am in no danger.'

Now light the four candles, asking them to form a protective perimeter so that whatever happens within this square will be contained and beneficial to both you and the abuser. For the next few minutes stand looking down at his photograph or symbol. From your new position of strength, he will be divested of his former power over you. Summon all the acceptance you can. Without it no progress will be made. This event *has* happened, and the only power you have over the events is to accept them, forgive them and then release them. Try to envisage the adult's higher self, so that with its help you can move beyond the personality whose despicable actions have blurred your life.

Repeat softly, over and over again, 'It is healing that he needs, not hatred. Healing, not hatred. Acceptance, acceptance, acceptance.'

Call up all the available strength from within yourself and forgive as deeply as you can. Place in front of the first candle your symbol for forgiveness.

If you cannot now go further with this ritual, don't worry. The processes of acceptance and forgiveness will have been set in motion and can continue at an almost unconscious level until you feel ready to repeat the ritual. Simply turn the photograph or symbol face downwards. Ask your helpers to leave the room. Dip your hands in the bowl of water, allowing this ritual cleansing to separate you from the events of the past. Remember once again that hatred is as strong a bond as love.

Blow out the candles and leave the room.

Undo the square.

If you wish to continue the ritual, either now or later, this is how you go about it.

If the concepts of reincarnation and karma are either unfamiliar or unacceptable to you, try at this juncture simply to accept that what you have undergone has a meaning and purpose which you may one day understand. If, however, you have already accepted the idea that the soul returns many times to earth in order eventually to achieve perfection, and that it is *you* who chose your present incarnation as necessary to your soul's evolution, you will be looking at the whole question of acceptance and forgiveness from an entirely different point of view. Had the adult concerned agreed with you before your incarnation to be the agent of your learning? If so, what was it that you needed to learn and why? You will have gone a long way towards freeing yourself of much of your resentment and pain if you can now face that question squarely. If you can, try to find a symbol for that new understanding. Write it on a slip of paper and place it beside the second candle.

Cleansing yourself of the past is as necessary to those who have been abused as to those who have been raped. Even after many years people still feel unclean from having their innermost being taken over without their consent. To have had the tenderness and love which should have accompanied the sexual act not only denied them, but replaced by ugly violence, is a supremely difficult fact to cope with. Should you want to cry out against this, once, symbolically, as you were not able to do as a child, do so. But if you fear this would destroy the centred feeling you achieved before entering the room, do it as part of your preparation rather than during the ritual itself.

Scoop up from the bowl a handful of water and sprinkle it over your head. If your gesture is done with real love for yourself, it will cleanse you as truly as a baptism.

As part of this purification of yourself, take off some object of clothing and replace it with a new one.

Write on a card your symbol for cleanliness, such as a fountain or a clear-running stream, and place it beside the third candle and the bowl of water.

It is now time to move a further step forward, so take the abuser's photograph or symbol and his chair out of the room. They no longer have any place here. If you feel that the photo should be burned or the symbol destroyed, and you are certain that they will not be needed for a repetition of the ritual, do so later on.

Return to the room and place beside the fourth candle the card on which you now write your symbol for the start to your new life. A ring, for instance, might serve well as a pledge to the future.

Remain for a few moments in the square, thoroughly absorbing the significance of each of the symbols you have chosen or been given. Feel yourself free and cleansed. Give thanks to all those, incarnate or discarnate, who have helped you.

When you are ready, nod to your helpers to leave the room.

Blow out the candles, and leave yourself.

Undo the ritual site.

Preparation

Form a square with four candles.

Place in it two chairs opposite each other.

In front of one of the chairs place a photo or symbol of the abuser.

Place a bowl of water beside the third candle.

If needed, put chairs outside the square for the helpers.

Have ready a pencil and slips of paper on which to write the symbols you will find during the ritual.

Have ready an article of clothing with which to replace the one you will discard.

Checklist

The helpers go into the room and seat themselves.

Centre yourself before entering the room and affirm your safety.

Light the candles.

Place the abuser's photo or symbol on his chair and dialogue with it.

Place in front of the first candle your symbol for forgiveness.

If you can go no further at this point, ask the helpers to leave the room. Turn the photograph or symbol face downwards on the chair.

Sprinkle yourself with water from the bowl.

Blow out the candles.

Leave the room.

Undo the square.

If you continue:

Place beside the second candle your symbol for the understanding you have achieved.

Cry out, if you wish.

Sprinkle yourself with a handful of water from the bowl.

Replace an old object of clothing with a new one.

Place beside the third candle and the bowl of water your symbol for cleanliness.

Remove his photograph or symbol and his chair from the room. Burn the photo or symbol later on if you like.

Return to the room and place beside the fourth candle your symbol for a start to a new life.

Remain quietly in the square for a few minutes, and give thanks.

Nod to the helpers to leave the room.

Blow out the candles, and leave the room yourself.

Undo the ritual site.

BEFORE UNDERGOING SURGERY

In Atlantis, ancient Egypt and some other cultures, the healers were also priests. The spiritual element, now almost entirely absent in modern Western medicine, was then so much a part of healing that a surgical operation was conducted as a religious ceremony. While one priest/healer withdrew the patient's spirit and held his astral and mental bodies safely (see p. 16), the other priest/healer was able to operate in tranquillity. No suppressants such as our modern anaesthetics were needed. In fact there is strong reason to suppose that in this state the patient was able to direct the operation himself, producing out of his own reactions an immediate diagnosis, an on-going commentary during the surgery itself, and later a post-operative report. Even the most sophisticated modern technology cannot compete with this performance, as it has no access to the patient's psychological or emotional reactions.

Alas, this is now no longer possible – not only because the roles of doctor and priest have long since separated, but also because our bodies have become so dense, and our vibrations so low, that an operation conducted like this would now kill us.

During an operation under anaesthetic, we do not consciously feel any pain. Yet our body remembers and records. Every fear and feeling of violation is inscribed into our muscles and nerve centres. These traumas may not surface for years; indeed, they may never do so unless deliberately called forth in therapy or by a further operation which evokes images of the first one. But they are none the less there, and around them cluster those aches and pains which go far deeper than their physical manifestation.

those aches and pains which go far deeper than their physical manifestation.

In our ritual we will attempt to acknowledge this fact to our body and seek to mitigate the harm done to it by the operation. Although we are not our physical body – at death it will be reabsorbed into the Earth and the essential I will return to the Source – while we are on Earth it is the vehicle for our mind and soul, and as such must be respectfully treated. A surgical operation is one of the best opportunities for experiencing directly this relationship between body and soul.

The Ritual

The main participants are (1) the surgeon, (2) the anaesthetist, (3) your physical, astral and mental bodies, and (4) you as a whole. Helpers are not really needed, although a witness could sit beside your 'operating table' if you so wished.

In the centre of the room place several comfortable cushions to be used as the operating table. On one side of it put some flowers, on the other a familiar object – preferably one that usually stands on your bedside table. This will declare to your body that it is to be lovingly cared for during the operation.

Lie down on your operating table and begin a dialogue with yourself. Tell your body that during the operation the anaesthetist will separate the physical from the astral/mental bodies to prevent you feeling any pain. Be sure that your conscious mind knows that there is no cause for alarm. Remembering that the physical body will be able to communicate its suffering to the unconscious during the operation, reassure your self that, as soon as you can, you will take it through a guided imagery so that these painful memories are released instead of remaining imprinted on the physical body at a subconscious level.

Next speak reassuringly to the astral and mental bodies. Tell them that the anaesthetist is a competent technician who will see that their separation from the physical and their subsequent re-entry into it will be achieved with the minimum of shock. Assure them that you are focusing consciously on this process in advance.

Still lying on your 'operating table', visualize to yourself the surgeon and his anaesthetist. Be sure that you feel completely at ease with both of them. Know that you are no longer a passive figure at this forthcoming event, not simply a number on a hospital trolley. You too will be participating. Your peace of mind and confidence are essential ingredients to the outcome of the operation.

If you are to have an organ removed, this is a good time to bid it goodbye. Thank it for what it has done for you. If it has caused you physical suffering in the past, reassure it that you no longer resent this. If you are having a hysterectomy, for instance, try to find some symbol which you can offer to your body as a substitute for what is being removed.

Now turn to the future and know with absolute conviction, that whatever the outcome of the operation, it is the right one. It is what your higher self has chosen.

When you feel ready, get down from the table and leave the room.

Undo the ritual site.

Preparation

Place a row of comfortable cushions in the centre of the room.

On one side of it put some flowers; on the other side a treasured object.

Checklist

Lie on the 'operating table'.

Dialogue with your physical, astral and mental bodies.

Visualize the surgeon and anaesthetist.

Remind yourself that you will be an active participant in the operation.

If an organ or limb is to be removed, dialogue with it.

Find a symbol for it and ask that it take the place, as far as possible, of the part to be removed.

Affirm that, whatever the outcome of the operation, it will be the right one.

Leave the room.

Undo the ritual site.

ABORTION FROM THE MOTHER'S POINT OF VIEW

Whatever the circumstances which lead a woman to have an abortion, she rarely emerges from the experience unscathed. Even if her first reaction has been relief at safely terminating the pregnancy, she is usually left with feelings that are very hard to assimilate, especially if she has to go through the experience alone. These feelings could include intense loneliness, resentment, guilt, anger at being abandoned, fear of discovery and great sadness at not being able to have the child.

All these emotions will have been intensified by the anxiety and physical fear associated with the operation itself. However commonplace abortion may have become, it is an operation like no other and evokes feelings in the mother which she may not even have suspected. If these are compounded by a sense of guilt, the results can be catastrophic, influencing her life, whether consciously or not, for many years.

In addition to the psychological trauma, there will also be strong physiological factors involved. 'The body remembers' is a saying which carries much truth (see p. 127). The body in this case will have been imprinted by two very distressing facts. First, the abrupt termination of the cycle that had been set in motion will cause it considerable shock. Second, this attack on its feminine self will probably overshadow its future sexual relationships, however unconsciously. If the woman is fortunate, she will find in a present or future affiliation the tenderness which can heal these shocks and scars. If not, she may well need the help of a therapist.

The fact that no official ritual exists for honouring the conception and death of that potential child is perhaps one of the main reasons why an abortion retains for so long such a prominent position in a woman's psyche. Most other occurrences of similar magnitude, whether happy or sad, are marked with some form of ceremony which helps to exteriorize and categorize the feelings evoked. If you have undergone an abortion, either recently or long ago, the following ritual is offered. It can be performed with or without words, and can be acted out as much or as little as you want.

The Ritual

What is presumably most needed by the soul of the aborted child is the loving care it would have received had it reached full term. For most mothers giving that love is their greatest need. The ritual, therefore, begins with you entering a beautifully arranged circle with an imaginary baby in your arms. Sit there in silence, asking Mother Earth to help you give this child the nourishment and love which your life circumstances prevented you doing at the time.

When you feel ready, lay the baby down on a blanket or a bed of softly coloured flowers. Surround it with sunshine, your favourite trees, the sound of birds, everything you most love about nature. By ceremonially acknowledging its existence as your child, you will be helping to make up for all that was formerly denied to it.

Giving the baby a name at this point could also be very helpful (see p. 41). It would add to your sense of its real and separate identity. If no name feels right, you might like to identify it by whatever quality you would wish for your child: Tenderness or Serenity, for instance.

When your feelings of love for the baby have been properly expressed, say to yourself that it is now time to release the child fully and joyfully. Sound aloud whatever note is in your heart.

Now turn to your own needs. It is essential that you start by forgiving yourself, whatever the circumstances and reasons for the abortion. Just sit quietly and allow compassion to flow over you. If it is helpful, cry – not for the baby but for yourself. When you feel really calm again, get up and walk about the room before starting on the next part of the ritual.

Once you are again seated, try to identify each of the heavy, soiled, unhappy or messy feelings that you associate with the abortion. Really look at them. Give them a shape or colour, or whatever most effectively represents them for you. Then consign them symbolically one by one to fire or to water, whichever seems to you the most purifying and final. These are feelings of which you want to be rid forever. Sprinkle your face and hands with water from the bowl.

The third step of the ritual for yourself seeks to connect you deeply with the Earth. This is as important for you as it was for the child. In order to make your feminine self whole from the assault to which it was subjected, it will need to receive the healing that only the Earth can give. So sit down, or lie down if you prefer, and breathe deeply and rhythmically. Ask to be made whole. Imagine the Earth's abundance of warmth and love rising to surround you.

Sound has a very deep healing quality. If you feel that sounding the note of your pain would bring you even deeper release, look fully and without fear at the most horrible moment of your pregnancy or abortion. Liberate from the depths of your body whatever sound demands to come forth.

For those who feel happy and at home in water, you could also ask for help from the other feminine element. Imagine yourself lying in a gently running brook, with the flowing water purifying you and providing that soothing sensation which comforts hurt.

If you feel that this ritual would cause you too much grief to bear on your own, ask a close friend to enact it with you. Also remember that it is only a suggestion. Alter anything that would make it more effective for you.

The feelings surrounding a miscarriage are very different from those of an abortion, but the distress over the loss of a child is equally poignant. This ritual could therefore be equally suitable for both situations, with a few obvious omissions for those who have had a miscarriage.

Similarly the ritual could be adapted for a woman who has had a sterilization or a hysterectomy. The symbol used in these cases might be less personal – one that represents a more universal state of motherhood. If you like, you could also add a few words that would express the sadness you feel over your loss of potential.

Preparation

Prepare the room or outdoor space with flowers and greenery.

Put in the centre a large cushion for you to sit on, and a blanket or bed of flowers for the imaginary baby.

Put in a corner of the room a bowl of water.

Checklist

Place an imaginary baby on the blanket or bed of flowers.

Name the child.

When your love has been well expressed, release the child.

Sound a note.

Give compassion and forgiveness to yourself.

Identify the messy feelings around the abortion and give them a shape or colour.

Symbolically burn them, or consign them to water.

Sprinkle your hands and face with water from the bowl.

Sit or lie on the ground absorbing the Earth's healing.

Identify the most difficult moment of your pregnancy or operation and sound it.

Ask for help from the water kingdom, if you wish.

Leave the room.

Undo the ritual.

ABORTION FROM THE FATHER'S POINT OF VIEW

This ritual, like the one for the mother, is in two parts. As the first part is the same as in the mother's ritual, it is not repeated here.

Until very recently, society allowed most men to disregard the guilt and responsibility involved in an abortion carried out for social reasons. A positive pregnancy test could be regarded as a nuisance or a lamentable failure of the 'precautions' taken. Unless exceptionally deep love existed between the two people or a particularly sensitive man was involved, the emotional aspect of the event tended to pass him by. He was thought to have behaved honourably if he took care of the financial aspects; his main concern centred around a clean, safe operation.

This attitude seems to be slowly changing. An increasing number of men are finding that although abortion may solve the problem at a physical level, it raises a disquieting number of emotional, psychological and moral questions which refuse to disappear. So strong are these new trends that they are working retrospectively. Many of the men experiencing this disquiet were involved in an abortion many years ago, yet the event is disturbing them so profoundly that they now need to find the means for releasing it.

The reasons for this change are complex. The Women's Movement is partly responsible, but other significant factors are also at work. In the same way that women are exploring their masculine side, so men are becoming willing to discover their feminine aspects, and can now express their distress at having exposed a woman to this ordeal. They can also allow this violation to her body to become part of their own vivid vicarious experience. As we become more attuned to the new Aquarian energies, a greater sense of brotherhood is another relevant factor.

The Ritual

Form a circle of branches or flowers and perform the ritual for the child, perhaps adding a statement about your newly-found feelings and your regret at not having protected the baby's life. If you feel comfortable with the idea, also ask its forgiveness for having given it all the pain of descending to Earth.

Start the second part of the ritual with a quiet meditation in which you try to understand the reason for that soul's brief appearance. Was it primarily for its own spiritual evolution or was it also for one of its parents, or for the couple they formed? The spiritual law of economy is so strictly adhered to in all matters of incarnation that it is highly unlikely that this pregnancy was not significant for at least two of the souls concerned. Discovering and honouring the baby's motives for its partial incarnation will validate them enormously. It might, for instance, have needed a very brief contact with the Earth before embarking on a full-length life.

Now turn to the question of forgiveness for yourself. This is vital. To remain feeling guilty, even obsessive, can do no one any good. Once you have taken responsibility for your action and expressed real regret for it, affirm aloud that you forgive yourself.

The next part of the ritual involves your ancestors –

and, if you like, those of the baby's mother. If, as so often happens, this unfulfilled pregnancy has awakened your sense of continuity and family, the following ceremony could help you to see the abortion from a wider perspective.

Stand in the centre of the circle and place your ancestors in a semi-circle around you, naming and greeting those of them whom you knew.

As you contact them, remember that those who were already discarnate at the time of the abortion knew that this child was not awaited by the ancestors to continue your family line. Keeping this fact well to the fore will help you to dispel a great many vain regrets and to be more receptive to whatever the ancestors may want to convey about families in general and about this child in particular.

The final part of this ritual seeks to disentangle you from the baby so that it can be allowed full release. Sit holding the symbol you have chosen for it, and acknowledge quietly any anger you still have for whatever circumstances prevented the baby's birth. Admit to your grief and disappointment. Deal conclusively with the emotions that remain over this issue between you and the child's mother. Spend a few minutes sending the baby your love. Then leave the room and undo the ritual.

Preparation

Make a circle of flowers or branches and place in it your symbol for the baby.

Checklist

Do the first half of the mother's ritual, adding to it anything you wish.

Meditate on the baby's reasons for choosing a foreshortened life.

Ask for forgiveness for yourself and affirm aloud that it has been given.

Invoke your ancestors, whom you imagine to be sitting in a semi-circle around you.

Name and greet those you know and dialogue with them.

Holding the symbol for the baby, acknowledge any remaining anger and grief.

Disentangle yourself from the baby so that it can find full release.

Leave the room.

Undo the ritual.

A PUBLIC TRAGEDY

When a national or world-scale tragedy occurs, our first reaction is often one of helplessness. Whatever opportunities there may be to express our sympathy through communal prayer or through giving money, food or clothing to the survivors, there remains a gap. There seems to be no way in which to state that 'We are one another', that because their pain is ours, some of it can be diffused through us. Some deep strength can be given to them by virtue of the fact that we are all droplets of the same divine Source.

This solidarity and compassion can however be expressed through a ritual and because our planet is already so pock-marked by undispersed sites of violence and tragedy, anything we can do to defuse a new one is well worth while.

The Ritual

As this ritual is being offered to a large group of people, the sense of brotherhood which it generates would probably be enhanced by having others participate in it. But if you know no one with whom you would feel comfortable sharing a ritual, use appropriate symbols for the other people from whom you are asking telepathic help. These could if necessary be public figures of such spiritual standing as Mother Teresa or the Dalai Lama. The symbols for them should be placed in a small basket so that they can be easily moved from one section of the room to the other.

Next, choose three further symbols. The first will

represent the tragedy itself, the second the survivors, while the third stands for all those who have been touched by the event. If you feel able to work with a fourth symbol representing those who have died, this would be very helpful. Place each of these symbols in a separate section of the room to form either a triangle or a square. As you do so, name each one clearly.

Now stand in a circle around the symbol representing the tragedy itself. (If you are alone, complete the circle with the symbols representing other human beings.) Imagine the disaster as vividly as you can. Smell the fire or feel the water engulfing you. Listen to the screams, the crashing of metal, the falling buildings or the machine gun fire. Really be there. Summon all your spiritual force to help disperse this ball of concentrated fear and pain, so that it be transformed from a destructive canker into pure energy which can be put to creative use.

Call on the four elements to help you: earth to absorb and transmute the tragedy, air to scatter it, water to wash it away, and fire to burn off any remaining dross. Ask that peace and stillness return to this area.

Before moving away from this first circle, separate yourself physically from the tragedy. You may want to return to it at a later date, but for the moment you have done all you can. To remain interlocked with it would not only affect you adversely but would also prevent you from playing your part in the rest of the ritual.

Your next circle is formed around your symbol for the survivors. Your main object here is to express compassion and a feeling of unity with your fellow human beings. This can be done in any number of ways: the participants should agree beforehand on their procedure. In a situation as emotional as this one it is particularly important to keep to the plan of a ritual. If anything unexpected occurs it could disturb the

entire proceedings. Whatever form your expression of
compassion and unity takes – song, silence, a dance or
a speech – be sure to separate afterwards from those you
have been helping.

The next circle you form focuses on assisting the
victims' families and friends to achieve the first vital steps
of detachment from the horror surrounding the death of
their loved ones. Grouped around the third symbol, try
to still the nightmares and the searing images tearing at
them. Help lay to rest their fear and fury. When you have
given them all the support you can, stand back and
separate yourself from them as before.

Whether or not you perform the fourth section of the
ritual depends on whether you feel able to help those who
have died. If you do, your support will be particularly
valuable because those who die in dramatic circumstances without warning nearly always have great
difficulty in passing over. Many of them awake in the
after-life believing themselves to be still on Earth, and
can only wander aimlessly until some form of assistance
is given to them. Compassion and love are very potent
healers and releasers. With the help of all those beings on
whom you can call, express these qualities to your
utmost.

Now move into the centre of the room, away from all
the symbols with which you have worked. Once again
clear yourself of fear and despair. Close each of your
chakras according to the 'closing down' exercises
described on p. 185. Visualize a blue cloak and draw it
around yourself. Seal it at the throat.

Leave the room, and undo the ritual site.

Preparation

Place in a basket the symbols you have chosen to
represent the other helpers.

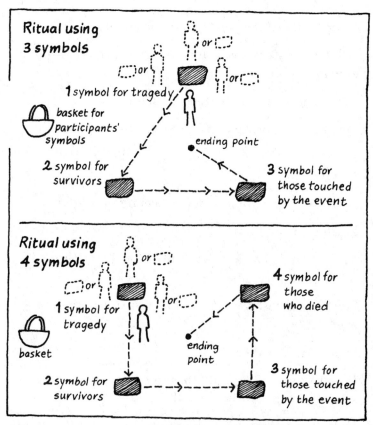

Settings for public tragedy ritual

Place in a triangle or square the three or four symbols for (1) the tragedy, (2) the survivors, (3) the victims' family and friends, and (4) the dead if they are to be included in this ritual.

Agree on your guidelines for offering help to the survivors.

Checklist ✐

Stand in a circle around your symbol for the tragedy. If you are alone, always complete your various circles with the symbols representing your fellow participants.

Imagine the tragedy as vividly as possible.

Ask for the pain and fear to be transformed into pure energy.

Ask for the help of the four elements.

Separate yourself psychically from the tragedy.

Form another circle around the symbol for the survivors.

Express your compassion and feeling of solidarity.

Separate from them.

Form a circle around the symbol for the victims' families and friends.

Help lay to rest the fear and fury surrounding the event.

Separate from them.

If you want to continue, form a circle around your symbol for those who have died.

Help them to release from Earth.

Separate yourself from them.

Stand in the centre of the room and detach yourself from the tragedy.

Do the closing down exercise described on p. 185.

Leave the room.

Undo the ritual.

THE DEATH OF
AN ANIMAL

The death of an animal, whether as a result of an accident, illness or natural causes, can leave us with a great sense of loss. The animals for which we mourn generally fall into two categories. Either they were pets, or else they were part of our working life, such as farm animals or performing animals. In all these cases, the animal's presence has been intertwined with the lives of the individual or family with which it lived or worked. The gap left by its death needs a ritual which declares how much the animal's contribution was appreciated and how much it is now missed.

The outward form of this ritual must be left as flexible as possible since it could be used for the death of a solitary old person's cat at one extreme or that of a performing elephant at the other. The cat's owner would probably feel intensely private about his grief, whereas the circus people might find a flamboyant group ritual the only satisfactory way of expressing their intense involvement. It should be possible to adapt the following basic ritual to cover a wide spectrum of possibilities.

The Ritual

The death of a child's pet is often insufficiently honoured by the adults in the household. Even if the pet was not immediately and obviously lovable – for instance, a frog or a rat – it was a creature with whom the child shared a whole imaginative world. Its disappearance, therefore, can bring overwhelming desolation. To compound this sadness, he may also be facing for the first time the irrevocability of death. However hard he cries and pleads, no one can bring back his pet. Most children find this fact almost as difficult to accept as the actual death. One of the purposes of this ritual is then to be an initiation which will influence the child's whole future attitude towards things that are irrevocable.

The answers to the questions which a child asks at this time may well be contradicted by what he later comes to believe, but you should nevertheless give firm answers. Where has his dead friend gone? Is it happy? Does it miss him and know that he still loves it? Answer these questions as openly and truthfully as you can, however difficult you find them. Any attempts to prevaricate or protect him will be spotted immediately and will cause him even greater bewilderment.

If you yourself accept the concept that animals belong to groups having a common soul, and that the child's pet will now have returned to its group, be sure to explain this to him. Nothing could reassure him more than to know that a reunion with close friends has taken place.

Because his imagination and empathy will already be so involved with the animal's death, the child will probably need only a few general guidelines for creating a ritual. But do make sure its practical aspects are dealt with in such a way that he experiences as little trauma as possible. If the death has been caused by an accident with visible results, it is better for the child not to see the animal's body. Give him the already-sealed receptacle of his choice for him to decorate as he wishes. Adorning a bare box with coloured paper or flowers or stickers or drawings can help him express his love for the animal. After the ritual, the receptacle should if possible be buried; if this is impracticable, dispose of it with care. If this feels too much for the child to bear, do it for him, preferably when he is asleep.

Let the child choose whether or not he wants to

perform the ritual alone and also where he would like it to take place – preferably in a sheltered spot where he will not be disturbed. Some of his sadness may be relieved through making a goodbye speech to his pet, but if he is too choked or shy to do this, a silent goodbye can be equally effective.

In any ritual to be performed by adults rather than children the above guidelines can be followed, with the possible addition of candles which most people feel are a necessary part of any ceremony concerned with death.

When preparing the receptacle for burial don't feel shy at decorating it: the special link between you and the animal can often be best expressed through colour and design.

Writing a few words about the animal could also help ease your distress. This could be specially useful if the size of the animal means that it has to be taken directly to its burial site or, because of public health regulations, has to be disposed of in a disrespectful way and your ceremony performed elsewhere.

Try to create through the ritual a focal point outside your home where the affection felt for the animal can be centred.

Do not replace a pet, especially a child's, until all sense of disloyalty to the dead animal has been overcome. If it was a working companion that has died and it has to be immediately replaced, be sure to explain this situation to the deceased animal, reassuring it that no one will ever take its place in your affections.

The usual instructions apply for the setting up and undoing of the ritual.

Preparations 🖋

If appropriate, decorate the animal's 'coffin'.

If you are to bury the animal yourself prepare a burial site.

Have candles ready if desired.

Have writing material on hand.

Checklist

Say goodbyes in whatever way you feel appropriate.

Light candles if required.

Write a few words about your animal if this would help.

Choose a focal point outside of the home where your affection for animal can be centred.

If a working animal has to be replaced immediately, explain this to the deceased animal.

Undo the ritual.

A BURGLARY

However much we try not to attach too much importance to material objects, being robbed of something for which we have worked hard, or which has great sentimental value, causes considerable distress. This in turn will probably be compounded by fear and a sense that our self and – in the case of a break-in – our home have been violated. Dispelling these emotions is vital to our psychic health.

The Ritual

The first part of the ritual aims to detach you as conclusively as possible from the stolen objects. For each of them draw or write on a card as accurate a description as you can. Then place them on the floor in a pattern which illustrates their relative importance to you. Tell them, collectively or individually, what you feel about them and how much you mind their disappearance. Really mourn them, which can be in words or through a chant or just by communicating with them in silence. Explain to them that because the likelihood of recovering them is very small, you would now like to release them and the constant nagging pain they would otherwise cause.

Do not relegate these cards to a dustbin; either bury them or burn them. Either of the elements involved (earth and fire) will complete the ceremony for you, though each will do so in a slightly different way. If you prefer to dispose of them in water and have access to a stream (running water is preferable), use leaves or flowers instead of cards to represent the stolen objects and float them away.

In the event of your stolen goods being returned to you, be sure to welcome them back with as much ceremony as you used to mourn their loss.

The second part of the ritual seeks to clear you and your home of that sense of invasion which makes a robbery so difficult to handle. However irrational it may seem, most people experience a theft as a personalized attack. Why have they been chosen for this outrage? What might happen to them next? How can they ever feel safe again? Some very fundamental trust in life is shaken by this kind of experience and unless something is done about it, the feeling persists.

The first thing to do is to make certain that all traces of the burglars' presence have been removed, and all fingerprints and dirt cleared away. If necessary, repaint a wall or room before doing the ritual.

Choose a time of day when you are certain not to be disturbed. Then process with lighted candles, either alone or with friends, around the entire house, garage, garden shed and so on. If you feel that incense would help disperse the intruders' presence, use it. Sprinkling water at the four corners of each room is also a powerful way of spiritually cleansing a space. In each room, quietly and undramatically banish the burglars.

If during the robbery you yourself were subjected to physical attack, it is vital that you free your body of the robbers' presence (see the ritual for rape on p. 114). Try also to forgive them as unconditionally as you possibly can, remembering that hatred and resentment form links just as potent as love, so that forgiving them will be of practical personal benefit to you as well as being spiritually desirable.

Send love and protection all around the buildings, and fill them with light.

If at the end of the ceremony you still feel yourself burdened with hatred and a sense of personal affront, write a letter to the burglars expressing everything you feel. Then burn it as calmly as possible.

Whenever you leave the house from now on, you might like to mentally place the sign of the cross encircled by light on your front door. Then send a beam of purple light (the colour having the highest and most spiritual vibration) all around the house.

Preparation

Prepare your slips of paper with descriptions or drawings of the stolen objects.

Have a container in which to burn them or a spade with which to bury them.

Remove all physical traces of the robbers.

Have available a candle for each person who is processing.

Have incense available if you want it.

Checklist

Place the slips of paper or leaves and flowers on the floor in appropriate patterns.

Dialogue with them.

Release them.

Bury or burn them, or consign them to water.

Process through the house and any outhouses.

If necessary, do a ritual for physical violence (see p. 114).

If you wish, do a short ritual for cutting the ties that bind (see p. 19).

If you wish, write a letter to the burglars and then burn it.

End the ritual by sending love and protection to the house.

RITUALS
FOR
NEW
BEGINNINGS

INTRODUCTION TO THE RITUALS

The rituals in this chapter are for marking endings and new beginnings. They will help you to leave the past behind so that you can step forward positively into the future.

They are based on the premise that it is undesirable to drag dead wood behind us when we move from one cycle into another. The more psychically clear and unburdened we can be at the start of a new phase, the better chance we have of both benefiting from it and of giving our best to it.

ENDING THERAPY

However difficult, even painful, therapy may be, ending it can often be just as hard. Indeed, many people in therapy continue far longer than is sensible for this very reason. It is only too easy to become therapy-dependent in the same way that one can become addicted to drugs or alcohol. But even when therapy has been brought to a close according to all the rules, life without it may well prove to be difficult at first.

One of the main reasons for this is that it entails a basic change in the way you have been relating to yourself and the outer world during the past months or years. Therapy is by its very nature an introverted occupation, purposely turning you in on yourself in order to help you dissect your actions and reactions, your feelings and your motives. It is concerned with detail and symbols which seek to bring understanding of wider issues. At the conclusion of therapy, you are being asked to replace this inward-looking mode with an outgoing one.

You are also being robbed of that star role which was quite rightly yours during all your therapy sessions. Only by total concentration on *you* could the knots gradually be unravelled so that you could be integrated with the world as a more whole person. That was the contract between you and the therapist. But once that contract was concluded and you were thought ready to call on your own inner strength rather than on an external figure, the intricacies of your psyche ceased to be a central focus. Unless your attention now turns to the outer world, and you apply to it all that you have learned, much of the effort and pain of the therapy sessions will have been wasted.

To relinquish anything familiar is always difficult, because patterns and habits form so quickly. Whether your therapy was interesting or excruciating, tiresome or fantastic, if it has lasted for any length of time it will have become a part of your life from which you will require careful weaning. The changeover will not only entail doing without regular support and confirmation of your self, but will also require a final break from the outworn patterns with which you have been dealing. These, it is hoped, will have been gradually dropped during the course of the therapy, but even if they have, this time of review and summing up demands a real freedom from these encumbrances.

Voicing your appreciation for whatever it is that therapy has given you is another important aspect of this ritual. Whether you feel it to have been a failure, a temendous success or something in between, you will presumably have gained some useful insights. Enumerating them will help to make them more concrete and accessible. In acknowledging that the time devoted to this search for clarity and integration has been worthwhile, you will also be laying the foundations for further growth.

The Ritual

Before embarking on this ritual you should have three symbols ready. The first represents the issues on which you have worked and which you now feel to be resolved. When choosing this symbol consider carefully the quality, weight, shape and colour of the issues. Time spent on finding the perfect symbol will be well rewarded.

For those questions that have not been resolved, or possibly not even touched upon, find a second symbol and try to define the reasons for their non-resolution. Consider also how solutions might be found in the future. Above all, assure your psyche that these matters will be dealt with as soon as possible. The third symbol represents all that you have learned during therapy.

If we consider the therapy period of your life as being justifiably self-centred and the future as being more outward-turned, this ritual requires two spaces of quite different sizes. One should be only large enough for two people, while the other comprises the rest of the room. The division between them can be formed by cushions. In the small section put chairs for yourself and the 'therapist', who is represented by a photograph or some object. Place a waste paper basket between you.

In the rest of the room, which represents your whole outer world, place symbols or printed cards for each section of your life: work, home, church, clubs, friendships etc. By placing these in such a way that you can visually grasp their relationship to one another and their positions of relative importance in your life, you will gain interesting insights.

Sit first in the smaller of the two spaces opposite your 'therapist' and express your thoughts or emotions, however eulogistic or negative, about the work you have done together. Then pick up your symbol for the issues resolved and drop it into the waste paper basket, thanking the therapist for his help in achieving this.

Now take the symbol for the unresolved issues and declare aloud what you intend to do about them. Will you return to therapy after a suitable period of assimilation? Will you deal with them yourself through what you have learned? Or are you so fed up with introspection that you propose to bury this symbol and pray that none of its problems ever surfaces. If this is your intention, be completely honest about it, otherwise you will undo some of the therapy's gains. Whatever your decision, drop this symbol into your left-hand pocket with a clear intent.

After giving thanks for it, place your third symbol in your right pocket; all that you have learned is now closely part of you.

Next, move into the 'world' part of the room and consider how each section of your life has been changed by your therapy. Try to express precisely each one's particular quality of change. Now that you have discarded what is resolved and committed yourself to dealing with what is still unresolved, you can really make use of what has been learned.

Leave the room, and then return it to its normal state.

Preparation 🖋

Divide off with cushions one small space. Place two chairs in it.

Place a waste paper basket between the two chairs.

Put your chosen three symbols in front of your chair.

In the rest of the room site the symbols/cards you have chosen for work, home, church etc. in such a way as to show their relative importance to you and their relationship to one another.

Put a photo or symbol on the therapist's chair.

Checklist 🖋

Sit opposite your therapist.

Express your opinion of the therapy period.

Drop into the waste paper basket your symbol for resolved issues, thanking your therapist for his help.

Holding the symbol for unresolved issues, declare your intentions towards them.

Put this symbol in your left pocket, promising to deal with it one way or another.

Put the third symbol in your right-hand pocket and give thanks for it.

Move into the 'world'.

Consider how therapy has changed your relationship to each area. Express the quality of each change.

Leave the room.

Undo the space.

THE END OF
AN ILLNESS

Many people believe that we draw to ourselves the disease or accident needed for some aspect of our spiritual/psychological growth. So understanding our need for illness and unravelling the message of the particular disease we have contracted is vital in helping us come to terms with it and banishing it definitively.

A common reason for attracting illness is that many people's spiritual lives at this time are developing so rapidly that they need a lot of time alone. Being unable to obtain this space for reflection and growth in their normal everyday lives, they may unconsciously call to themselves some form of accident or disease which forces them to spend time quietly on their own.

Another reason is connected with our past lives. As stated earlier, there is far more to us than our physical body. We have other, finer bodies vibrating at ever higher frequencies, all with one aim: to reach the light or the divine. That part of us which is eternal and returns time after time to Earth in order to continue its learning is subject to karma, the law of cause and effect. Because we reap what we sow, we are born into the environment where we will meet again those we have wronged and those who have wronged us. This gives us the opportunity to repay our karmic debts.

Similarly, if something concerning our health remained unresolved in an earlier life, falling ill now could be the most natural and direct way of bringing about a resolution. The same would apply to physical harm done to someone else – past karma could be redeemed by a present illness.

As to why a particular disease is attracted, there are

many aspects to consider. Was it a psychological need to which the illness responded? Were love and attention so desperately required? If so, why could they not be obtained by gentler means? Or was the reason for the illness a spiritual one? Did the possibility of death need to be faced before an advance on the path could be made? Were a temporary period of immobility or some other incapacity required in order to arouse compassion for others?

If we are to learn any lessons from a disease we must analyse its precise effects on the body. Where, for instance, is it located? If on the left side, it is drawing attention to one's feminine nature; if on the right, to one's masculine nature. At what chakra level is it? Which of the four elements is involved? Our circulation, for example relates to the water element, the lungs to air, the bones to earth and the emotions to fire. And what function is being pinpointed? A damaged hand could represent impaired action, a diseased breast could be related to nurturing, malfunctioning feet could be pointing to a lack of groundedness, while a diseased heart could be speaking about the person's vital centre.

A concentrated exploration of the particular condition will provide many clues, ranging from a simple request for rest to a violent warning of disaster. The messages could also be more subtle. If, for instance, you are constantly suffering sore throats, it could be very rewarding to consider how successfully your creativity is being allowed to manifest itself. If your breathing is shallow and painful, your lungs are not being filled with the breath of life or Spirit; what is being refused from life?

Modern medicine has lost the concept of disease as a teacher, and its only criterion is speed of recovery. But the suppression of symptoms does not equal healing, and very often modern drugs not only deprive us of the opportunity for rest and growth but also rob us of invaluable clues about our psychological and spiritual states. It is unwise to allow this to happen, if for no other reason than the fact that a disease which is merely suppressed, not cured, will nearly always re-emerge.

So even if the symptoms have disappeared and you have been declared physically sound, do not ask your illness to leave finally until you are satisfied that you have learned from it all the wisdom you can.

The Ritual

All that is needed for this ritual is a circle within which you place a large ball of cotton wool that you have fluffed out so that it becomes especially absorbent. A witness can be invited to the ritual if you like, but no helpers are necessary.

Enter the circle and stand beside the ball of cotton wool. Pour into it all the symptoms and anxieties you have experienced during your illness. Allow all the headaches, the indigestion, the cramps and the coughing to be absorbed by it. These fears and pain have now been outworn; you no longer need to carry them.

If your illness was a life-threatening one, bid farewell to the fear of death. Thank your disease for the new awareness it has brought to you.

Take the cotton wool and place it in a closed container just outside the circle, affirming that at the end of the ceremony you will either burn it, or run it under a tap, squeeze it out and then bury it.

Put a clean wad of cotton wool in the centre of the circle. Walk slowly around the outside of the circle three times, affirming your freedom from the need for that particular disease.

Leave the room.

Undo the circle.

Preparation 🌿

Make a circle.

Place a large ball of fluffed-out cotton wool inside it.

Have another wad of cotton wool available.

Put a closed container just outside the circle.

Checklist 🌿

Step into the circle.

Pour into the cotton wool all the symptoms you have experienced during your illness.

Thank the illness for the learning received.

Put the cotton wool outside the circle in the closed container, promising to dispose of it as soon as the ritual is completed.

Put a new wad of cotton wool in the centre of the circle.

Walk three times around the circle, affirming your freedom from the need for that particular disease.

Leave the room.

Undo the ritual site.

LEAVING AN ORGANIZATION

Whether or not you have left an organization voluntarily, the process of disentangling yourself from it is never easy. If the departure was further complicated by feelings of injustice or bitterness, it will be even more difficult. The term 'organization' as used here includes businesses, charitable foundations or any other group with which you have been seriously involved in terms of career, time, money or emotions.

The word 'disentanglement', evoking an untidy spider's web, is the clue to this ritual. Your every thought and emotion since you joined the organization has emitted tiny etheric threads which are now entwined not only around you, your colleagues and your boss but also around the fabric of the organization itself. With the passage of time these threads have expanded and grown clusters of thought-forms. Your reactions to the aims and objects of the organization and the methods by which they are achieved have also built strong links between you and it. Unless these ties are consciously broken, they will continue to affect you long after you want to be free of them. Remaining entangled in them would be at best confusing, at worst completely stultifying.

The Ritual

Place two chairs opposite each other with a waste paper basket between them. One chair represents the organization; the other is yours. Next to the latter place a pile of different-coloured balls of wool.

Sit down and tie one of the balls of wool to some part of the organization's chair, declaring it to be you in the organization. Where exactly you place it is probably as significant as the colour wool you have chosen. Have you fixed the wool underneath the seat of the chair because you felt yourself to be 'unseen' at work? Or have you tied it to the chair's right arm because you were the boss's 'right hand'? If you give your position no specific importance don't worry, it may not be significant in this case, or else the answer may come to you later in the ritual.

Continue to attach the different-coloured strands to the chair, naming each of them aloud as persons, problems, skills you brought to the organization or issues in which you were involved and so on. After tying each strand, lay the ball of wool carefully on the floor so that it does not get tangled with any of the others.

Be sure to question such factors as the way you were treated. Did this ever make you angry? Was there ever any sense that the ideals of the organization were betrayed? Are you feeling jealous of any of your colleagues? Were you disappointed, even bitter, because an illness forced you to leave?

Where two distinct factors co-exist, as in the last possibility, be sure to give each of them a separate strand of wool. Your illness would be one factor, your disappointment another.

Once you have finished this part of the ritual, try to establish the connections between the different strands by crossing them over each other. If, for instance, you are jealous of the person who replaced you, that person and your jealousy need to overlap.

As you interweave these elements and persons, define to yourself as clearly as possible the way in which you are still joined to the organization and what you now want your relationship with it to be. Should all the links be cut?

Or are there people there whom you would still like to see? The clearer you can be about this, the more effective will be the next stage of the ritual.

As you start the untangling process, be very discriminating. Those strands which appear to you worthless should be precisely and definitively cut from the chair and from their ball of wool and dropped into the waste paper basket. However, those which you value and want to retain need to be untied, rolled back on to their ball and put into a box.

Sit for a moment offering thanks for all you have been given by the organization. Now that all these positive factors have been isolated, you will be able to benefit from them without having to be sucked back into the past in order to reach them.

Preparation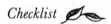

Put out two chairs with a waste paper basket between them.

Place by your chair several balls of wool.

Put out a box into which some of the balls of wool will later be placed.

Checklist

Sit down.

Tie to the appropriate part of the chair facing you a ball of wool for each person, problem, skill, or issue you wish to represent in the organization.

Consider which of these ties you want to keep.

Cut off each unwanted strand of wool and put it in the waste paper basket.

Untie the wanted ones and roll them back on to their balls. Put them in the box.

Give thanks for all you have received.

Leave the room.

Undo the ritual.

MAKING NEW YEAR'S RESOLUTIONS

As the New Year is rung in, a spate of good resolves flies about. Gluttony, laziness, arrogance, jealousy, pride, envy and a whole crowd of other undesirable qualities are foresworn. Resolutions about money also abound: less will be spent; more will be earned; better accounts will be kept. It's all star-spangled and glowing – for about ten days.

Then langours and frailties begin to creep in. A box of chocolates left over from Christmas is consumed 'because it would be wrong to waste them'. The rigorous timetable devised for writing one's world-shaking book is broken for 'just this once'. The slippery slope opens up. Then jealousy peeps out and gets you; a nasty row ensues. Temptation pops up at the Sales; it would be short-sighted not to succumb. And so it goes on. By the end of January this year's crop of resolutions has been branded idiotic and impracticable. Luckily the whole ridiculous subject can be forgotten until next year.

But isn't this rather a waste? By combining that wonderful New Beginning quality with a ritual, could we not anchor at least one or two desirable changes?

The Ritual

Although serious in its intent, this ceremony is basically festive as it is part of New Year's Day. So take as many brightly coloured candles as you have resolutions and form them into a serpent shape on the floor. Decorate your room with greenery. Place on a table some object or a poem that expresses change: a picture of a butterfly, an iceberg, or an autumn tree about to shed its leaves. Next to this put a symbol representing what you hope to be by the end of the year. If you cannot find anything which satisfactorily defines that quality, take a photograph of yourself and attach to it a slip of paper stating your aims. A commitment made to your own image is hard to retract or cheat over.

If several people are taking part in this ritual, they should place their personal objects in separate sections of the room and perform the ceremony in turn, while the others participate as much or as little as has been previously agreed. If there is not enough room for this, simply replace the candles and the symbols after each person has completed his ritual.

As you enter the room, light all the candles in the serpent, naming them as you do so. Take your time. Really consider each quality or resolve. Put all your energy into each one, but beware of being over-ambitious because nothing is more discouraging and undermining than falling short of a resolution. One small failure could make you give up on everything, whereas if you had been less demanding you could have succeeded.

When the candles are all lit, take your symbol for change and hold it in your hands. Ask aloud or in silence for the will necessary to effect this change. Ask only for that which will flow harmoniously with the rest of your life.

Now take your second symbol and express aloud exactly what you want of yourself in the next twelve months. Imagine as vividly as possible the you who will be standing here next year. Greet that embryonic you.

Blow out your candles one at a time.

Leave the room.

Undo the ritual.

Preparation

Make a serpent of candles.

Decorate the room with greenery.

Put on a table an object, poem or picture expressing change.

Next to it place a symbol for your intentions for the coming year.

Checklist

Light all the candles, naming them.

Hold the symbol for change and ask for the necessary will to effect it.

Holding your second symbol, express your aspirations in detail.

Greet the new you.

Repeat the process for each participant.

Blow out the candles.

Leave the room.

Undo the ritual.

A BIRTHDAY

Most of us retain from childhood the feeling that our birthday is a time for celebration, a special day on which everyone will be trying to make us happy. For these people a birthday ritual presents no problem. They will simply want to make it as fun and triumphant as possible, to affirm what they already know to be true.

But this is not so for everyone. For some people their birthday is surrounded by sad memories and a myriad of fears whose cause and duration vary. Will anyone remember that it is their birthday? What have they accomplished in the past year? Why must they be painfully reminded that their life is slipping away? Questions of self-worth in all its forms come very much to the fore as birthdays roll around.

For those who find birthdays difficult, a ritual will need more imagination. It will be attempting to reverse a deep-seated pattern which is fundamentally suspicious of celebration. It could be helpful to precede it by an initiation ritual (see pp.84 or 91), because many people who shun birthday celebrations are those who recoil from taking root on the planet.

If this idea does not appeal try, before the ritual is to take place, to remember all the good things about the past year and to anticipate what is positive about the coming year. Try also to recall memories of past happy birthdays. Few people have none.

The Ritual

For those who enjoy their birthday, getting dressed up in something special is a good way to add to the festive feeling of this ritual.

Make a really pretty circle with flowers and attractive objects in harmonious colours. Fill the circle with streamers or ribbons. If this would be a good place for the birthday person to receive his presents, pile them up at one end of the circle. You could also place the cake beside them. Lighting its candles and blowing them out later could be joyful focal points of the ceremony.

If the birthday person has some particular interest or hobby, it might be fun to have a theme running through the decorations. As this is an occasion when you will all be moving around and expressing yourself with joy rather than with solemnity, don't use any formal props.

Most people who rejoice in their birthday will probably prefer this ritual to be performed with as many friends as possible, so make the circle really large. The birthday person enters first and is then encircled. From this star position he expresses anything he wants to say: his joy at being alive, his happiness through friendships, his prospects for the coming year . . . whatever he feels. If anyone wants to give an answer, they should do so.

Hugging everyone, singing, receiving presents, lighting the cake, all these can be part of the occasion. Whatever suits the birthday person's mood and affirms that this is his special day is fine. If you all entered the room dancing, you may want to leave it in the same way.

Undo the circle.

A ceremony for someone wanting to reverse the pattern of sadness surrounding his birthdays will have to be quite different from the one described above. It calls for a simpler setting and fewer participants, as the emphasis will be on inner change.

Enter the circle and begin by addressing your parents, whose photographs you may wish to have present. If it is they who originated your feelings, tell them that you no longer wish your progress through life to be annually overshadowed by this sadness.

Now address the 'you' of former years. Start by placing around the circle numbered cards representing each year of your life. Add to them, where appropriate, a symbol for each important birthday. Address these years if you wish. Allow the will for change to flow through you. Let whatever sadness or indifference surrounded your birthdays fall away. Walk slowly around the circle, as many times as you need, deeply contemplating your life.

Giving yourself a present of something you really want but would not in the normal course of events buy for yourself is a good way of declaring that you value yourself and that you recognize this day as special.

If you would like to sing anything before leaving the circle, do so. This could start to establish the feeling of celebration that you now want to be present at your birthdays.

Leave the room.

Undo the circle.

Preparation

For the first version of this ritual, make a circle with an emphasis on beauty.

If you wish, put the presents and the cake in the circle.

Have matches ready for the candles.

For the second version, make a simple circle.

Have photographs of your parents available, if you wish.

Place around the circle numbered cards for each year of your life, plus any symbols you need for the special years.

Prepare a present to give to yourself.

Checklist 🖋️

In the first version, walk or dance into the circle with your friends.

Stand in the centre of the circle with everyone around you. If so desired, speak to them.

Open your presents and light the candles on the cake.

Go out dancing and/or singing.

Undo the circle.

In the second version, enter the circle. Address your parents and those years which need special attention.

Give yourself your present.

Sing something if you want to.

Leave the circle and the room.

Undo the circle.

STARTING A
NEW PROJECT

No matter how rational we imagine ourselves to be, we all secretly hope that magic is alive and well and not too far away, and that if we call on it there will be an enthusiastic response. At no time is this hope more active than when we are starting a new project. By gathering together in a ritual all available assistance, including good luck charms, our new project is given a sense of confidence that will go a long way towards making it a success – providing of course that the project itself is sound.

The Ritual

For this ceremony, all those who are participating in the new beginning, whatever its nature, should be present. It is their combined energy, enthusiasm and faith that will bring to the ritual, and thence to the project, that irresistible quality of certainty.

The circle you prepare should be festive and at the same time as magic as you feel happy with. Any amulets, charms or lucky objects that any of you possess could be interwoven with the flowers or stones of the circle. You could hang up a new moon, have a photo of a chimney sweep, draw a four-leaf clover or represent any traditional bringers of good luck.

Place in the centre of the circle whatever you consider to be a suitable symbol for the project. Put a lot of thought into your choice, because it should be an inspiration to all of you as well as your focal point and uniting factor. Standing at the centre throughout the ritual, it will draw to itself all the love and energy you can give it.

Enter the circle and stand around it. This is a group ritual where no one is the leader, so anyone can speak in whatever order. The first thing to establish is the nature of the project, including all the expectations and hopes which are being put on it.

The next thing to affirm is what each of you is prepared to bring to the project in terms of time, money and effort. Hearing these commitments – both yours and those of the others – made in this sacred place will bestow on them far greater weight than they would otherwise have.

Now call on everything that can help your enterprise in any way. Break your circle and go around it one at a time, touching each of the charms that has been placed there. If you want to say anything, do so. You may also want to make some special request or affirm something to a particular talisman or symbol. The energy of the good luck charms will unite the group and give you great faith in the success of your project.

You could end by each going to the centre of the circle and touching a piece of wood that you have laid there. If that feels too superstitious, then end the ceremony by bowing to each other and to the project's symbol. You may feel like giving a shout of triumph as you go out.

Undo the circle.

Preparation ✐

Make a very festive circle containing the amulets, charms and lucky objects of all the participants.

Put in the centre a symbol for the project and, if you like, a piece of wood.

Checklist

Everyone enters the circle and stands around the symbol for the project.

Each declares the expectations and hopes being put on it.

Each says what he is prepared to give to the project.

Each goes around the circle touching the charms and invoking their aid.

Each touches the centre piece of wood, if he so wishes.

Bow to each other and to the project symbol and leave the circle.

Leave the room.

Undo the circle.

RITUALS
FOR
HEALING
THE CHAKRAS

INTRODUCTION
TO THE
RITUALS

We have already seen how important the chakras and the subtle bodies are to ritual, which bears testimony to the invisible as well as the visible influences in our lives. The chakras also bring us understanding of the energy systems constantly interweaving around us. Until quite recently the chakric system was unknown in the West; now it is becoming increasingly important in physical, psychological and spiritual work.

In order for the chakric system to function at full strength, it needs to have each of its chakras working harmoniously both individually and with each other. At the end of this section there is a ritual to correct an over-emphasis on the thinking function (the brow chakra). Using this as an example, rituals for the many other possible imbalances can easily be invented.

In this section, which deals with each of the chakras individually, the most important thing to remember is that the overall system is a whole, and each of its parts is closely inter-related with all the others. It is therefore vital to consider it as an entity. To work on an individual chakra in an isolated manner can lead to yet more imbalances within the system. To reduce this risk, construct a complete set of symbolic chakras which can be laid out on the floor for all chakra rituals. This can be done with cushions, each of which should be labelled with its name and given its proper colour. Starting at the base of the trunk and ending at the crown of the head, the chakras' names are: root, sacral, solar plexus, heart, throat, brow and crown. Their colours follow those of the rainbow. Starting at the root they are red, orange, yellow, green, blue, indigo and violet. (See below.)

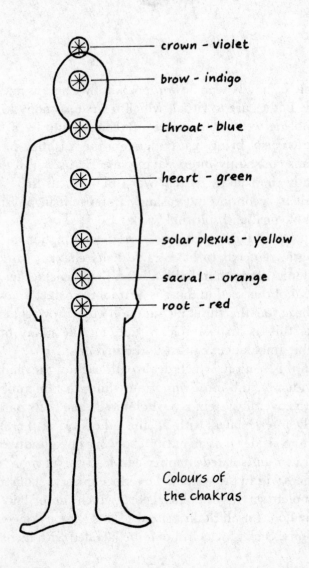

crown – violet

brow – indigo

throat – blue

heart – green

solar plexus – yellow

sacral – orange

root – red

Colours of
the chakras

Many other chakras exist all over the body, but for the sake of these rituals we will confine ourselves to the seven major ones.

Unless blockages between them have for some reason occurred, energy should be flowing freely throughout the whole system, connecting and activating the various chakras. To ensure as clear a passage of energy as possible, all chakra work should be preceded by the exercise described on p. 184. In doing this, you not only clear the channel between all your chakras but also help to establish your connection with both the Earth and the Heavens.

Each chakra is endowed with specific functions and develops at a particular age, starting at the root and working upwards. The malfunctioning of an individual chakra is frequently caused by its inadequate development during the appropriate years. Alternatively the cause may lie in our present lifestyle. It is important to differentiate between these two before embarking on any of these rituals.

The connections between certain of the chakras must also be carefully considered before deciding which of them needs the healing or re-memberment offered by these rituals. Some of them are so closely twinned that it is not always evident which of them is causing the problem. At times these 'twins' may both need healing. In order to create a visual representation of these intimately linked energies, suggestions will be made later for connecting the appropriate cushions.

As we have seen, the chakras develop at clearly defined periods of our lives. If a person suffers a trauma or illness, or lacks love and encouragement during one of these periods, the chakra which should then be developing will not do so properly. A review of your life with these developmental periods in mind is a very rewarding way of gaining insight into the strengths and weaknesses of each chakra. Try to remember as much as possible about each of those periods. What was happening to you? What did you lack? Did you experience sadnesses? What were your ambitions and talents? What were the expectations placed on you?

The ages given for the development of each chakra are as follows. For the root, it was said until about twenty years ago that it developed between birth and five years old; now that children are maturing more rapidly, that time-span has been shortened to three years. The sacral now develops between the ages of three and eight; the solar plexus between eight and twelve; the heart between twelve and fifteen; and the throat between fifteen and eighteen. As it is possible for the brow and crown chakras not to manifest, while still allowing the person to lead a socially acceptable life, no developmental age is given for these two chakras; on the other hand, if enough work is done on them they can become active at any period of one's life.

Opening and closing the chakras

The more open and receptive your chakras are, the more powerful will be the effect of a ritual. Doing the following exercise before every chakra ritual will ensure this desired openness, but remember to close down at the end of every ceremony. Openness becomes vulnerability when it is taken out into everyday life.

Either standing, or sitting on a straight-backed chair, breathe quietly and deeply for two or three minutes. When you feel calm and centred, become aware of your root chakra. Feel its earthy, stabilizing quality. See the deep rich red in which it is bathed. Ask it to unfold gently, ready to welcome what will be given to it by the ritual. Then move up to the sacral with its warm orange colour. See its steady motion working in harmony with the root chakra.

Travel thus up your body, each time bringing in the next appropriate colour and linking that chakra with the others. In this way your whole body will become a mediator between Heaven and Earth, the lower chakras rooting you in the planet, the higher ones making available to you as much of the spiritual world as you are currently able to contact. The heart centre will join the two.

At the close of the ritual the exercise should be performed in the reverse order, starting at the crown and ending at the root. As you work downwards, place a cross encircled with light onto each chakra.

Enfold yourself in a cloak of light with its hood drawn gently over your head.

Healing for the chakras

The following functions which are commonly attributed to each chakra form the basis of the seven rituals in this section.

Through the root chakra we experience our attachment to the Earth, our desire to be incarnate. Its raw energy provides us with our sense of self-preservation and gives us the desire to 'get up and go'.

Our sacral chakra is concerned with creativity in the widest sense and includes our sexuality. It is closely paired with the throat chakra through which that creativity, at whatever level, can be expressed. An unfulfilled relationship between these two chakras can lead to immense frustration and waste.

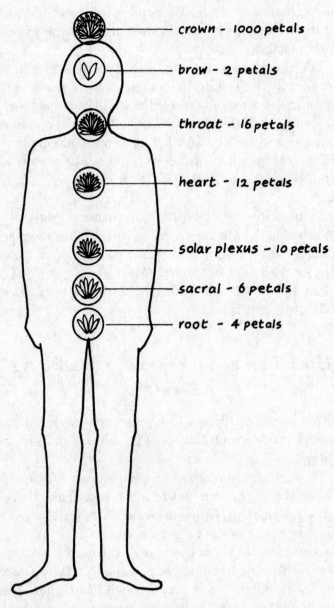

Number of petals in the seven major chakras

crown - 1000 petals

brow - 2 petals

throat - 16 petals

heart - 12 petals

solar plexus - 10 petals

sacral - 6 petals

root - 4 petals

In the solar plexus lies our identity, our little ego. Unless this is allowed to develop during the appropriate period of our childhood, immense difficulties will result. It will churn uncontrollably as our entire character becomes subjugated to its unreasonable demands. It will also be unable to expand and link with the transpersonal self in the brow chakra, with which it should be closely twinned. It is also in the solar plexus that our psychic ability is born. If that ability is to grow and eventually be drawn upwards for use as a spiritual tool, it must learn to work with the brow, where willpower can become devoted to service.

The heart, as the central chakra mediating between the three lower and the three higher ones, is vital to the wellbeing of the whole. If new energies are to enter it without causing great pain, possible disease and even death, we must do all we can to ensure it is in good functioning order. Where acute suffering has occurred in a person's life, especially when he was a child, the heart chakra is usually damaged or has been deliberately closed down – a disastrous state of affairs for the whole system. The ultimate aim of the heart is to transform personal love and affection into unconditional love for all creation.

Our throat chakra expresses our creativity of all kinds. In order for it to function well our talents, however humble, must be allowed to emerge. A blocked throat chakra is the source of enormous frustration and anger, whereas a smoothly flowing one can generate great joy. Here again, as when the solar plexus joins to the brow, if the sacral links with the throat the energies can be raised from the personal to the transpersonal.

Clarity, knowledge and wisdom find their home at the brow. It deals also with the higher levels of intuition and all activities of the mind. If allied with the heart, wisdom is born. It is important here to differentiate between the brow chakra and the 'third eye' which is above the brow chakra and does not form part of the major chakra system. It is primarily concerned with psychic powers.

The crown is the centre through which our higher self gains access to the spiritual worlds. The most sensitive and complex of the chakras, it is to be treated with great reverence. Known in the East as the thousand-petalled lotus, it is the polar opposite of the root chakra whose composition is extremely simple. From the root to the crown each chakra becomes increasingly complex and has vibrations of a higher frequency.

When working well, the chakras turn lightly and evenly. Except for the root and the crown, all of them lie horizontally in our bodies, their stems facing towards our back, their petals towards our front. The root chakra's petals on the other hand are turned downwards, emphasizing our status as Earth beings. The crown's petals face towards the higher worlds to which we equally belong.

It cannot be emphasized too strongly that in all chakra work we are seeking not only the optimum health of each individual chakra, but also to have them all functioning in harmony with each other.

THE ROOT CHAKRA

Many of those who complain of chronic lack of energy are suffering from an underactive root chakra. The wheel that should be constantly turning, drawing in energy and sending it up the spinal column to feed all the other chakras, is as lethargic as the person feels. When working on this problem, remember that this energy is freely available to us if we will only learn how to use it.

Another prime role of the root chakra is to maintain our sense of self-preservation. People who have attempted suicide, or those who are seriously accident-prone because they attribute little importance to their own life, need to strengthen this part of themselves. It is through the root chakra that we are joined both to the human race and to the thread of all our other lives, past and future. To refuse these connections is to waste much of our incarnation. Those who feel part of a whole, supportive of themselves and others, no longer need to opt out of life either consciously or unconsciously.

Many people whose root chakra is defective will, for one reason or another, have experienced difficulty incarnating (in the incarnation rituals described on pp. 84 and 91, various reasons are suggested why full incarnation could have appeared to them difficult and dangerous). Where people have been reluctant to become part of Earth life, their root chakra is almost certainly under-developed and would show up as pallid pink in the aura instead of a rich red. Their sacral and solar plexus chakras will probably also have very tenuous connections with their root. Establishing a really good grounding or rooting in the element of earth is the best way to combat this condition.

When researching your root chakra's developmental

period (from birth to five or from birth to three, depending on when you were born, see p. 184) you will be mainly dependent on other people's memories of you; yet looking carefully at photographs of yourself will often give very relevant clues. It can also be helpful to review the conditions in which your family found itself during those years. A dramatic but illuminating example would be, for instance, if your mother had died at your birth. Your most fundamental point of attachment to the human race would have been snatched from you; your nourishment would have been a substitute. You would have experienced sadness all around you – your world would in fact have been a most unsatisfactory place. Instead of your mother contributing to the formation of your first chakra, her death could easily have driven you almost entirely out of your body. If, on the contrary, you were born into a warm and contented family who displayed every sign of joy at your arrival, your root chakra would be so well grounded that if any other chakra later failed to develop satisfactorily, righting this would be comparatively simple.

The Ritual

Start this ritual, and all the others in this chapter, by laying out the entire chakra system on the floor to make your visual concept of its inter-relatedness vivid. A weakness or over-development in one chakra can create disharmony in them all.

Place below the seven cushions a semi-circle of large stones representing the Earth, within which the root chakra should feel thoroughly at home. Put a horizontal line of small stones on each side of the half-moon to denote humanity, to which you are also attached. Above the

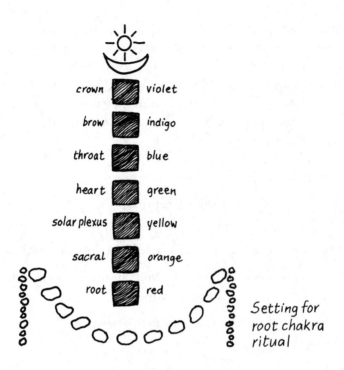

crown		violet
brow		indigo
throat		blue
heart		green
solar plexus		yellow
sacral		orange
root		red

*Setting for
root chakra
ritual*

crown chakra place a symbol for the sun and the moon.

Standing barefoot on your root chakra cushion, feel into all the connections which exist – or certainly should exist – between that chakra, your entire body, the Earth and humanity. You will very soon sense the key importance of this chakra's position. Start breathing into it a deep rich red colour. With each inbreath seek to turn the wheel of your root chakra, steadily, at the speed with which it is comfortable. As you sense the energy enter it in rhythmical waves, make a link with your other six chakras and practise sending energy up and down your spinal column – gently and evenly so as not to unbalance any of the other chakras. Finish with the energy moving downwards. Feed your root with anything you feel it lacks: courage, strength, the will to live etc.

When you have done all you can for the time being,

close down the chakras starting at the crown, imagining them as many-petalled flowers which are to fold gradually inwards, though never to become tight buds. Over each of them make the sign of the cross within a circle of light. This will ensure that they are protected and that when you go out into the world you will not be over-vulnerable to outside influences.

Preparation

Lay out the seven cushions representing your seven chakras.

Make a semi-circle of stones below the lowest cushion.

Place two horizontal lines of small stones on each side of the semi-circle to denote humanity.

Put a symbol for the sun and moon above the crown chakra.

Checklist

Stand on the root chakra and feel into your connections with your body, the Earth and humanity.

Breathe into it a deep rich red.

On each inbreath see your root chakra wheel turning at a comfortable pace.

Link the root to the other six chakras.

Send energy up and down your spinal column, ending on a downward movement.

Feed your root anything it lacks.

Close down all chakras.

Leave the room.

Undo the ritual.

THE SACRAL CHAKRA

The colour of the second chakra, the sacral, is orange and its main concerns are creativity and sexuality. Both of these should be seen as encompassing wide areas: creativity includes all activity which contributes something positive to the universe; sexuality encompasses everything contributed to an intimate relationship.

The majority of our contemporary problems arise from imbalances in the individual and collective sacral chakras. This in turn affects our throat chakras, which cannot express themselves when our sacral is not in good working order. Proof of this fundamental imbalance can be seen in the violent frustration and anger all around us.

The developmental period for this chakra is between the ages of three and eight or five and eight, depending upon the age at which the root chakra's development was completed (see p. 184).

When reviewing those years of your life when your sacral chakra was forming, relate your personal growth to the context of a wider setting. The impact of World War II on a child, for instance, was enormous and would account for many aspects of his sacral strengths and weaknesses. Include in this review considerations such as your feelings at that age about your creativity. Was it disregarded, allowed, or actively encouraged by your family and schoolteachers? Was your voice heard in matters such as decorating your room or choosing your subjects at school? Were those things which 'made your heart sing' taken seriously? Explore also the origins of your attitudes towards sexuality. Was sex a forbidden subject, a butt for jokes, or something natural and joyful? What message was given out by your parents about their own relationship? If they divorced during that period of your life, how did this affect your feelings about marriage and the possibility of a happy/creative association between two people? Try to follow these questions on through the rest of your life in order to gain further insights into the growth and healing needed by your sacral chakra.

The Ritual

Lay out the props for this ritual as for the root chakra. Then link together the sacral and throat chakras by two thick pieces of wool, one laid on each side of the 'body'. Each piece of wool should consist of an orange and a blue strand intertwined, to recall the colours of each of the chakras in question. As you do this, bypass the solar plexus and heart chakras and note that all work done on the sacral will very specifically help the throat.

On either side of the sacral chakra place two symbols, one to represent what has already been achieved by that chakra and the other to express your future hopes for it.

Give considerable thought to a third symbol which will denote the relationship already created between your sacral chakra and the outside world. It is your sense of identity through your creativity and sexuality which you are describing here. Place this symbol anywhere in the room that feels appropriate.

Standing barefoot on your orange cushion, bring together all the wounded, inadequate parts of your sacral chakra and flood them with a beautiful strong orange light, asking for them to be strengthened and integrated into the whole.

After expressing gratitude for the fruits of this chakra, assure it that you have become more conscious of its needs and will try your best from now on either to feed or disengorge it, to release or untangle it, whichever is required.

Finish by closing all your chakras and drawing a cloak of light around yourself.

Leave the room and undo the ritual.

Preparation

Lay out the chakra system as before.

Link the sacral and the throat with two intertwined pieces of wool, one on each side of the cushions.

Put a symbol on each side of the sacral to represent this chakra's achievements and your hopes for it.

Put somewhere in the room a symbol to represent the sacral's relationship with the outside world.

Checklist

Stand barefoot on the sacral cushion.

Flood the wounded parts of your sacral with a beautiful orange light.

Express gratitude for the fruits of this chakra.

Reassure it.

Close all the chakras.

Draw a cloak of light around yourself.

Leave the room.

Undo the ritual.

THE SOLAR PLEXUS CHAKRA

Begin as usual by laying out your whole chakra system. Then, in the same way that you earlier linked your sacral and throat chakras, join together your solar plexus and your brow with two pieces of thick wool – yellow and indigo intertwined. Be careful to bypass the heart and throat.

The linking of these chakras pinpoints two of the solar plexus's most important potentials. One is for it to become so clear and purposeful that your brow can function transpersonally – that is to say uncluttered by the prejudices and anxieties of the personality. The second is that through training and dedication you can draw up the rudiments of your psychic ability from the solar plexus into your brow chakra, where it can become a transcendent intuition manifesting the teachings of your higher self.

The solar plexus, whose colour is a warm golden yellow, is the seat of our will and of our emotions. These we can either express with clarity or else experience as a muddled blur. It is interesting to note how many popular expressions acknowledge the chaos created by a disturbed solar plexus. 'Butterflies in your stomach' is a typical one.

To help you understand any problems related to your solar plexus, look at what was happening in your life between the ages of eight and twelve. What opportunities did you have for manifesting your will? Did you have to assert yourself aggressively in order to get what you wanted? Could you gradually assume your power at home and at school? During those years were you aware of your intuition and your psychic ability? If so, were they encouraged or repressed? Or have you concealed them so successfully that it is now extremely difficult for these talents to emerge? In what emotional climate were you then living?

As answers come to these questions, write them down on cards and place them around your solar plexus cushion. Now answer on further cards the following group of questions about relationships, a prime concern of the solar plexus. What is the general pattern of your relationships? Do you bully people or try to control them? Can you easily be made to feel guilty or at fault? Are your friendships long-lasting? Do you sit through official meetings in silence or do you take the lead? Do you walk into parties with confidence? There may well be other questions you also want to explore.

Now take some more cards and note on them your driving emotions, both positive and negative. By forming various patterns with these cards try to establish what your emotional blueprint is so that you are aware of the recurring patterns brought about by these emotions. Place these too beside your cushion.

The Ritual

Stand on your solar plexus cushion, barefoot, and ask again and again for your clarity of will and clarity of emotions to become ever stronger, so that *you* rather than your solar plexus are in charge of your life.

End the ritual as for the others.

Preparation

Lay out the seven cushions.

Join the solar plexus and the brow with intertwined yellow and indigo strands of wool.

Write on cards the answers to the questions given in this chapter.

Checklist 🍃

Stand barefoot on the solar plexus cushion.

Ask for clarity of will and emotions.

End the ritual as before.

THE HEART CHAKRA

It is at the heart chakra that we experience all the permutations of love. Unlike any of the other chakras, it is said to be subdivided: one part expresses our personal love, while the other aspires to that most difficult of concepts, unconditional love. If you feel this subdivision to be too complicated for the moment, leave your heart chakra cushion as it is. But if you want to convey this idea, place another cushion above the existing one; this will show you symbolically that unconditional love, which makes no stipulations and exacts no bargains, resides at a spiral above personal love.

The colour attributed to the heart is a clear green tinged with neither yellow nor blue. This is the central colour of the rainbow, as the heart is the central chakra in the human body. Be very aware of this as you consider its importance and role. If at any time it becomes frozen through fear or pain, it can create havoc with the entire system; a lot of intensive work will be needed to free its vital power.

The heart is the mediator between what are known as the three 'lower' chakras and the three 'higher' ones. These terms do not, however, denote any qualitative judgment. The 'higher' chakras are in no way superior to the 'lower' ones; both sets are equally needed. Yet misapprehensions have caused many seekers after the spiritual path to develop their throat, brow and crown chakras excessively, to the detriment of their root, sacral and solar plexus – and their lives have, as a result, become a total shambles. It could even be argued that the opposite is true: the more harmoniously the 'lower' chakras are working, the greater are the achievements possible to the 'higher' chakras.

Before doing any work on the heart chakra, go through the same exercise as for the other chakras, reviewing your life during its developmental stage – in this case between the ages of twelve and fifteen. Were they years in which you could express and receive love? Were you encouraged to devote yourself idealistically to some cause? Did you learn to care for animals? Was love for God part of your heart development? Try to view dispassionately the foundations on which you were building at the time. Many people are already deeply flawed and off-centre by the age of twelve. Have subsequent events changed the quality of energy which flows through your heart?

When you have remembered as much as you can about those important three years, write on some cards the relevant factors and place them beside one of your heart cushions. Then write on further cards your heart connections with the world. As you do so, analyse scrupulously whether your love for these individuals, groups and ideals has judgments or strings attached to it. 'I would love them *if* . . .' is a sure sign that – at present anyhow – your love does not qualify as unconditional.

When this particular map of your life is laid out in front of you, consider what changes need to be made to any of your individual relationships or to your heart chakra itself. Check also whether its connections to the other chakras are satisfactory or whether there are impediments to a free flow between them. Do any ill-defined lines of demarcation between the chakras cause energy muddles? Can you see from these patterns how detrimental pain and sadness are to the heart? And how beneficial forgiveness and release are?

The Ritual

When your cards are all in place, stand barefoot on your heart cushion and flood your heart with a beautiful calm green.

End the ritual as for the others.

Preparation 🖋

Lay out the cushions.

If you feel ready, place another cushion above the existing heart cushion to represent the unconditional love centre.

Consider the developmental years of your heart chakra.

Write on cards the answers to the various questions posed and place them beside the appropriate heart cushion.

Do the same for your heart connections with the world.

Check out the connections and the lines of demarcation between the heart and the other chakras.

Checklist 🖋

Stand on the heart cushion and flood your heart with a beautiful calm green.

End the ritual as before.

THE THROAT CHAKRA

As we have seen, the throat chakra is so closely linked with the sacral that in order for them to work at their full potential they must be functioning well not only on their own but also as a pair. Another prerequisite to this successful twinning is that the heart chakra should be open to allow an energy-flow through it from one to the other.

The colour of the throat is a pure blue, tinged with neither green nor purple.

This centre develops between the ages of fifteen and eighteen. If progress on the chakras has been good up to that point, at about fifteen years old the creativity of the sacral will begin to express itself quite naturally in whatever way is right for the person. The first spiritual aspirations will also start forming at this time because the throat is a chakra of expansion.

As you review your life between fifteen and eighteen, pay particular attention to the help which that creative side of you was given at that time. Did your family allow/encourage you to be heard? Were the beginnings of that transpersonal you treated seriously? Did anything or anyone shatter that embryonic chakra so that its development had to be postponed? If it is not functioning fully at present, what are its needs?

Remember that if this tool for self-expression has not become a well-tuned instrument, no amount of latent creativity will serve you because it has no means of reaching the outer world. Write on cards the answers to the following questions. Do you communicate well through speech, song, the written word? What about body language, telepathy and guidance? Can you express your emotions and thoughts clearly?

Look also at what diseases, if any, assail your throat.

Have you had to have your tonsils removed? Do you often suffer from a sore, rasping throat? Do you lose your voice at times? If so, on what occasions? When you have to express something difficult or disagreeable? Does your throat constrict during arguments? Does breathlessness prevent you from speaking out? Interpret these outer symptoms as symbolically as possible.

The more your life includes meditation, healing and all manner of communication which goes beyond the spoken and written word, the wider must be the area involved in your answers. Don't be afraid to 'think big'. The more conscious you are of influencing and being influenced by a wide spectrum of ideas and people, the more quickly you will grow. But, equally, don't disregard the fact that there is a lot of fear and negativity around us at the moment. The more sensitive to growth you become, the more you will need to learn to protect yourself against these detrimental influences. As your throat chakra gains power, you must also acquire the self-discipline to protect others from those gestures, pauses or silences with which it hopes to unburden itself when unable to do so clearly and directly.

The Ritual

When you have formed your throat chakra map, stand barefoot on its cushion and send healing and light to everything with which you are in contact through your throat.

Sound the note which you feel your throat could, or does, emit to the world.

End this ritual as for the others.

Preparation

Consider your life between the ages of fifteen and eighteen.

Write on cards the answers to the questions about this period.

Write down the key words concerning the way your creativity expresses itself.

Write down the key words to your throat's physical symptoms.

Checklist

Stand barefoot on the throat chakra cushion and send light and healing to everything with which you are in contact through your throat.

Sound your note.

End this ritual as for the others.

THE BROW CHAKRA

The colour of the brow chakra is indigo, that beautiful, mysterious colour which lies between blue and purple. It is the colour of pure thought and of that non-attachment which, although deeply involved, stands back and assesses dispassionately. It is in the brow chakra that the will born in the solar plexus can transcend the personal to become transpersonal and bring through those ideas and ideals contacted via the higher self.

Because this chakra frequently remains dormant, no developmental age is ascribed to it. In a life where material considerations are given priority over the mind and soul, it will remain unexpressed, its inactivity condemning the crown chakra also to remain dormant. Its evolution can, however, occur at any time when you are ready.

In exploring your brow chakra, differentiate clearly between your intellect and your mind. The intellect is that limited section of intelligence which acts on practical levels through facts and figures. The mind – the concern of the brow chakra – is far greater. When working in co-operation with the soul, the mind can link us to the creator and the universe – not as a mystic, which would occur through the crown chakra, but as a person of expanded consciousness. The mind is that which makes us *know*.

If, in addition to this activation of our brow chakra, our heart and brow centres are acting together in power and harmony, our understanding and wisdom will grow to great depth.

When assessing the state and needs of your brow chakra, try to define what encouragement it has received from yourself and others. Was it considered important?

Was its existence even recognized? Were your studies directed at expanding or contracting your brow? Do you now think of yourself as someone whose mind and soul have value? Do your mind and your creativity work well together? Consider carefully how you can help your brow to be more satisfactorily nourished by your lower chakras.

Committing yourself to exploration of the brow is a decisive step and not to be taken lightly. If the time is right for this exploration, it is also a necessary step.

When writing on cards the answers to all these matters and many others you may want to consider, try to think as expansively and universally as possible. The brow chakra is profoundly concerned with expansion and transformation. To restrict it is to kill it.

The Ritual

Stand barefoot on your brow chakra cushion and feed into it all the clarity you can summon. If this chakra is already active in you, imagine beautiful indigo waves being sent out from it in an ever-wider field.

End this ritual as for the others.

Preparation

Differentiate between the intellect and the mind.

Define the importance that you and others have given to your brow.

Consider the role of the lower chakras in expanding the brow.

Consider your commitment to the brow and your relationship with the sacred.

Place on the brow cushion the cards on which you have written key words for all these matters.

Checklist 🖋

Stand barefoot on your brow chakra cushion and feed into it all the clarity you can summon.

If this chakra is active in you, send out indigo waves from it.

End this ritual as for the others.

THE CROWN CHAKRA

The colour of the crown chakra, the thousand-petalled lotus, is royal purple, the vibrations of which are the highest that human beings can at the moment perceive. It is the chakra of the spirit, our direct link with the higher worlds. This chakra remains undeveloped even more frequently than the brow. For those who are 'called' to spiritual growth, however, its expansion is crucial. Within the crown are mirrored the six other centres, so that, before it can come to life, their imbalances will need to be at least in part resolved.

When considering this chakra's condition, think back first to your childhood. Were you then so involved in the other worlds that you took them for granted? Were fairies and nature spirits at times more real – possibly preferable – to the everyday world? Did you as an adolescent ever have moments of total 'knowing' which shaped your entire life? Although the crown chakra cannot develop during childhood and adolescence, it already exists then in embryo form and rituals such as baptism can open it to such experiences. If they were not trampled by self-doubt or the ridicule of others, are they now ready to be the building blocks for your crown chakra? What you could not at that time express because your throat and brow chakras were silent could now become significant factors in your development.

It may, on the other hand, have been much later in life that you had your first insight or altered state of consciousness, or made contact with your guides or other beings. Have you, for instance, known the mystic experience of oneness with all creation? If so, what kind of psychological climate did you live in at the time? Did it make you repress those moments, so that you neither spoke of them nor attempted to renew them? Or did more pressing interests and considerations push them aside? Although neglected, these experiences have nevertheless established the climate in which your crown chakra could now grow.

Write on cards the answers to as many of these questions as you can, and then place them around the crown chakra cushion.

The Ritual

Stand barefoot on your crown chakra cushion and state clearly what links you would like to have with spiritual matters. Open yourself to the higher worlds. If you feel ready, dedicate yourself to them.

End your ritual as you did the others.

Preparation

Review the elements that could serve as building blocks for your crown chakra.

Consider your response to them so far.

Place on the crown chakra cushion the cards on which you have noted your self-assessment.

Checklist

Stand barefoot on your crown chakra cushion and state your desired links with spiritual matters.

Open yourself to the higher worlds and dedicate yourself to them if you wish.

The map of your chakra system

If you have been working on your chakras systematically from root to crown, now would be a good moment to take one long last look at the map of your chakra system. See how each is dependent on all the others. Note the progression of their colours, each one rising in frequency. Observe again the importance of the heart as a centre and mediator. Think deeply about the pairing of the sacral with the throat and the solar plexus with the brow. If you have not already ascertained which of your chakras needs further attention, consider that now, remembering that work on an individual chakra must always be integrated into the whole, otherwise fresh imbalances will be created.

Now take a large sheet of paper, date it, and copy on to it your chakra system, making sure to label all your symbols and cards very clearly. If you later repeat these rituals, this sketch will be an invaluable help in showing you what changes have come about and what still needs to be done.

Send healing and love to the overall picture, maintaining a strong sense of balance between the various parts.

As you put away the seven cushions, be sure to divest them of their role as chakras and see them once again as everyday objects.

CORRECTING
OUT-OF-BALANCE
CHAKRAS 1

This and the following ritual are designed to correct the type of problem that arises when the chakra system is out of balance. Using these two as examples, further rituals for other specific problems of this kind can easily be invented.

The first ritual is for those who live predominantly at a mental level and tend to despise, or at best disregard, their bodies. By largely ignoring their three lower chakras they lose touch with the Earth and become increasingly unbalanced within themselves. At some point in their lives this top-heaviness usually becomes intolerable, if only for health reasons.

People take to 'living in their heads' for a variety of reasons, the most common being that their professional training forces them to concentrate so hard on intellectual work that they have no energy left for their heart centre and lower chakras. With their throat used almost entirely for the expression of ideas and their crown probably felt to be non-existant, they end up as one enormous brow.

Another reason for living in this way is that something has happened to make the person deliberately disregard his functions of feeling, sensation and intuition. Having declared thinking to he the only reliable and interesting form of self-expression for the human race, he retires into an ivory tower. There his lack of compassion (heart function) and sense of solidarity with his fellow humans (lower chakras) can lead to danger for others and grave relationship problems for himself.

A further frequent cause of people being taken over

by their brow chakra is that they have been deeply wounded in some way. To close, or even freeze, their heart chakra may have seemed to them the only way to make themselves impervious to pain. The subsequent loss of richness to their life will appear unimportant compared to the safety acquired by living in their intellect.

The Ritual

Lie on the floor surrounded by your helpers, each of whom is holding a cushion. Ask them to place their cushions on your face. If it does not frighten you and helps convince you that your hitherto omnipotent head centre has been truly demoted, ask them to press down on the cushions. Become really aware of each chakra in your body, including your crown if that is a reality to you.

After a few moments stand up, scattering the cushions all around you and declaring: 'I am no longer predominantly my head.' With your feet firmly planted on the ground, and your arms outstretched, recite slowly the names of the seven chakras starting at the root, and affirming as you do so that you will no longer ignore the existence of any one of them – however difficult or unpleasant you may find its problems.

Do not, however, commit yourself to making this major change too fast or too drastically. Instead of speeding things up, it would slow them down.

If your excessive brow development has stemmed from an experience which made you freeze your heart centre, the final section of this ritual may strike you as threatening. If this is so, end the ceremony by simply assuring your helpers that you will allow your heart to unfold slowly.

If, however, you want to continue, stand with your helpers in a circle around you. Go to each one in turn and, maintaining eye contact, place your hand on his heart with his hand on your heart. This can be done either in silence or else accompanied by a phrase such as: 'My heart is the means through which I shall now express myself. It awakens to the heart of others.' If you would like your helpers to respond, they could say something such as, 'My heart welcomes your newly awakened heart.'

When this is completed, leave the room.

Undo the ritual.

Preparation

Place in the room a blanket for you to lie on.

Put out as many cushions as there are helpers.

Checklist

Lie down on the blanket.

The helpers put cushions on your head.

Become aware of each of your chakras.

Stand up and scatter the cushions.

Recite the names of the seven chakras and commit yourself to developing them.

Either end the ritual here or continue with the final part.

Go to each of your helpers and declare that your heart is henceforth to be the centre of your being.

Leave the room.

Undo the ritual.

CORRECTING
OUT-OF-BALANCE
CHAKRAS 2

Although it is perfectly possible to live a socially acceptable life without developing your brow chakra, once your solar plexus expands beyond a certain point it needs a broader-visioned chakra to counterbalance it.

People who have not yet provided this counterbalance will experience problems, especially if their hearts are also closed. Working exclusively from their personality and will, they will be rigid, power-seeking and possibly even cruel. If, on the other hand, their heart chakras are functioning in conjunction with their solar plexus but they have no brow chakra to provide them with good sense and vision, that heart energy will be expressed as sentimentality and their decisions will be dictated by whim or even hysteria. They will act with impulsive warmth but without thought for the consequences.

Both these groups will despise intellectuals as 'dreamers', valuing only those who 'get things done'. All of them will create constant difficulties through their lack of wholeness.

The Ritual

Lie on the floor and ask your helpers to cover your solar plexus with cushions. Lie there for a few minutes trying to imagine yourself acting from a more balanced combination of chakras. Breathe deeply into each of them, reciting its characteristics. When you stand up, scatter the cushions and make a statement such as: 'It is through my brow and throat chakras that I now want to communicate with my fellow men.' If you feel it is now also time to become aware of your crown chakra, you could state something like: 'It is through my crown that I aspire to God.'

If you feel ready to perform the second part of the ritual, go to each of your helpers in turn and, placing your hands on each other's brow, acknowledge that broader mind quality you now want to start manifesting.

Leave the room and undo the ritual.

Preparation 🖋

Put out a blanket for you to lie on.

Put out as many cushions as there are helpers.

Checklist 🖋

Lie on the floor.

Your helpers cover your solar plexus with cushions.

Imagine yourself acting from different chakras; recite all their characteristics.

Stand up and scatter your cushions, making a statement of intent.

If you want to end the ritual here, leave the room.

If you want to continue, go to each helper in turn and, placing your hands on each other's brow, make a statement about the mind quality you now want to manifest.

Leave the room.

Undo the ritual.

INDEX

READING LIST

CRYSTAL, Phyllis:
Cutting the Ties that Bind, Weiser, US, 1993

FERRUCCI, Piero:
What We May Be, Aquarian Press, 1993

FREEDOM LONG, Max:
The Secret Science Behind Miracles, De Vross, US, 1988
The Secret Science at Work, De Vross, US, 1988

HARNER, Michael:
The Way of the Shaman, Mandala Books

JUNG, C G:
Memories, Dreams and Reflections, Collins, 1983
Man and His Symbols, Collins, 1983

ST AUBYN, Lorna:
The New Age in a Nutshell, Gateway, 1990
Today Is a Good Day to Die, Gateway, 1991

Ma...

FOR

DUMMIES®

PORTABLE EDITION

by Greg Brooks, Ruth Mortimer, Craig Smith and Alexander Hiam

WILEY

A John Wiley and Sons, Ltd, Publication

Marketing For Dummies®, Portable Edition
Published by
John Wiley & Sons, Ltd
The Atrium
Southern Gate
Chichester
West Sussex
PO19 8SQ
England

E-mail (for orders and customer service enquires): cs-books@wiley.co.uk

Visit our Home Page on www.wileyeurope.com

Copyright © 2011 John Wiley & Sons, Ltd, Chichester, West Sussex, England

Published by John Wiley & Sons, Ltd, Chichester, West Sussex

British Library Cataloguing in Publication Data: A catalogue record for this book is available from the British Library.

ISBN 978-1-119-97435-2 (paperback), ISBN 978-1-119-97463-5 (ebk), ISBN 978-1-119-97464-2 (ebk), ISBN 978-1-119-97465-9 (ebk)

Printed and bound in Great Britain by TJ International, Padstow, Cornwall

10 9 8 7 6 5 4 3 2 1

WILEY

About the Authors

Greg Brooks is Content Strategy Director at C Squared, publisher of *M&M* magazine, creative media website www.cream global.com and producer of the Festival of Media. He is also a freelance journalist and digital media consultant with ten years experience covering the global digital industry. He has been a regular contributor to UK national titles such as *Marketing, New Media Age, Brand Strategy, Broadcast, Future Media, The Guardian* and Channel 4's *4Talent* online portal. He is also co-author of *Digital Marketing for Dummies*. In a consultancy role he has worked with Sky, McDonald's, News International, BT, Red Bull, Camelot (UK Lottery operator), EnergyWatch, Visit Britain and OfCOM (UK communications regulator), advising on the future strategic use of digital media.

Ruth Mortimer is associate editor for *Marketing Week* magazine. In charge of a team of dedicated features writers at the publication, she appears regularly in national press such as *The Independent* and the *Daily Express* discussing issues relating to business, marketing and branding. She also appears on TV and radio as an expert commentator in this field for multiple programmes, including those on the BBC and Sky.

Previous to joining *Marketing Week*, Ruth was editor of global business title *Brand Strategy*, as well as writing for Channel 4's '4talent' service to let young people know about new talents in music, design, arts and digital techniques. At *Brand Strategy*, she took the magazine through a full redesign and repositioning, introducing a new range of supplements and a conference programme, while contributing articles to sister titles *Design Week* and *New Media Age*. Before writing about marketing for a living, Ruth was an archaeologist, working mainly in the Middle East.

Craig Smith is the former editor of *Marketing*, the UK's highest circulation weekly magazine, and PPA Weekly Business Magazine of the Year, serving the marketing and advertising industries. He has worked as a business journalist for many years and is a regular commentator on marketing issues to the national press and broadcast media.

Craig works closely with industry trade bodies the Association of Publishing Agencies and Business in the Community to promote best practice in the areas of customer magazines and cause-related marketing.

Alex Hiam is a consultant, corporate trainer, and public speaker with 20 years of experience in marketing, sales, and corporate communications. He is the director of Insights, which includes a division called Insights for Marketing that offers a wide range of services for supporting and training in sales, customer service, planning, and management. His firm is also active in developing the next generation of leaders in the workplace through its Insights for Training & Development. Alex has an MBA in marketing and strategic planning from the Haas School at U.C. Berkeley and an undergraduate degree from Harvard. He has worked as marketing manager for both smaller high-tech firms and a *Fortune* 100 company, and did a stint as a professor of marketing at the business school at U. Mass. Amherst.

Alex is the co-author of the bestseller, *The Portable MBA in Marketing* (Wiley) as well as *The Vest-Pocket CEO* and numerous other books and training programmes. He has consulted to a wide range of companies and not-for-profit and government agencies, from General Motors and Volvo to HeathEast and the U.S. Army (a fuller list of clients is posted at www. insightsformarketing.com).

Alex is also the author of a companion volume to this book, the *Marketing Kit For Dummies* (Wiley), which includes more detailed coverage of many of the hands-on topics involved in creating great advertising, direct mail letters, Web sites, publicity campaigns, and marketing plans. On the CD that comes with the *Marketing Kit For Dummies*, you'll find forms, checklists, and templates that may be of use to you. Also, Alex maintains an extensive Web site of resources that he organised to support each of the chapters in the book.

Dedication

From Craig: For my partner Amanda and children, Leon and Bibi, who graciously forgave me my absence while working on this project.

From Greg: For my family and my friends who have seen much less of me because of this project and to my colleagues and especially Ruth, who has had to put up with seeing much more of me as a result.

From Ruth: To all my friends, family and workmates who have put up with me spreading myself too thin over the last year, thank you all. Also to Greg, who is never slow to spot a good idea.

Authors' Acknowledgments

From Greg: I couldn't have completed this project without the steadying hand, eagle-eye and encouraging words of my partner in crime Ruth. It's been a hectic few months and thanks to your drive and enthusiasm the finished article is every bit as good as we wanted it to be. That is down to you.

Also to the Wiley team, never slow to help us along the way if we needed a prod, or a helping hand. As always you have been a perfect foil and vital reality check, to ensure this book is as useful to 'Joe public' as possible.

Thanks to everyone for their input on this project, be you a creative, online or media agency, a brand, social network, research company or one of our valuable contacts. This book wouldn't exist without your help.

Publisher's Acknowledgements

We're proud of this book; please send us your comments through our Dummies online registration form located at www.dummies.com/register/.

Some of the people who helped bring this book to market include the following:

Acquisitions, Editorial, and Media Development

Project Editor: Jo Jones

Development Editor: Simon Bell

Commissioning Editor: Samantha Spickernell

Assistant Editor: Ben Kemble

Copy Editor: Kate O'Leary

Proofreader: Helen Heyes

Technical Editor: John Bills

Publisher: David Palmer

Production Manager: Daniel Mersey

Cover Photo: © Manor Photography/ Alamy

Cartoons: Ed McLachlan

Composition Services

Project Coordinator: Kristie Rees

Layout and Graphics: Melanee Habig, Corrie Socolovitch

Indexer: Potomac Indexing, LLC.

Contents at a Glance

Contents

Introduction

●●

*M*arketing is the most important thing that you can do in business today, even if your job title doesn't have the word *marketing* in it. Marketing, in all its varied forms, focuses on attracting customers, getting them to buy, and making sure that they're happy enough with their purchase that they come back for more. What could be more important? Ever try to run a business without customers?

About This Book

We wrote this book to help you do that critical job of marketing as well as you possibly can. We wrote with a variety of marketers in mind, including small business owners and entrepreneurs who wear the marketing and sales hat along with several other hats. We also wrote for managers and staffers of larger organisations who work on marketing plans, product launches, ad campaigns, printed materials, Web sites, and other elements of their organisation's outreach to customers and prospects.

We kept in mind that some of our readers market consumer products, others sell to businesses, and some market physical products, while others offer services. The different types of organisation have many important distinctions, but good marketing techniques can work wonders anywhere.

Marketing can be a great deal of fun – it is, after all, the most creative area of most businesses. In the long run, however, marketing is all about the bottom line; if it doesn't have the potential to translate into profits somewhere down the line, you shouldn't be doing it. So, although we had fun writing this book, and we think you can enjoy using it, we take the subject matter very seriously. Any task that brings you to this book is vitally important, and we want to make sure that the advice you get here helps you perform especially well.

Conventions Used in This Book

We refer to any organised, coordinated use of product development, price, promotion, distribution and sales as your *marketing plan*. There is an important distinction between a marketing plan and your *marketing campaign* – some people start off down the campaign route thinking that marketing is all about advertising and promotion. It isn't. We want you to have a marketing plan. Creating a plan means avoiding random or disconnected activities. It also means thinking about how everything the customer sees, whether that be your prices, premises or staff, interlinks and contributes to achieving your marketing goals. Whether you work in a large organisation or own a small business, you need a coherent, well-thought-out marketing plan!

We refer to whoever buys what you sell as the *customer*. This customer can be a person, a household, a business, a government department, a school, or even a voter. We still call them your customers, and the rules of sound marketing still apply to them.

What you sell or offer to customers we refer to as your *product*, whether it's a good, service, idea, or even a person (such as a political candidate or a celebrity). Your product can be animate or inanimate, tangible or intangible. But if you offer it, it's a product in marketing jargon, and using just one term for whatever the reader wants to sell saves us all a lot of time and wasted printer's ink.

We also treat person-to-person sales as one of the many possible activities under the marketing umbrella. You need to integrate selling, which is its own highly sophisticated and involved field, into the broader range of activities designed to help bring about sales and satisfy customers. We address ways of managing sales better as part of our overall efforts to make all your marketing activities more effective.

Foolish Assumptions

In writing this book, we made a few assumptions about you:

✔ You're clever, caring, and persistent, but you don't have all the technical knowledge that you may need to do great marketing. Not yet, anyway.

✔ You're willing to try new ideas in order to improve sales results and grow your organisation. Marketing is challenging, after all, and requires an open mind and a willingness to experiment and try new ideas and techniques.

✔ You're willing and able to switch from being imaginative and creative one moment to being analytical and rigorous the next. Marketing has to take both approaches. Sometimes, we ask you to run the numbers and do sales projections. Other times, we ask you to dream up a clever way to catch a reader's eye and communicate a benefit to them. These demands pull you in opposite directions. If you can assemble a team of varied people, some of them numbers orientated and some of them artistic, you can cover all the marketing bases more easily. But if you have a small business, you may be all you have, and you need to wear each hat in turn. At least you will never get bored as you tackle the varied challenges of marketing!

✔ You have an active interest in generating new sales and maximising the satisfaction of existing customers. This sales orientation needs to underlie everything you do in marketing. Keep in mind that the broader purpose on every page of this book is to try to help you make more and better sales happen!

How This Book Is Organised

This book is organised into parts that we describe in the following sections. Check out the Table of Contents for more information on the topics of the chapters within each part.

Part 1: Where You Are, Where You're Going

Military strategists know that great battles must be won first in the general's tent, with carefully considered plans and accurate maps, before the general commits any troops to action on the field of battle. In marketing, you don't have any lives at stake, but you may hold the future success of your organisation in your hands! We advocate just as careful an approach to analysis and planning as if you were a general preparing on the eve of battle.

In this part, we show you how to make the most of your marketing by focusing on your customers and what your organisation delivers to them and give you strong, aggressive marketing strategies that can maximise your chances of sales and success. You'll also get the help you need to put a plan of action together that you can be reasonably confident will actually work.

Part II: Creating Thinking, Powerful Marketing

Great marketing requires a wide range of special skills. If you don't already have all of them, this part shores up any gaps and helps you take advantage of specialised tools and techniques.

We cover an essential marketing skill: Where can you find the best customers? What do they respond to? What is the competition up to? Imagining, communicating and researching make up the power skills of great marketers, and we want to make their insights available to you!

We share with you that most precious and hard-to-capture of marketing skills: the marketing imagination. When marketers can bottle up a little of this magic and work it into their marketing plans, good things begin to happen. We also address another fundamental marketing skill: communicating with customers. Good ideas plus clear, interesting communications add up to better marketing.

Part III: Advertising Everyone Can Do

Advertising is the traditional cornerstone of marketing. Back in the early days of marketing, firms combined advertisements with sales calls and great things happened to their revenues. In this part, we show you how to create compelling, effective on paper – the traditional medium of marketing. You can run full-page, colour ads in national magazines if you have a big budget, or you can place small, cheap black-and-whites in a local newspaper – and either one may prove effective with the right creativity and design. Everyone can access radio and TV these days, too, regardless of budget, if you know how to use these media economically and well. However, you may also want to use perhaps the simplest – and most powerful – form of advertising: the simple sign - from signs on buildings, vehicles, doors to posters at airports and advertising hoardings next to main roads. You can put advertising to good use in your business in so many different ways.

Part IV: Powerful Alternatives to Traditional Advertising

Digital marketing – search, display, social and mobile – is becoming more important in a global economy, so we cover the basics in this section. We offer advice to get your company Web site to appear when people search online for your product or similar ones, ensure that you always reach the right customers with powerful emails and even give you some tips on the latest powerful online tool – social marketing using social networks. Many marketers also value the power of publicity and we discuss how to help the media cover your stories to get more exposure at far less cost than if you had advertised. Special events also provide you with a powerful alternative or supplement to ad campaigns and can bring you high-quality sales leads.

Part V: Connecting With Your Customers

The classic marketing plan has seven components (the 7 Ps – see Chapter 1), but much of what marketers do (and what is covered throughout Parts II to IV) falls into the fourth P: promotion. In this part, we go deeper into the other Ps: branding, pricing and discounting to create incentives for purchase; the aggressive use of distribution strategies to place your product in front of consumers when and where they are most likely to buy; and selling and servicing customers. We draw your attention to the all-important product and make sure yours is naturally brilliant enough to shine out and beckon customers to you. We also encourage you to examine your distribution, sales, and service, because these can make or break a marketing plan (and a business), too.

Part VI: The Part of Tens

The Part of Tens is a traditional element of *For Dummies* books, and it communicates brief but essential tips that didn't fit easily into the other parts. We recommend that you look at this part whenever you need insights or ideas because it encapsulates much of the essential philosophy and strategies of good marketing practice. And reading this part also helps you avoid some of the dead ends and traps that await the unwary marketer.

Icons Used in This Book

Look for these symbols to help you find valuable stuff throughout the text:

This icon flags specific advice that you can try out in your marketing plan straight away. The icon uses a pound sign for the filament of the light bulb because the acid test of any great idea in business rests in whether it can make you some money.

Sometimes, you need the right perspective on a problem to reach success, so this icon also flags brief discussions of how to think about the task at hand. Often, a basic principle of marketing pops up at this icon to help you handle important decisions.

All marketing is real-world marketing, but this icon means that you can find an actual example of something that worked (or didn't work) in the real world for another marketer.

In marketing, lone rangers don't last long. Successful marketers use a great many supporting services and often bring in graphic artists, ad agencies, digital agencies, research firms, package designers, retail display designers, publicists, and many other specialists. You can't do it all. Sometimes, the best advice we can give you is to pick up your phone and make a call. And this icon marks a spot where we give you leads and contacts.

You can easily run into trouble in marketing because so many mines are just waiting for you to step on them. That's why we've marked them all with this symbol.

When we want to remind you of essential or critical information you need to know in order to succeed, we mark it with this icon. Don't forget!

Where to Go from Here

If you read only one chapter in one business book this year, please make it Chapter 1 of this book. We've made this chapter stand alone as a powerful way to make the most of your marketing and upgrade or enhance the things that you do to make profitable sales. We've packed the rest of the book with good tips and techniques, and it all deserves attention. But whatever else you do or don't get around to, read the first chapter with a pen and action-list at hand!

Or maybe you have a pressing need in one of the more specific areas covered by the book. If fixing your Web site is the top item on your to-do list, go to Chapter 6 first. Or are you working on a letter to customers? Then Chapter 7 on marketing communications and direct mail can really help out your project. Planning an event? Read chapter 8 first. Whatever you're doing, we have a feeling that this book has a chapter or two to help you out. So don't let us slow you down. Get going! It's never too early (or too late) to do a little marketing.

Part I
Where You Are, Where You're Going

'It was a marketing company's suggestion, and it's also a great help to the school finances.'

In this part . . .

Management's job is to see the company not as it is, but as it can be. Helping you recognise that vision is the purpose of this part. Whatever your current business or service is and does, this part helps you to imagine and plan what it may become in the next quarter and year. How do you do that?

You need, first, to understand your marketing programme – the integrated ways in which you reach out to motivate customers and win their loyal support. Next, we highly recommend that you come to grips with the big strategy questions in a marketer's life – who are we and what makes us so special that our sales and profits deserve to grow? A plan, even a simple one-page plan, can help you a lot as you make marketing decisions throughout the coming year.

In this part we also help you ground your marketing efforts by sharing ways of increasing your knowledge of your customers, competitors, and market.

Chapter 1

Making the Most of Your Marketing

*E*ven though you're reading Chapter 1 of a book called *Marketing For Dummies*, you're probably already 'doing' quite a bit of marketing, maybe without even knowing it. Many companies, and even some of the biggest ones, mistake marketing for just advertising. But promotion is just one aspect of marketing; many of the other elements that go into doing good marketing are things that you may think of as essential and everyday parts of doing business, such as setting prices and getting your product into the hands of your customers.

You may be good at doing some or all of these things, but unless you're co-ordinating all of these activities under a formal marketing framework, your efforts aren't nearly as efficient or effective as they could be.

Your Marketing Strategy: A Map to Success

Any marketing you do ought to be based on a *marketing strategy*, which is the big-picture idea driving your success. In order to make your marketing strategy happen you need to work out how you're going to achieve it, which involves writing up a *marketing plan*.

The ultimate campaign

At the end of 2008, Barack Obama was elected president of the United States of America. While we're not going to pretend that marketing alone was behind this victory for the Democratic candidate, there is no doubt it played an important part. Obama cleverly used multiple marketing methods – particularly online ones popular with younger voters – to help build support for his campaign. By embracing these techniques, he was able to show youthful Americans that he was relevant to their lives today and show older voters that he was on top of new trends and developments.

Obama made sure he had a presence on all the big social networks, such as Facebook, as well as some smaller versions too. This way his supporters could stay in touch with his campaign easily as the content was updated regularly. It helped make people feel closer to Obama as a person than is usual in political campaigns.

Obama also kept a regular blog, used micro-blogging service Twitter, which announced his thoughts or feelings to online 'followers' and made use of search marketing optimisation to ensure positive results popped up whenever people searched for his name or policies online. He even posted videos of speeches on YouTube.

While there were many other elements to Obama's marketing campaign too, including more traditional types of advertising on TV and radio, there is no doubt that using the most relevant and innovative techniques helped put the now-president on the world stage. If someone as time-pressed and intelligent as Obama thinks marketing is important enough to spend his energy and effort on, then it's certainly worth you spending your time learning how best to do it.

Knowing Your Customer

Many definitions of marketing have been created by experts with too much time on their hands. The Chartered Institute of Marketing (CIM), the international body for marketing and business development, defines marketing as 'the management process responsible for identifying, anticipating and satisfying customer requirements profitably'. Wow. We prefer our own, simpler version – 'selling more stuff to more people'. But you don't get very far in business these days by just making stuff and then finding people to buy it. Instead, you've got to find out what customers want from you and then create a product to meet those needs. This view is the difference between being what the experts call product-orientated and customer-orientated.

Whether you're product- or customer-orientated, however, the first and most important principle of marketing is this: know your customer. When you understand how customers think and what they like, you can develop products or services that meet those needs and come up with appropriate and appealing ways to communicate them.

You need to understand your customer on two levels: the rational, functional dimension of making a purchase decision, and the irrational, emotional dimension. To truly know your customer, you need to explore two primary questions:

- ✔ **How do they feel about your product?** Does it make them feel good? Do they like its personality? Do they like how it makes them feel about themselves?

- ✔ **What do they think about your product?** Do they understand it? Do they think its features and benefits are superior to those of the competition and can meet their needs? Do they think that your product is good value given its benefits and costs?

Sometimes, one of these dimensions dominates. In other instances, all dimensions are equally important. Which is true of your customers? Depending on your customers, you need to take one of the three following approaches:

✔ **Informational approach.** The approach you use if your customers buy in a rational manner. This approach involves showing the product and talking about its benefits. Use this approach when you think buyers are going to make a careful, thoughtful, informed purchase decision.

✔ **Emotional approach.** This approach pushes emotional instead of rational buttons. For example, a marketer of virus-scanning software may try to scare computer users by asking them in a headline, 'What would it cost you if a virus destroyed everything on your computer right now?' Use an emotional approach when your customers have strong feelings you can tap into and relate to your product or service, or when you think people are going to make an impulsive decision.

✔ **Balanced mix.** This approach uses a combination of informational and emotional appeals. It engages both the rational and emotional sides of the buyer's mind. For example, after a scare-tactic (emotional) headline asking, 'What would it cost you if a virus destroyed everything on your computer right now?', we'd follow up with a few statistics such as, 'One out of every ten computer users suffers a catastrophic virus attack each year.' The facts reinforce the nervous feelings the headline evoked, helping move the prospect toward purchase.

Decide which of these three approaches to use and then use it consistently in all your communications. When in doubt, use the balanced mix to hedge your bets.

Getting focused

You begin to organise and focus your marketing activities when you define as clearly as possible who you're targeting with your marketing.

To help you focus, write a detailed description of this customer, as if you were developing their character for use in a novel or screenplay you plan to write. (The plot of this story is, of course, that the character falls in love – with your product or service.)

If your customers are other businesses, then you can group them by the type of product or service they offer or by the industry sector they're in. If your customers are people, the common ways to define them are by demographics (age and location), socio-economic status or by attitudes and behaviour. Whichever way you try to identify the group or groups of customers most likely to buy from you, the objective is the same: to create a specific product and tailored marketing message that will have the best effect on them.

You further increase your focus when you decide whether your target customers prefer marketing that takes a rational, information-based approach, an emotional, personality-based approach, or a balanced mix of the two. Then you know whom to target, and you have an important clue as to how to target them and communicate with them in every element of your marketing.

Another aspect of your customer focus is whether you want to emphasise attracting new customers, or retaining and growing existing customers. One or the other may need to dominate your marketing, or perhaps you need to balance the two. Marketing to new prospects is usually a different sort of challenge from communicating with and satisfying existing customers, so knowing what is most important helps you to improve the effectiveness of your marketing.

Finding out why customers like you

In marketing, always think about what you do well, and make sure you build on your strengths in everything you do.

You can't be all things to all customers. So now we want you to clearly and succinctly define (notes, please!) what your special strength or advantage is. Start your sentence like this: 'My product (or service) is special because . . . '

 For example, if you're known for good customer service, make sure to train, recognise and reward good service in your employees and to emphasise good service in all communications with your customers and prospects. A photo of a friendly, helpful employee could be featured in your advertising, brochures or web page, because friendliness personifies your excellence in customer service. You can also quote customer testimonials that praise your service. You may want to offer a satisfaction guarantee of some sort, too. Focus on your strength in all that you do and your marketing becomes more profitable.

Working out the best way to find customers

Take a look at the following list to see some of the most common answers – things that businesses often say are most effective at bringing in the customers:

- ✔ **Referrals.** Customers sell the product or you.

- ✔ **Trade shows and professional association meetings.** Contacts sell the product .

- ✔ **Sales calls.** Salespeople sell the product.

- ✔ **TV, radio or print ads.** Advertising sells the product.

- ✔ **Product demonstrations, trial coupons or distribution of free samples.** Product sells itself.

- ✔ **Websites and newsletters.** Internet information sells the product.

- ✔ **Placement and appearance of buildings/shops.** Location sells the product.

As the preceding list indicates, each business has a different optimal formula for attracting customers. Many successful businesses put one-third to two-thirds of their marketing resources into their top way of attracting customers and then use other marketing methods to support and leverage their most effective method. Successful businesses don't spend any time or money on marketing activities inconsistent with their best method or that rob resources from it.

Defining Your Marketing Methods

Peter Drucker, who passed away in 2005 and was one of few justly famous management gurus, defined marketing as the whole firm, taken from the customer's point of view.

Your own view is totally irrelevant to customers. The success of any business comes down to what customers do and they can only act based on what they see. That's why marketing and advertising gurus often say, 'perception is everything'. You must find ways to listen to your customers and to understand their perceptions of your firm and offerings, because your customers (not you) need to define your marketing methods.

This section requires you to think about and write down some ideas, so get out a pencil and some paper to jot down notes while you're reading.

Finding your customer touchpoints

From the customer's point of view, identify the components of your marketing. (The components include everything and anything that the customer sees, hears, talks to, uses or otherwise interacts with.) Each customer interaction, exposure or contact is what we call a touchpoint, where good marketing can help build customer interest and loyalty.

Remember, some of the people who sell your product, such as a wholesaler, may not be in your plan or even on your company's payroll. Are they all representing your firm and product properly – with the focus and professionalism you want?

Analysing your seven Ps

In marketing, points of contact between the customer and your communications, products and people are the only things that really matter. These are *touchpoints*, and we find that most of them aren't itemised in a firm's marketing budget or plan.

 When does your customer interact with your people or product, or information about your people or product? Take a few minutes to make up your master list of touchpoints, which will form the basis of a more extensive and accurate marketing plan. To help you create this list, we suggest you use the seven Ps of marketing: product, price, place, promotion, people, process and physical presence. Now think about your touchpoints using these seven Ps.

There used to be just four Ps of marketing (product, price, place and promotion), which are sometimes referred to as the *marketing mix*. Every marketing expert seems to have his or her own set of Ps, but don't get too hung up on which set of Ps is the right one. The list we give here is the most up to date and covers all the key touchpoints.

Product

What aspects of the product itself are important and have an influence on customer perception or purchase intentions? List the tangible features that relate to how well the product is meeting current and future customer needs, and intangibles like personality, look and feel and also packaging. Remember that first impressions are important for initial purchase, but that performance of the product over time is more important for repurchase and referrals.

Price

What does it cost the customer to obtain and use your product? The list price is often an important element of the customer's perception of price, but it isn't the only one. Discounts and special offers are part of the list of price-based touchpoints, too. Don't forget any extra costs the customer may have to incur, such as the cost of switching from another product to yours.

Place

When and where is your product available to customers? Place is a big influence, because most of the time, customers aren't actively shopping for your product. Nobody runs around all day, every day, looking for what you want to sell. Getting the place and timing right is a big part of success in marketing and often very difficult. When and where do you currently make your product available to customers?

Promotion

This fourth P incorporates any and all ways you choose to communicate with customers. Do you advertise? Send mailings? Promotion includes all aspects of communicating with customers: advertising, personal selling, direct marketing, sales promotion and public relations. Do distributors or other marketing partners also communicate with your customer? If so, include their promotional materials and methods because they help shape the customer's perception too. What about other routine elements of customer communication, such as bills? Routine admin forms part of the impression your marketing communications make too.

People

Almost all businesses offer a variety of human contacts to customers and prospective customers, including salespeople, receptionists, service and support personnel, collections, and sometimes shipping, billing, repair, or other personnel, too. All these points of human contact are important parts of marketing. People need to be trained and motivated to put across the right image for your marketing and that's down to you, not them.

Process

You need to think not only about the point when customers buy your product, but everything that happens before and after that. These are the processes through which you connect the product with the customer. Do you keep them informed about deliveries and can you avoid delays? Do you have a proper complaints procedure? All these issues aren't as back-office as many companies believe, and they all affect the way your customers perceive your business.

Physical presence

Not all businesses make a tangible product and this latest addition to the list of marketing Ps covers those organisations and the image they portray to customers. Physical presence means your company's premises and vehicles and even the appearance of your staff. If you offer services rather than tangible products, you need to provide prospective customers with an image communicating what your organisation represents (you do anyway, you probably just haven't thought about it or formally planned it).

Deciding which P is most important

Ask yourself which of the seven Ps needs to be most important in your marketing. If you've already identified what customers like about you (for example, your special quality or a distinct point of difference from competitors), this may point you toward one of the Ps.

The company that sells the quality of its service, for example, obviously needs to emphasise people and processes in its marketing and business plan. In contrast, the company whose products are technically superior needs to make sure its marketing investments focus on maintaining the product edge.

Don't be tempted to make price the main focus of your marketing. Many marketers emphasise discounts and low prices to attract customers. But price is a dangerous emphasis for any marketing activity; you're buying customers instead of winning them. That approach is a very, very hard way to make a profit in business. Price reasonably, use discounts and vouchers sparingly and look for other things to focus on in your marketing.

Clarifying Your Marketing Expectations

When you make improvements to your marketing, what kind of results can you expect? As a general rule, the percentage change in your marketing activity will at best correspond with the percentage change you see in sales. For example, if you only change 5 per cent of your marketing from one year to the next, you can't expect to see more than a 5 per cent increase in sales over whatever their natural base would be.

Projecting improvements above base sales

Base sales are what you can reasonably count on if you maintain the status quo in your marketing. If, for example, you've seen steady growth in sales of 3 to 6 per cent per year (varying a bit with the economic cycle), then you may reasonably project sales growth of 4 per cent next year, presuming everything else stays the same. But things rarely do stay the same, so you may want to look for any threats from new competitors, changing technology, shifting customer needs and so on, and be careful to adjust your natural base downward if you anticipate any such threats materialising next year. Your base, if you don't change your marketing, may even be a negative growth rate, because competitors and customers tend to change even if you don't.

When you have a good handle on what your base may be for a status quo sales projection, you can begin to adjust it upward to reflect any improvements you introduce. Be careful in using this tactic, however, because some of the improvements are fairly clearly linked to future sales, while others aren't. If you've tested or tried something already, then you have some real experience upon which to project the improvement's impact. If you're trying something that is quite new to you, be very cautious and conservative about your projections at first, until you have your own hard numbers and real-world experience to go on.

Planning to fail, understanding why and trying again

Start small with new ideas and methods in marketing so that you can afford to fail and gain knowledge from the experience and then adjust and try again. In marketing, you don't have to feel bad about making mistakes, as long as you recognise what went wrong and take away useful lessons.

We're positive pessimists in relation to marketing. Our philosophy is, 'what can go wrong, will go wrong . . . and we'll be fine!' Avoid being too heavily committed to any single plan or investment. Keep as much flexibility in your marketing as you can. Favouring monthly commissions for salespeople and distributors is also wise, because then their pay is variable with your sales and goes down if sales fall, which means you don't have to be entirely right about your sales projections.

Flexibility, cautious optimism and contingency planning give you the knowledge that you can survive the worst. That way, you have the confidence to be a creative, innovative marketer with the courage to grow your business and optimise your marketing. And you can afford to profit from your mistakes.

Don't expect to solve all your company's problems through your marketing. If the product is flawed from the customer's perspective, the best thing you can do as a marketer is to present the evidence and encourage your company to improve the product. Don't let others in your company try to tell you otherwise.

Marketing activity needs to constantly evolve and improve. Most companies fall far short of their full potential, which is why for every hundred businesses, only a few really succeed and grow. The others don't have the right marketing needed to maximise their success. Think big in your marketing. You can always do something more to improve your effectiveness and your results.

Chapter 2

Your Marketing Strategy and Plan

*S*trategies are the big-picture insights that guide your marketing activity and make sure all its elements add up to success. A good strategy gives a special kind of high-level direction and purpose to all you do. This chapter shows you how to take your focus to an even higher level, by centring your marketing on a single, core strategy that gives you an overarching goal. With this strategy, your marketing begins to fall into place naturally.

Benefiting from a Core Strategy

Key to using a core strategy is making sure that your strategy is the hub around which all your marketing activities rotate.

In Figure 2-1, you can see how a strategy provides an organising central point to a range of marketing activities. This example is for the gift shop at an art gallery; its strategic goal was to get gallery visitors to come into the shop and make a substantial purchase. Gift-shop staff developed a variety of tactics for their marketing, each of which is clearly helpful in achieving the strategy or the goal.

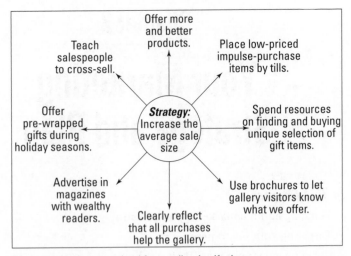

Figure 2-1: A strategy wheel for a gallery's gift shop.

As you create your own core strategy, make sure you can draw a solid arrow from your chosen strategy to each of the activities on the rim. Also try to explain in simple words how the activity helps implement your strategy and achieve your strategic goal. If the link to the big-picture strategy isn't clear, modify or eliminate the activity.

If you have more than one strategy, draw more than one wheel. But avoid too many or your resources get spread so thinly that you can't achieve *any* of your goals. Also, try to select strategies that have some synergy. The strategy wheels need to belong on the same wagon or they can't move you forward.

Expanding with a Market Expansion Strategy

Market expansion is the most common strategy in marketing and the idea is disarmingly simple. Just pick some new territory and head out into it. Oh, and don't come back until you've struck gold.

Expanding sales within your territory

The drinks company Innocent is expanding its market without expanding its geographic territory. In fact, as the company makes fruit smoothies, expanding geographically is difficult, as the fresh nature of its products mean they don't store or ship particularly well. Innocent's expansion plans are based on increasing the range of products it offers. As well as offering single-serve smoothies, it sells family-size packs, fruit-flavoured waters, smaller cartons for kids and even little snack-sized 'veg pots'. With a larger product line, Innocent can occupy more shelf space in the supermarkets, cafes and sandwich bars where it sells and get a larger 'share of throat' as a result. But how much have Innocent's sales goals increased to reflect this market expansion strategy? The answer to that question depends not only on the increase in Innocent's potential market due to its product expansion, but also on the strategic risks of growing its market. The main risks are that new sales won't really be new, but may be replacement sales for its original smoothies, and that customers won't like the new products as much as the old. Innocent needs to make sure it keeps product quality high and that the new range is different enough from its original product line not to cannibalise its sales.

The market expansion strategy has two variants: you can expand your market by finding new customers for your current products (often this means going into new geographic territory to do so), or you can try to sell new products to your existing customers and market.

If you choose to adopt a market expansion strategy as your main focus – the hub of your marketing wheel – make sure most of your marketing activity is working toward this goal. For example, if you seek publicity, make sure most of it is about your new product or in your new market, not about the old. All of your resources may be needed to effectively expand your market. And the faster you get through the transition and achieve your growth goal, the better, because extra costs are usually associated with any expansion.

Risk increases if you experiment with new products – defined as anything you're not accustomed to making and marketing. So you need to discount your first year's sales projections for a new market by some factor to reflect the degree of risk. A good general rule is to cut back the sales projection by 20 to 50 per cent, depending upon your judgement of how new and risky the product is to you and your team.

Risk also increases if you enter any new market – defined as new kinds of customers at any stage of your distribution channel. You should also discount those sales projections by 20 to 50 per cent if you're entering a new market to reflect your lack of familiarity with the customers.

What if you're introducing a new product into a new market? *Start-up firms* – those just setting out in business – often run both these risks at once, and need to discount sales projections even further to reflect them. Sometimes a market expansion strategy is so risky that you really shouldn't count on any revenues in the first year. Better to be conservative and last long enough to work out how to correctly handle the marketing than to over-promise and have your marketing die before it succeeds.

Specialising with a Market Segmentation Strategy

A *market segmentation strategy* is a specialisation strategy in which you target and cater to (specialise in) just one narrow type or group of customer. If you're in the consulting business, you can specialise in for-profit businesses or not-for-profit businesses. You can even design and market your services to individuals – as, for example, a career development consultant does. Each of these types of customer represents a subgroup, or segment, of the larger consulting industry. And you can drill down even further to define smaller segments if you wish. You can specialise in consulting to the healthcare industry, or to manufacturers of boxes and packaging, or to start-up firms in the high-tech sector. Certain consultants use each of these strategies to narrow down their markets.

A segmentation strategy has the advantage of allowing you to tailor your product and your entire marketing effort to a clearly defined group with uniform, specific characteristics. For example, the consulting firm that targets only the healthcare industry knows that prospective clients can be found at a handful of industry conferences and that they have certain common concerns around which consulting services can be focused. Many smaller consulting firms target a narrowly defined market segment in order to compete against larger, but less specialised, consulting firms.

Specialising to outdo the competition

Use the segmentation strategy if you think your business can be more profitable by specialising in a more narrowly defined segment than you currently service. This strategy works well when you face too many competitors in your broader market and you can't seem to carve out a stable, profitable customer base of your own. Also use the specialisation strategy if it takes better advantage of things you're good at. This strategy sits well with the idea of focusing better, based on your unique qualities (see Chapter 1).

Adding a segment to expand your market

If you're running out of customers and market and need to expand (see the 'Expanding with a Market Expansion Strategy' section earlier in this chapter), targeting a new segment is one way of doing so. For example, the consultant specialising in coaching executives in the healthcare industry could decide to start offering a similar service to not-for-profit organisations. A different approach and different marketing may be needed because the two industries are different in many ways and have only partial overlap (much of the healthcare industry is not-for-profit, but many not-for-profit organisations are not hospitals). By specialising in two segments instead of just one, the consulting firm might be able to grow its total sales significantly.

Developing a Market Share Strategy

Another common and powerful strategy is to increase your market share through your marketing activities. In essence, this means taking some business from your competitors. *Market share* is, very simply, your sales as a percentage of total sales for your product category in your market (or in your market segment if you use a segmentation strategy too).

Calculating your share of the market

If you sell £2 million worth of inflatable paddling pools and the world market totals £20 million per year, then your share of the global inflatable paddling pool market is 10 per cent. The calculation is almost that simple. Or is it? Not quite. To accurately identify your market share, you need to consider what units to use to measure sales, the total sales in your market, your product category and more. The following sections explain.

Choosing a unit

What unit should you measure sales in? Sterling, euros, dollars, units, containers or grams are fine, as long as you use the same unit throughout. You can calculate your share of the European market for fibre optic cable in metres sold, so long as both your sales and industry sales are measured in metres sold, and euro sales or metric tonnes aren't mixed into the equation by mistake. Just pick whatever seems to make sense for your product and the information you have access to.

For example, if you're a distributor of salad cream to UK supermarkets and grocery shops, you can buy a market intelligence report on the salad sauces sector (the figures we use here are from a Mintel report) to discover that the total salad cream and mayonnaise market was worth £146 million in 2007. If your sales are £7.8 million, then your market share is 7.8 ÷ 146 or 5.3 per cent.

The report may also tell you that Brits spend almost twice as much on mayonnaise as traditional salad cream, a market segment that doesn't compete directly with you, in which case you can calculate your market share of the 34 per cent of total sales that are solely salad cream: $15.9 \div (0.34 \times 474)$ or 9.8 per cent – a much bigger share, based on a narrower definition of the market. Which calculation is right?

Defining your product category

What is your product category? This may be the most important strategic question you ever ask or answer. If you sell salad cream, are you competing with the mass-market mayonnaise brands such as Hellmann's and Kraft, or not? Should you count these products' sales in your market share calculations and try to win sales from them?

Ask your customers. Are they choosing among all the salad sauce options, or just some of them? What matters is *customer perception*: how the customers see the category. So watch your customers or ask them to find out what their purchase options are. Get a feel for how customers view their choices – then include all the likely or close choices in your definition of the market. With salad sauces, you may find that a majority of consumers do sometimes buy mayonnaise as well as salad cream. And you may also find that you must, as a distributor, fight for grocery shelf space and room on supermarket aisles against the mass-market brands. So you probably do need to use total salad sauce market sales (including mayonnaise) as your base, not salad cream sales alone.

Researching the total sales in your market

To calculate market share, you need to estimate the total sales in your market. Doing so requires some research on your part. (Sorry, you can't avoid the research.) While you're at it, why not try to get some historical data – the sales in your market for the past five or ten years, for example? This information allows you to look at the growth rate of your market – which is an indicator of its future potential for you and your competitors.

Such data is most easily obtained from industry trade associations or marketing research firms, many of which track sales by year in different product categories. Many companies offer these market reports, but some of the best known are Mintel (www.mintel.com), Euromonitor (www.euromonitor.com) and Datamonitor (www.datamonitor.com). Market reports will cost you between £200 and £20,000, depending on the source, geographic scope and size of the report. A cheaper option for more rudimentary data is the trade magazines for the industry of your choice (that generally cover industry size and trends at least once a year). *Marketing Week*, for example, publishes analysis and research on a different consumer goods sector every week. Trade magazines are often the best source for the B2B marketer.

Such data is increasingly available on the web, too. For keyword searches, enter the name of your product combined with 'sales figures' or 'market size' into a search engine such as Google and see what you can find. Sites with marketing information abound.

Using the napkin method for estimating market share

Take a look at this simple method for estimating market size and share that you can sketch on the back of a napkin if you haven't the time or money for fancier approaches:

1. **Estimate the number of customers in your market (how many people in your country are likely to buy toothpaste, how many businesses in your city buy consulting services?).**

2. **Estimate how much each buys a year, on average (six tubes, fifteen hours of consulting service).**

   You can check your sales records, or ask some people what they do, to improve this estimate.

3. **Now, just multiply the two figures together to get the total size of the annual market, and then divide your unit sales into it to get your share.**

Setting market share goals

Market share gives you a simple way of comparing your progress with your competitors from period to period. If your share drops, you're losing; if your share grows, you're winning – the calculation's that simple. Most marketing plans are thus based at least partly on a *strategic market share goal*, such as: 'Increase share from 5 to 7 per cent by introducing a product upgrade and increasing our use of trial-stimulating special offers.' A salad cream wholesaler, for example, whose product competes primarily with speciality salad cream brands and secondarily with mass-market mayonnaise products, may develop strategic goals that look something like this:

- Increase value sales of our products to end consumers of salad sauces from 5.3 to 8 per cent.

- Protect our share of the speciality salad cream market by keeping it at 15 per cent or higher.

- Differentiate our product even more from Hellmann's, Kraft, Heinz and other mass-market salad sauce brands by emphasising what makes our salad cream special to avoid having to compete directly against much larger marketers.

Post mortems on last year's marketing plan should always be based on an examination of what market share change accompanied it. If you don't already do routine post mortems, or careful analyses of what happened and why it differed from your plans, you should. If the past period's marketing doubled your market share, seriously consider replicating it. But if share stayed the same or fell, you're ready for something new. So whether you make share gain the focus of your marketing or not, at least keep it in mind and try not to lose any share.

Should you invest in growing your share?

In addition to its use as a benchmark, market share may also give you insights into the realities of your potential success or at least into the future profitability of your product and business. Many experts believe that market share is a good long-term predictor of profitability, arguing that market-share leaders are more profitable and successful than other competitors. This belief is taken so seriously in some companies that brands with low market share are dropped so as to focus spending on those brands with a chance at category leadership.

If this theory is correct, you need to build market share aggressively. We favour share-growth strategies because some good studies are showing that high-share businesses have higher returns on investment on average. The Strategic Planning Institute (a consulting firm in Cambridge, USA) has extensive data on market share and financial returns in its PIMS (Profit Impact of Marketing Strategy) database. We like its database because it looks at *business units* (divisions or subsidiaries in a single market) rather than whole companies and is thus more marketing orientated. And those business units with higher market shares have higher pre-tax *returns on investment* (or ROI; the percentage yield or the amount earned as a percentage of the amount invested). The relationship is roughly as shown in Table 2-1.

Table 2-1   Profiting from Market Share

Market Share (%)	ROI (%)
Less than 7	10
7 to 15	16
15 to 23	21
23 to 38	23
38 or more	33

Also impressive is some PIMS data suggesting that a gain in market share seems to lead to a corresponding gain in ROI (although the ROI gain is a half to a quarter as large on a per-centage basis). You can visit www.pimsonline.com for more details of its research on effective marketing strategies.

Oh, by the way, we must warn you that loss of share leads to loss of ROI. So defending existing market share is a good strat-egy. You can accomplish this by keeping your brand's image well polished, by innovating to keep your product fresh and by designing good marketing campaigns in general. We gener-ally advise marketers to defend leading shares, and to try to grow their low shares into leading positions. For example, if you're a strong third-place finisher in the share race, you should probably consider investing in a growth effort in order to leapfrog the number-two player and get within striking distance of the number-one slot.

But not all studies say the same thing about market share. If you're a small firm with a narrow market niche, trying to grow your share by expanding aggressively can get you in trouble. Balance share growth with the need to avoid excessive risks.

Achieving your market share goals

How can these market share goals be achieved? Consider the salad cream wholesaler example For starters, a distributor needs retail shelf space, so you may need to push to win a larger share of shelf space from retailers, especially if you're dealing with large supermarkets. To earn the right to this shelf space, you may need to do some consumer advertising or publicity, provide the stores with good point-of-purchase displays or signs, improve your product packaging or do other things to help ensure that consumers take a stronger interest in buying your products.

This plan needs to revolve around the goal of increasing share by 1½ percentage points. Each point of share is worth £4.74 million in annual sales (1 per cent of the total sales in the market), so a plan that involved spending, say, an extra £250,000 to win a 1.5 per cent share gain can provide an extra £7.1 million if it works. But will it work? To be cautious, the marketer may want to discount this projection of £7.1 million in additional sales by a risk factor of, say, 25 per cent, which cuts it back to a projected gain of £5.3 million.

Now consider timing. Remember that the plan can't achieve the full gain in the first month of the year. A sales projection starting at the current level of sales in month one and ramping up to the projected increase by, say, month six, may be reasonable. Dividing £5.3 million by 12 to find the monthly value of the risk-discounted 1.5 share point increase gives you £444,375 in extra monthly sales for the sixth month and beyond. Lower increases apply to earlier months when the marketing is just starting to kick in. But the marketing expenses tend to be concentrated in the early months, reflecting the need to invest in advance in order to grow your market share.

Everything about your marketing follows from these simple strategies. And you can tell when you need them by looking at where you are in your product's life cycle, which makes your strategic thinking fairly simple.

Now, you should have some idea what your marketing strategy is and which markets you need to expand in order to grow your business. But with every good strategy comes a good marketing plan to set that strategy into real achievable actions.

Writing a marketing plan

You don't have to write a marketing plan to use this book or even to benefit from this chapter. But you may want to, because doing so isn't as hard as you may think, and, most important, a good plan increases the odds of success. In fact, most of the really successful businesses we know – small or large, new or old – write a careful marketing plan at least once a year.

Marketing combines lots of activities and expenditures in the hope of generating or increasing sales and maintaining or increasing market share. You won't see those sales numbers rise without a coherent plan linking a strategy based on the strengths of your position to your sales and marketing activities that can convince targeted customers to purchase. Marketing can get out of control or confused in a hurry unless you have a plan. Every successful business needs a marketing plan. (Yes, even if you're in a small or start-up business. In fact, especially if you are; you don't have the resources to waste on unplanned or ineffective marketing.)

Identifying Some Planning Rules and Tips

Marketing plans vary significantly in format and outline from company to company, but all have core components covering:

✔ **Your current position** in terms of your product, customers, competition and broader trends in your market.

- ✔ **For established businesses, what results you achieved in the previous period** in terms of sales, market share and possibly also in terms of profits, customer satisfaction or other measures of customer attitude and perception. You may want to include measures of customer retention, size, frequency of purchase or other indicators of customer behaviour, if you think them important to your new plan.

- ✔ **Your strategy** – the big picture that will help you get improved results.

- ✔ **The details of your marketing activities**, including all your company's specific activities, grouped by area or type, with explanations of how these activities fit the company's strategy and reflect the current situation.

- ✔ **The numbers**, including sales projections and costs. Consider whether knowing these additional numbers would help your business: market share projections, sales to your biggest customers or distributors, costs and returns from any special offers you plan to use, sales projections and commissions by territory or whatever helps you quantify your specific marketing activities.

- ✔ **Your *learning plans*.** You may want to test the waters or experiment on a small scale if you have a new business or new product or if you're experimenting with a new or risky marketing activity. You need to determine what positive results you want to see before committing to a higher level. Wisdom is knowing what you don't know – and planning how to work it out.

The more unfamiliar the waters, the more flexibility and caution your plan needs. If you're a start-up, for example, consider a step-wise plan with a timeline and alternatives or options in case of problems. Especially if you're writing a marketing plan for the first time, make flexibility your first objective. Avoid large advance purchases of media space or time, use short runs of marketing materials at the copy shop over cheaper off-set printing of large inventories and so on. Optimising your plan for flexibility means preserving your choice and avoiding commitments of resources. Spending in small increments allows you to change the plan as you go.

If your business has done this all before, however, and your plan builds on years of experience, you can more safely favour *economies of scale* over flexibility. (Advertising, for example, is cheaper and more efficient if you do it on a large scale, because you get bigger discounts on design of ads and purchase of media space or airtime.) If you know a media investment is likely to produce leads or sales, go ahead and buy media in larger chunks to get good rates. You don't have to be as cautious about testing mailing lists with small-scale mailings of a few hundred pieces. A good in-house list supplemented by 20 per cent or fewer newly purchased names probably warrants a major mailing without as much emphasis on advance testing. Adjust your plan to favour economies of scale if you feel confident that you can make sound judgements in advance.

But always leave yourself at least a *little* wiggle room. Reality never reflects your plans and projections 100 per cent of the time. Aim for an 80 per cent match in marketing, and plan accordingly.

The following sections share a few other suggestions to follow if you want to increase your marketing plan's chances of success.

Avoiding common mistakes

Marketing campaigns end up like leaky boats very easily, so be sure to total up your costs fully and carefully. Each activity seems worthy at the time, but too many of them fail to produce a positive return – ending up like holes in the bottom of your boat: too many of those holes, and the water starts rising. To avoid the costly but all-too-common mistakes that many marketers make, follow these suggestions:

- ✔ **Don't ignore the details.** You build good plans from details like customer-by-customer, item-by-item or territory-by-territory sales projections. Generalising about an entire market is hard. Your sales and cost projections are easier to get right if you break them down to their smallest natural units (like individual territory sales or customer orders), do estimates for each of these small units, and then add those estimates up to get your totals.

✔ **Don't imitate the competitors.** Even though everyone seems to market their products in a certain way, you don't have to imitate them. High-performing plans clearly point out what aspects of the marketing are conventional and why – and these plans also include some original, innovative or unique elements to help differentiate your company from and outperform the competition. Your business is unique, so make your plan reflect your special talents or advantages.

✔ **Don't feel confined by last period's budget and plan.** Repeat or improve the best-performing elements of the past plans, but cut back on any elements that didn't produce high returns. Every plan includes some activities and spending that aren't necessary and can be cut out (or reworked) when you do it all over again next year.

✔ **Don't engage in unnecessary spending.** Always think your plan through and run the numbers before signing a contract or writing a cheque. Many of the people and businesses you deal with to execute your marketing activities are salespeople themselves. They want your marketing money and they don't care as much as you do whether you get a good return or not.

Breaking down your plan into simple sub-plans

If all your marketing activities are consistent and clearly of one kind, a single plan is fine. But what if you sell services (like consulting or repairs) and also products? You may find that you need to work up one plan for selling products (perhaps this strategy aims to find new customers) and another plan for convincing product buyers to also use your services. Follow the general rule that if the plan seems too complicated – divide and conquer! Then total everything up to get the big picture with its overall projections and budgets.

If you have 50 products in five different product categories, writing your plan becomes much easier if you come up with 50 sales projections for each product and five separate promotional plans for each category of product. (Believe it or not, this method sounds tricky but will make life much simpler.) We've included some methods to break down your planning, making it easier and simpler to do:

✔ Analyse, plan and budget sales activities by sales territory and region (or by major customer if you're a business-to-business (B2B) marketer with a handful of dominant companies as your clients).

✔ Project revenues and promotions by individual product and by industry (if you sell into more than one).

✔ Plan your advertising and other promotions by product line or other broad product category, as promotions often have a generalised effect on the products within the category.

✔ Plan and budget publicity for your company as a whole. Only budget and plan publicity for an individual product if you introduce it or modify it in some way that may attract media attention.

✔ Plan and budget for brochures, websites and other informational materials. Be sure to remain focused in your subject choices: one brochure per topic. Multipurpose brochures or sites never work well. If a website sells cleaning products to building maintenance professionals, don't plan for it to broker gardening and lawn-mowing services to suburban homeowners as well. Different products and customers need separate plans.

Writing a Powerful Executive Summary

An executive summary is a one-page plan. This wonderful document conveys essential information about your company's planned year of activities in a couple of hundred well-chosen words or less. If you ever get confused or disorientated, this clear, concise summary can guide you back to the correct strategic path. A good executive summary should be a powerful advertisement for your marketing, communicating the purpose and essential activities of your plan in such a compelling manner that everyone who reads it eagerly leaps into action and does the right things to make your vision come true.

Draft the executive summary early in the year as a guide to your thinking and planning. But revise this document often, and finish it only after finishing all the other sections, because it needs to summarise them.

Help yourself (and your readers, if others in your company are going to be involved in approving or implementing the plan) by giving an overview of what's the same and what's different in this plan, compared with the previous period's plan. Draft a short paragraph covering these two topics.

Summarise the main points of your plan and make clear whether the plan is:

- ✔ **Efficiency orientated:** For example, your plan introduces a large number of specific improvements in how you market your product.

- ✔ **Effectiveness orientated:** For example, your plan identifies a major opportunity or problem and adopts a new strategy to respond to it.

Make sure that you summarise the bottom-line results – what your projected revenues will be (by product or product line, unless you have too many to list on one page) and what the costs are. Also show how these figures differ from last year's figures. Keep the whole summary under one page in length if you possibly can.

If you have too many products to keep the summary under a page, you can list them by product line. But a better option is to do more than one plan. If a plan can't be neatly summarised in a page, it probably needs more thought. We've worked with many businesses in which marketing prepares a separate plan for each product.

Clarifying and Quantifying Your Objectives

Objectives are the quantified, measurable versions of your strategies. For example, if your strategy involves raising the quality of service and opening a new territory in order to grow your sales and market share, you need to think through how you'll do all that and set a percentage increase goal for sales and a new, higher goal for market share. These numbers become your objectives. The objectives flow from your thinking about strategies and tactics, but put them up near the front of your plan to help others quickly understand what you're saying.

 What objectives do you want your plan to help you accomplish? Will the plan increase sales by 25 per cent, reposition a product to make it more appealing to upmarket buyers or launch a new product? Maybe the plan will combine several products into a single family brand and build awareness of this brand through print and radio advertising. Address these sorts of topics in the objectives section of the plan. These points give the plan its focus.

If you write clear, compelling objectives, you'll never get too confused about what to write in other sections – when in doubt, you can always look back at these objectives and remind yourself what you're trying to accomplish and why.

 Try to write this part of the plan early, but keep in mind that you'll rewrite it often as you gather more information and do more thinking. Objectives are such a key foundation for the rest of the plan that you can't ever stop thinking about them. However, for all their importance, objectives don't need a lot of words – half a page to two pages, at most.

Preparing a Situation Analysis

The context is different for every marketing plan. A *situation analysis* examines the context, looking at trends, customer preferences, competitor strengths and weaknesses and anything else that may impact sales. The question your situation analysis must answer is, 'What's happening?' The answer to this question can take many forms, so we can't give you an easy formula for preparing the situation analysis. You should analyse the most important market changes to your company – these changes can be the sources of problems but also potential opportunities.

What are the most important changes that have occurred since you last examined the situation? The answer depends on the situation. See the difficulty? Yet somehow you have to gain enough insight into what's happening to see the problems and opportunities clearly.

Seeing trends more clearly than others do

Your goal is to see the changes more clearly than the competition. What you want from your situation analysis is:

- **Information parity:** When you know as much as your leading competitors. If you don't do enough research and analysis, your competitors will have an information advantage. Therefore, you need to gain enough insight to put you on a level playing field with your rivals. (That includes knowing about any major plans they may have. Collect rumours about new products, new people and so on. At a minimum, do a weekly search on a web-based search engine for any news about them. You can also customise web pages such as Google News to highlight any stories about specific brands or businesses and have them delivered to your email inbox.)

- **Information advantage in specific areas:** This is insight into the market that your competitors don't have. Information advantage puts you on the uphill side of an uneven playing field and that's an awfully good place from which to design and launch a marketing campaign. Look for new fashions, new technologies, new ways to segment the market – anything that you can use to change the rules of the game even slightly in your favour.

Most marketing plans and planners don't think about their situation analysis in this way. We're telling you one of our best-kept secrets because we don't want you to waste time on the typical *pro forma* situation analysis, in which the marketer rounds up the usual suspects and parades dull information in front of them without gaining an advantage from it. That approach, although common, does nothing to make the plan a winner.

Building a competitor analysis table

Develop a format for a generic competitor analysis table. Make entries on the following rows in columns labelled for Competitor #1, Competitor #2, Competitor #3 and so on:

- ✔ **Company.** Describe how the market perceives it and its key product.

- ✔ **Key personnel.** Who are the managers, and how many employees do they have in total?

- ✔ **Financial.** Who owns it, how strong is its *cash position* (does it have spending power or is it struggling to pay its bills?), what were its sales in the last two years?

- ✔ **Sales, distribution and pricing.** Describe its primary sales channel, discount/pricing structure and market share estimate.

- ✔ **Product/service analysis.** What are the strengths and weaknesses of its product or service?

- ✔ **Scaled assessment of product/service.** Explore relevant subjects such as market acceptance, quality of packaging, ads and so on. Assign a score of between 1 and 5 (with 5 being the strongest) for each characteristic you evaluate. Then add the scores for each competitor's row to see which seems strongest, overall.

- ✔ **Comparing yourself to competitor ratings.** If you rate yourself on these attributes, too, how do you compare? Are you stronger? If not, you can include increasing your competitive strength as one of your plan's strategic objectives.

Explaining Your Marketing Strategy

Many plans use this section to get specific about the objectives by explaining how your company will accomplish them. Some writers find this task easy, but others keep getting confused about the distinction between an objective and a strategy. The objective simply states something your business hopes to accomplish in the next year. The strategy emphasizes the big-picture approach to accomplishing that objective, giving some good pointers as to what road you'll take.

An objective sounds like this: Solidify our leadership of the home PC market by increasing market share by 2 points.

A strategy sounds like this: Introduce hot new products and promote our brand name with an emphasis on high quality components, in order to increase our market share by 2 points.

Combining strategies and objectives

Some people view the difference between objectives and strategies as a pretty fine line. If you're comfortable with the distinction, write a separate *Strategy* section. If you're not sure about the difference, combine this section with the objectives section and title it *Objectives and Strategies*; what you call the points doesn't matter, as long as they're good.

Your strategies accomplish your objectives through the tactics (the seven Ps) of your marketing plan. (See Chapter 1 for a discussion of the seven Ps, sometimes also known as the *marketing mix.*) The plan explains how your tactics use your strategies to accomplish your objectives.

Don't pull a Napoleon. If you're currently the tenth-largest competitor, don't write a plan to become the number one largest by the end of the year simply based on designing all your ads and mailings to claim you're the best. Make sure that your strategy is achievable. Would the average person agree that your strategy sounds attainable with a little hard work? (If you're not sure, find some average people and ask them.) And do you have enough resources to execute the strategy in the available time?

Also, be realistic about what marketing can achieve for you. If you plan to get employers to give their employees every other Friday off so those employees can attend special workshops that your firm sponsors, well, we hope you have a back-up plan. Employers don't give employees a lot of extra time off, no matter how compelling your sales pitch or brochure may be. The same is true of consumer marketing. You simply cannot change strongly held public attitudes without awfully good new evidence.

Additionally, don't simply copy the strategy of a rival or plan to do too many things you don't really know about. There's no point being a 'me-too' competitor rather than unique or launching a cheese factory if you're better at producing computer chips.

Is your strategy flaky?

What do you do if you're the leading producer of breakfast cereals, but the total market for breakfast cereals is declining? Find new and exciting ways for people to consume breakfast cereals, obviously. When Kellogg decided to launch its Cereal Mates product, it thought it was following changes in customer behaviour rather than asking people to radically change their ways. The pattern of breakfast consumption had changed, with fewer people having the time or inclination for a sit-down breakfast at home. The trend was for breakfast on the go, so Kellogg created cereal to go.

Cereal Mates was an all-in-one single serve version of Kellogg's most popular breakfast cereals. It came with its own spoon and was sealed in such a way that the milk didn't need refrigerating. Mistake number one – consumers didn't want warm milk on their cereal. So Kellogg changed tactic and situated Cereal Mates in supermarket chill cabinets. Mistake number two – who looks in the chill cabinets for breakfast cereal?

Consumers were even more confused by the advertising, which showed kids helping themselves at home while their parents slept. Finally, the price was prohibitive (certainly too high to encourage trial) at around 65p. At the time, you could buy a family-sized box of cereal for not much more than that.

Cereal Mates was eventually killed off when Kellogg finally realised they had mistaken a change in consumer eating habits with a change in the way people wanted to consume breakfast cereal – not the same thing at all. The company got the strategy right when it eventually launched a product that could be eaten on the go but was only dimly related to cereal – its NutriGrain bars. You have to sense-check your strategy, especially when you're asking your customers to try something radically different.

Summarising Your Marketing Mix

Your *marketing mix* is the combination of marketing activities you use to influence a targeted group of customers to purchase a specific product or line of products. Creating an integrated and coherent marketing mix starts, in our view, with an analysis of your *touchpoints* – in other words, how your organisation can influence customer purchases. And the creative process ends with some decisions about how to use these touchpoints. Usually you can come up with tactics in all seven of the marketing Ps: product, price, place (or distribution), promotion, people, process and physical presence.

Prioritising your touchpoints and determining cost

Prioritise by picking a few primary touchpoints – ones that will dominate your marketing for the coming planning period. Make the choice carefully; try to pick no more than three main activities to take the lead. Use the other touchpoints in secondary roles to support your primary points. Now begin to develop specific plans for each.

Say that you're considering using print ads in trade magazines to let retail store buyers know about your hot new line of products and the in-store display options you have for them. That's great, but now you need to get specific. You need to pick some magazines. You also need to decide how many of what sort of ads you'll run, and then price out this advertising campaign.

Do the same analysis for each of the items on your list of marketing components. Work your way through the details until you have an initial cost figure for what you want to do with each component. Total these costs and see if the end result seems realistic.

A spreadsheet greatly helps this process. Just build formulas that add the costs to reach subtotals and a grand total, and then subtract the grand total from the projected sales figure to get a bottom line for your campaign. Figure 2-2 shows the format for a very simple spreadsheet that gives a quick and accurate marketing campaign overview for a small business.

In this figure, you can see what a campaign looks like for a company that wholesales products to gift shops around the UK. This company uses personal selling, telemarketing and print advertising as its primary marketing components. The company also budgets some money in this period to finish developing and begin introducing a new line of products.

This company's secondary influence points don't use much of the marketing budget when compared with the primary influence points. But the secondary influence points are important too. A new web page is expected to handle a majority of customer enquiries and act as a virtual catalogue, permitting the company to cut back on its catalogue printing and postage costs. Also, the company plans to introduce a new line of floor displays for use at point of purchase by selected retailers. Marketers expect this display unit, combined with improved see-through packaging, to increase turnover of the company's products in retail stores.

Overview of Campaign to Target Retail Store Buyers	
Components	**Direct Marketing Costs (£)**
Primary influence points:	
– Sales calls	£265,100
– Telemarketing	162,300
– Ads in trade magazines	650,000
– New product line development	100,000
	Subtotal: £1,177,400
Secondary influence points:	
– Quantity discounts	£45,000
– Point-of-purchase displays	73,500
– New Web page with online catalogue	15,000
– Printed catalogue	30,500
– PR	22,000
– Packaging redesign	9,200
	Subtotal: £195,200
Projected Sales from This Programme	£13,676,470
Minus Campaign Costs	– 1,372,600
Net Sales from This Marketing Campaign	**£12,303,870**

Figure 2-2: A campaign budget, prepared on a spreadsheet.

Marketing plans for multiple groups

If your marketing plan covers multiple groups of customers, you need to include multiple spreadsheets because each group of customers will need a different marketing mix.

For example, the company whose wholesale marketing campaign you see in Figure 2-2 sells to gift shops. But the company also does some business with stationery shops. And even though the same salespeople call on both, each of these customers has different products and promotions. They buy from different catalogues. They don't use the same kinds of displays. They read different trade magazines. Consequently, the company has to develop a separate marketing campaign for each customer, allocating any overlapping expenses appropriately. (For example, if you make two-thirds of your sales calls to gift shops, then the sales-calls expense for the gift shop campaign should be two-thirds of the total sales budget.)

Exploring Your Marketing Components

In this part of your plan, you need to explain the details of how you aim to use each component of your marketing mix. Devote a section to each component. The more of your thinking you get on paper, the easier implementing the plan will be later – as will rewriting the plan next year.

Although this portion is the lengthiest part of your plan, we're not going to cover it in depth here.

At a minimum, this part of the plan should have sections covering the seven Ps – the product, pricing, place (or distribution), promotion, people, process and physical presence. But more likely, you'll want to break these categories down into more specific areas.

Don't bother going into detail in your marketing plan on components that you cannot alter. Sometimes, the person writing the marketing plan can't change pricing policy, order up a new product line or dictate a shift in distribution strategy. Acknowledge in writing any issues or challenges you have to cope with, given that you can't change other factors. Now write a plan that does everything you can reasonably do given your constraints.

Managing Your Marketing

This section summarises the main activities that you, your employees or your employer must perform in order to implement the components of your marketing mix. The section then assigns these activities to individuals, justifying the assignments by considering issues such as an individual's capabilities and capacities, and how the company will supervise and control that individual.

Sometimes this section gets more sophisticated by addressing management issues, such as how to make the sales force more productive or whether to decentralise the marketing function. If you have salespeople or distributors, develop plans for organising, motivating, tracking and controlling them. Also create a plan for them to use in generating, allocating and tracking sales leads. Start these subsections by describing the current approach, and do a strengths/weaknesses analysis of that approach, using input from the salespeople, reps or distributors in question. End by describing any incremental changes/improvements you can think to make.

Make sure that you've run your ideas by the people in question *first* and received their input. Don't surprise your salespeople, sales reps or distributors with new systems or methods. If you do, these people will probably resist the changes, and sales will slow down. People execute sales plans well only if they understand and believe in those plans.

Projecting Expenses and Revenues

Now you need to put on your accounting and project management hats. (Perhaps neither hat fits very well but try to bear them for a day or two.) You need these hats to:

- ✔ Estimate future sales, in units and by value, for each product in your plan.

- ✔ Justify these estimates and, if they're hard to justify, create worst-case versions, too.

- ✔ Draw a timeline showing when your marketing incurs costs and when each component begins and ends. (Doing so helps with the preceding section and also prepares you for the unpleasant task of designing a monthly marketing budget.)

- ✔ Write a monthly marketing budget that lists all the estimated costs of your activity for each month of the coming year and breaks down sales by product, territory and month.

If you're a start-up or small business, we highly recommend doing all your projections on a *cash basis*. In other words, put the payment for your year's supply of brochures in the month in which the printer wants the money, instead of allocating that cost across 12 months. Also factor in the wait time for collecting your sales revenues. If collections take 30 days, show money coming in during December from November's sales and don't count any December sales for this year's plan. A cash basis may upset accountants, who like to do things on an accrual basis – see *Accounting For Dummies*, 4th Edition, by John A. Tracy (Wiley) if you don't know what that means; cash-based accounting keeps small businesses alive. You want a positive cash balance (or at least to break even) on the bottom line during every month of your plan.

If your cash-based projection shows a loss in some months, fiddle with the plan to eliminate that loss (or arrange to borrow money to cover the gap). Sometimes a careful cash-flow analysis of a plan leads to changes in underlying strategy. For example, getting customers to pay with credit cards rather than by cheque could make a big difference to cash flow.

Several helpful techniques are available for projecting sales, such as build-up forecasts, indicator forecasts and time-period forecasts. Choose the most appropriate technique for your business based on the reviews in this section. If you're feeling nervous, just use the technique that gives you the most conservative projection. Here's a common way to play it safe: use several of the techniques and average their results.

Build-up forecasts

These predictions go from the specific to the general, or from the bottom up. If you have sales reps or salespeople, ask each one to project the next period's sales for their territories and justify their projections based on what changes in the situation they anticipate. Then aggregate all the sales force's forecasts to obtain an overall figure.

If you have few enough customers that you can project per-customer purchases, build up your forecast this way. You may want to work from reasonable estimates of the amount of sales you can expect from each shop carrying your products or from each thousand catalogues sent out. Whatever the basic building blocks of your marketing, start with an estimate for each element and then add these estimates up.

Indicator forecasts

This method links your forecast to economic indicators that ought to vary with sales. For example, if you're in the construction business, you find that past sales for your industry correlate with *gross domestic product* (known as *GDP* or national output) growth. So you can adjust your sales forecast up or down depending upon whether experts expect the economy to grow rapidly or slowly in the next year.

Multiple scenario forecasts

You base these forecasts on what-if stories. They start with a straight-line forecast in which you assume that your sales will grow by the same percentage next year as they did last year. Then you make up what-if stories and project their impact on your plan to create a variety of alternative projections.

You may try the following scenarios if they're relevant to your situation:

- ✔ What if a competitor introduces a technological breakthrough?

- ✔ What if your company acquires a competitor?

- ✔ What if the government deregulates/regulates your industry?

- ✔ What if a leading competitor fails?

- ✔ What if your company has financial problems and has to lay off some of its sales and marketing people?

- ✔ What if your company doubles its ad spending?

For each scenario, think about how customer demand may change. Also consider how your marketing would need to change in order to best suit the situation. Then make an appropriate sales projection. For example, if a competitor introduced a technological breakthrough, you might guess that your sales would fall 25 per cent short of your straight-line projection.

The trouble with multiple scenario analysis is that . . . well, it gives you multiple scenarios. One way to turn all those options into one number or series of numbers is to just pick the option that seems most likely to you. Or take all the options that seem even remotely possible, assigning each a probability of occurring in the next year, multiplying each by its probability and then averaging them all to get a single number.

For example, the 'cautious scenario' projection estimates £5 million, and the 'optimistic scenario' projection estimates £10 million. The probability of the cautious scenario occurring is 15 per cent, and the probability of the optimistic scenario occurring is 85 per cent. So you find the sales projection with this formula: [(£5,000,000 × 0.15) + (£10,000,000 × 0.85)] ÷ 2 = £4,630,000.

Time-period projections

To use this method, work by week or month, estimating the size of sales in each time period and then add up these estimates for the entire year. This approach helps you when your marketing activity or the market isn't constant across the entire year. Ski resorts use this method because they get certain types of revenue only at certain times of the year. Marketers who plan to introduce new products during the year or to use heavy advertising in one or two *pulses* (concentrated time periods) also use this method because their sales go up significantly during those periods. Entrepreneurs, small businesses and any others on a tight cash-flow lead need to use this method because it provides a good idea of what cash will be flowing in by week or month. An annual sales figure doesn't tell you enough about when the money comes in to know whether you'll be short of cash in specific periods during the year.

Creating Your Controls

This section is the last and shortest of your plan but in many ways, is the most important. This section allows you and others to track performance.

Identify some performance benchmarks and state them clearly in the plan. For example:

- ✔ All sales territories should be using the new catalogues and sales scripts by 1 June.
- ✔ Revenues should grow to £75,000 per month by the end of the first quarter if the promotional campaign works according to plan.

These statements give you (and, unfortunately, your employers or investors) easy ways to monitor performance as you implement the marketing plan. Without these targets, nobody has control over the plan; nobody can tell whether or how well the plan is working. With these statements, you can identify unexpected results or delays quickly – in time for appropriate responses if you've designed these controls properly.

A good marketing plan gives you focus and a sense of direction, and increases your likelihood to succeed, but writing a good one takes time and many businesses don't have a lot of that to spare. A sensible rule is to spend time on your marketing plan, but not so much that you don't have a chance to look up and see whether the market has changed since you started writing it. If the plan you wrote at the start of the year is no longer relevant because business conditions have changed quickly, tear it up and start again – don't stick rigidly to something that's no longer relevant just because it's there.

Using Planning Templates and Aids

Referring to model plans can help you in this process. Unfortunately, most companies don't release their plans; they rightly view them as trade secrets. Fortunately, a few authors have compiled plans or portions of them, and you can find some good published materials to work from.

Several books provide sample marketing plans and templates. These texts show you alternative outlines for plans, and they also include budgets and revenue projections in many formats – one of which may suit your needs pretty closely:

- ✔ *The Marketing Kit For Dummies*, by Greg Brooks, Ruth Mortimer and Alex Hiam (Wiley), includes a five-minute marketing plan worksheet if you're the impatient sort

- ✔ *The Marketing Plan*, by William Cohen (Wiley), is a practical step-by-step guide that features sample plans from real businesses

- ✔ *The Marketing Planning Tool* is available online free to both members and non-members through the 'Marketing Shop' section of the Chartered Institute of Marketing's website (www.cim.co.uk)

Chapter 3

Researching Your Customers, Competitors and Industry

. . . .

In This Chapter

▶ Planning and doing original research

▶ Finding quick research techniques

▶ Profiting from existing information sources

. . . .

*W*hat makes your product or service better or worse than that of your competitors? That question, and more like it, can help you tighten up your strategy, make more accurate sales projections and decide what to emphasise (visually or verbally) in your marketing communications. A little research can go a long way toward improving the effectiveness of your marketing.

Research for better ideas and decisions

You don't need to buy in an expensive trendwatching service to keep a businesslike eye on new consumer developments that may affect your market. Instead, take subscriptions for a diverse range of publications, read free blogs on the Internet such as Trendwatching (www.trendwatching.com) and make a point of talking to people of all sorts, both in your industry and beyond it, to keep you in the flow of new ideas and facts. Also, ask other people for their ideas and interests.

Do you have any situations that you want more information about before making a decision? Then take a moment to define the situation clearly and list the options you think are feasible. Choosing the most effective advertising medium, making a more accurate sales projection or working out what new services your customers want are all examples of important decisions that research can help you make.

Suppose, for example, that you want to choose between print ads in industry magazines and e-mail advertisements to purchased lists. Figure 3-1 shows what your notes may look like.

Research for your strengths and weaknesses

So how do you find out what customers think? By asking customers to rank you on a list of descriptors for your business/product/service. The scale ranges from 1 to 10 (to get a good spread), with the following labels:

1	2	3	4	5	6	7	8	9	10
Very bad		Bad		Average		Good		Very good	

If you collect a rating of all the descriptive features of your product from customers, many of those ratings will prove quite ordinary. Consider the type of responses you'd get for a bank branch. The list of items to rate in a bank may include: current accounts, savings accounts, speed of service and the friendliness of banking staff, along with many other things you'd need to put on the list in order to describe the bank in detail. You're likely to discover that some items, like current accounts and saving accounts, get average ratings. The reason is that every bank offers those and, in general, each one handles such accounts in the same way. But a few of the features of a particular bank may be exceptional – for better or for worse.

Notable negatives, such as long queues at lunchtime when people rush out to do their banking, stand out in customers' minds. They remember those lines and tell others about them. Long queues at lunchtime may lead customers to switch banks and drive away other potential customers through bad word of mouth. Similarly, notably good customer service sticks in customers' minds, too. If that same branch has very friendly staff and express queues for simple transactions during busy periods, this warmth and efficiency can build loyalty and encourage current customers to recruit new customers through word of mouth.

With this information, you know what things your customers think you do brilliantly and what features you need to do some work on.

Decision	Information Needs	Possible Sources	Findings
Choose between print ads in industry magazines and email advertisements to purchased lists	How many actual prospects can print ads reach?	Magazines' ad salespeople can tell us.	Three leading magazines in our industry reach 90 per cent of good customers, but half of these are not in our geographic region. May not be worth it?
	What are the comparable costs per prospect reached through these different methods?	Just need to get the budget numbers and number of people reached and divide available money by number of people.	Email is a third of the price in our market.
	Can we find out what the average response rates are for both magazine ads and emails?	Nobody is willing to tell us, or they don't know. May try calling a friend in a big ad agency; they may have done a study or something.	Friend says response rates vary wildly, and she thinks the most important thing is how relevant the customer finds the ad, not the medium used.
	Have any of our competitors switched from print to email successfully?	Can probably get distributors to tell us this. Will call several and quiz them.	No, but some companies in similar industries have done this successfully.
	Conclusions? Seems like we'll spend less and be more targeted if we design special emails and send them only to prospects in our region. Don't buy magazine ad space for now; we can experiment with email, instead. But we need to make sure the ads we send are relevant and seem important, or people just delete them without reading them.		

Figure 3-1: Analysing the information needs of a decision.

Bright spark

Research can help you discover weaknesses and turn them into strengths. Comet, the chain of electrical stores, had been losing sales for several years to supermarkets and general retailers as they entered the market. It decided that some flashy destination stores would fix the problem and set about overhauling the layout, product ranges and signage to differentiate them from Comet's new competitors.

The size and design of the stores wasn't the main solution to the problem, though. A simple and, at £20,000, inexpensive research programme discovered that Comet's customers felt that its greatest weakness was the quality of its staff. This was a twofold problem as they also felt that the most important aspect of customer satisfaction was, you guessed it, the quality of the staff. Comet accepted the truth and acted on it by changing its criteria for customer satisfaction. Soon after, it achieved a record trading performance.

Here are a few tips to keep in mind as you gather customer ratings:

✔ Draw a graph of all the features of your product, rated from negative to neutral to positive. A graph will give you a visual image of how your customers perceive your business's strengths and weaknesses.

✔ Offer customers a reward for filling in a survey sheet (that's how important survey sheets are). You can offer a free prize draw for the returned survey sheets, a reduction on current fees or a discount on future products. Whichever option you choose, let your customers know that their views matter to you; that alone can improve your customer-service scores.

Planning Your Research

Start research with a careful analysis of the decisions you must make.

Then, for any uncertain or risky decisions, you need to pose questions whose answers can help you reduce the risk and uncertainty. And now, with these questions in hand, you're ready to begin your research!

You need to pose a series of questions that have the potential to reduce your decision-making uncertainty or to reveal new and exciting options for you as a decision-maker.

Take the question, 'Is the product positioned properly, or do we need to change its image?' To find out whether repositioning your product makes sense, you may ask how people currently perceive the product's quality and performance, how they view the product compared with the leading competitor's and what the product's personality is. If you know the answers to all these questions, you're far better able to make a good decision.

Measuring customer satisfaction

Try to design a customer satisfaction measure that portrays your company or product in a realistic light. You can measure customer satisfaction with survey questionnaires or with the rate of customer complaints; measures combining multiple sources of data into an overall index are the best.

To gauge customer satisfaction, ask your customers revealing questions, similar to the following list:

1. **Which company (or product) is the best at present?**

   (Provide a long list, with instructions to circle one, and give a final choice, labelled Other, where respondents can write in their own answer.)

2. **Rate [your product] compared with its competitors:**

Far worse		Same			Far better	
1	2	3	4	5	6	7

3. **Rate [your product] compared with your expectations for it:**

Far worse		Same			Far better	
1	2	3	4	5	6	7

You can find useful guidelines on how to design a questionnaire on the website of the Market Research Society (www.mrs.org.uk), under 'Guidance', within the Frequently Asked Questions section. The site also includes advice on how to select a research agency and lists sources of free statistical and demographic information.

Using the answers

Even the most rudimentary piece of research can throw up a range of different, and sometimes contradictory, findings. One customer may think the most important thing is for you to lower your prices; another may be prepared to pay more for greater staff expertise. You probably can't achieve both of these goals simultaneously. Here are a few strategies that can help you focus your response:

- ✔ **Your own instinct should allow you to sort the good research results from the bad.** This doesn't mean ignoring what you don't want to hear, but it does mean you shouldn't unquestioningly react to everything the research tells you.

- ✔ **Concentrate on just one of the strengths and one of the weaknesses.** If your product or service has a quality that's unique in your market, you need to exploit it to the full. If you have a real problem that may drive valuable customers away, you need to put it right fast.

 Pay attention to your most valuable customers. You can't please all of the people all of the time, so don't try.

Introducing Five Ideas for Low-cost Research

You don't have to spend thousands of pounds researching ideas for a new ad campaign (or anything else). Instead, focus on ways of gaining insight or checking your assumptions using free and inexpensive research methods.

Watching what your competitors do

When you compare your marketing approach to your competitors', you easily find out what customers like best. Make a list of the things that your competitors do differently to you. Now ask ten of your best customers to review this list and tell you what they prefer – your way or one of the alternatives. Keep a tally. You may find that all your customers vote in favour of doing something different to the way you do it now.

Using e-mail for single-question surveys

If you market to businesses, you probably have e-mail addresses for many of your customers. Try e-mailing 20 or more of these customers for a quick opinion on a question. Result? Instant survey! If a clear majority of these customers say they prefer using a corporate credit card to being invoiced because the card is more convenient, well, you've just gained a useful research result that may help you revise your approach.

Don't e-mail customers with questions unless they're happy to be approached. You don't want to be treated as an e-mail spammer!

Researching your strengths

Perhaps the most important element of any marketing plan or strategy is clearly recognising what makes you especially good and appealing to customers (we talk more about identifying your strengths in Chapter 1). To research the strengths that set you apart from the competition, find the simplest way to ask ten good customers this simple but powerful question: 'What's the best thing about our [fill in the name of your product or service], from your perspective?'

The answers to this question usually focus on one or, at most, a few features or aspects of your business. Finding out how your customers identify your strengths proves a great help to your marketing strategy. After you know what you do best, you can focus on telling the story about that best attribute whenever you advertise, create publicity or communicate with your market in any way. Investing in your strengths (versus your competitors' strengths or your weaknesses) tends to grow your sales and profits most quickly and efficiently.

Analysing customer records

Most marketers fail to mine their own databases for all the useful information they may contain. Studying your own customers with the goal of identifying three common traits that make them different or special is a good way to tap into this free data – because you already own it!

A computer shop we frequent went through their records and realised that its buyers are:

- ✔ More likely to be self-employed or entrepreneurs than the average person.

- ✔ More sophisticated users of computers than most people.

- ✔ Big spenders who care more about quality and service than the absolute cheapest price.

This shop revised its marketing goal to find more people who share these three qualities. What qualities do your customers possess that make them special and what would constitute a good profile for you to use in pursuing more customers like them?

Getting info from the web

Throughout this book, we include numerous websites, as these are the quickest and easiest places to find free information. For instance, the Internet Advertising Bureau (IAB) and the Interactive Media in Retail Group (IMRG) have more data on how many customers are connected to the Internet and who shop online than we can possibly include here. Look out for these website references, but more importantly remember that Internet search engines, such as Google, make finding free data simple – and the more you use them, the easier it is to filter out all the sites you're not interested in.

Say you want to set up a website where customers can buy your products directly. You want to know how many people have access to the Internet in the UK and how many are prepared to use their credit card details to buy things. You may also want to find a website developer who can create a secure and fully transactional site for you. Already you have three questions that need answers and you haven't even started your search.

Go to the Google search engine (www.google.co.uk) type in the key words 'internet access', and you'll get a list of 199 million sites, most of them trying to sell you something. You can narrow the information down by being more specific. The phrase 'online shoppers' will return just over 46.7 million sites; this number is better, but still too many. Type in 'online shoppers market size', however, and you get just 300,000 suggestions, which is better again. Explore these results but if you don't find the information you need, the IAB or IMRG have the answers to all three questions. You only need a bit of practice to be able to find relevant information on the web quickly and easily.

Tapping into government resources

Often, the best source of free information is national and local government. Many governments collect copious data on economic activity, population size and trends within their borders. In Britain, the UK Statistics Authority, now an independent, non-ministerial body accountable directly to Parliament, and its executive arm, the Office for National Statistics (ONS), are the best general sources of data on a wide range of demographic and economic topics.

We're always amazed at the sheer range and quantity of information available on the UK Statistics Authority site, and you probably will be too. Of course, we don't know whether you need to know crime statistics in a certain London borough, but if you do, this is the right place! Described as the 'home of official UK statistics', you can access the ONS at www.ons.gov.uk

Much of the data on the UK population is based on the Census. Although the Census only takes place every ten years, you'll find the information's very detailed and, usefully, can be broken down by neighbourhood. The statistics on inflation and prices, consumer spending, business investment – in fact, anything financial – are more up to date, usually to the last full quarter.

Getting media data

If you're doing any advertising, ask the magazine, newspaper, website or radio station you buy advertising space from to give you information about their customer base – snippets about the people exposed to your ads. This information can help you make sure you reach an appropriate audience. You can also use the exposure numbers to calculate the effectiveness of your advertising.

If you've yet to decide where to advertise, or even in which media, some useful media websites can give you the numbers on how many and what kind of consumers each title or station will deliver. You can trust these sources because in most cases they were set up and are supported by the media owners operating in that area to provide an independent verification of sales and audience profiles so that advertisers can see what they're getting – and hopefully buy more. For this reason, most of the data, for occasional users like you, is free.

The Audit Bureau of Circulations (ABC; www.abc.org.uk) has data on magazines, national and local newspapers and exhibition visitors. You can find out how many people are reading the titles, where they live and what type of consumers they are; for B2B magazines, you can find out what sector they work in and what their job titles are. For data about Online readers, visit the specific ABC site for electronic media (www.abce.org.uk). Most of the different media have organisations providing this sort of data: for TV, see BARB (www.barb.co.uk); for radio, see RAJAR (www.rajar.co.uk); and for outdoor media such as posters, see POSTAR (www.postar.co.uk).

Part II
Advertising Everyone can Do

'Are you sure this stunt is going to sell our
custard pies, Colin?'

In this part . . .

Advertising can be fun and we're going to ask you to have some serious fun. It also needs to be creative and have that special spark to work really well.

The essence of great advertising communications remains the same across all the dozens of possible media – from the lowly business card or the simple brochure to the sophisticated print ad, local television spot ad or Internet ad campaign.

You also have a lot of media choices – probably more than you realise – because you can always advertise in alternative ways and advertising doesn't have to be as expensive as most people assume.

So, read on to find out how you can pump up your marketing communications and put advertising to better effect in your business.

Chapter 4

Brochures, Signs and Posters

In This Chapter

▶ Designing the simplest print product of all – brochures

▶ Finding successful signs for your business

▶ Designing billboards and other large signs

Most marketers budget more for print advertising than any other type – the exception being the major national or multinational brands that market largely on television. But for most local and regional advertising, print probably provides the most flexible and effective all-around marketing medium, although internet advertising is fast eating into this lead. In this chapter we focus on a choosing the best content and format for all your print material to ensure you are marketing your company in the most effective way.

Producing Brochures, Fliers and More

You can get your print design out to the public in an easy and inexpensive way, using brochures, fliers, posters and many other forms – your imagination is the only limit to what you can do with a good design.

You can also do small runs (100 or less) straight from a colour printer. Buy matte or glossy brochure paper designed for your brand of printer and simply select the appropriate paper type in the print dialog box. Today's inexpensive inkjet printers can produce stunning brochures. But you have to fold these brochures yourself and the ink cartridges aren't cheap. So print as needed or try contacting your local copy shop. Kall Kwik and many other copy shops now accept e-mailed copies of files and can produce short runs of your brochures, pamphlets, catalogue sheets or other printed materials on their colour copiers directly from your file.

Many brochures foolishly waste money because they don't accomplish any specific marketing goals; they just look pretty, at best. To avoid creating an attractive, but pointless, brochure that doesn't achieve a sales goal, make sure that you know:

- ✔ Who will read the brochure.
- ✔ How they will get the brochure.
- ✔ What they should discover from and do after reading the brochure.

These three questions focus your brochure design and make it useful to your marketing.

Marketers often order a brochure without a clear idea of what purpose the brochure should serve. They just think a brochure is a good idea: 'Oh, we need them to, you know, put in the envelope along with a letter, or, um, for our salespeople to keep in the boots of their cars; maybe we'll send some out to our mailing list or give them away at the next trade show.'

With this many possibilities, the brochure can't be properly suited to any single use. It becomes a dull, vague scrap of paper that just talks about the company or product but doesn't hit readers over the head with any particular appeal and call to action, something that's become increasingly important as consumers can look up information about your company online at any time.

Listing your top three uses

Define up to three specific uses for the brochure. No more than three, though, because your design can't accomplish more than three purposes effectively. The most common and appropriate uses for a brochure are:

- ✓ To act as a reference on the product, or technical details of the product, for sales prospects.

- ✓ To support a personal selling effort by lending credibility and helping overcome objections.

- ✓ To generate leads through a direct-mail campaign.

Say you want to design a brochure that does all three of these tasks well. Start by designing the contents. What product and technical information must be included? Write the information down and collect necessary illustrations, so that you have the *fact base* (the essential information to communicate) in front of you.

Writing about strengths and weaknesses

After you create your fact base (see the preceding section), organise these points in such a way that they highlight your product's (or service's) greatest strengths and overcome its biggest challenges. Don't know what your product's strengths and weaknesses are? List the following, as they relate to sales:

- ✓ The common sales objections or reasons prospects give for not wanting to buy your product.

- ✓ Customers' favourite reasons for buying, or the aspects of your product and business that customers like most.

With your fact base organised accordingly, you're ready to begin writing. Your copy should read as if you're listening to customers' concerns and answering each concern with an appropriate response. You can write subheads in the format: 'Our Product Doesn't Need XXX' and 'Our Product Brings You XXX' so that salespeople or prospects can easily see how your facts (in copy and/or illustrations) overcome each specific objection and highlight all the major benefits.

Incorporating a clear, compelling appeal

Add some basic appeal communicated in a punchy headline and a few dozen words of copy, along with an appropriate and eye-catching illustration. You need to include this appeal to help the brochure stand on its own as a marketing tool when it's sent out to leads by post or passed on from a prospect or customer to one of his or her professional contacts.

The appeal needs to project a winning personality. Your brochure can be fun or serious, emotional or factual – but it must be appealing. The appeal is the bait that draws the prospect to your hook, so make sure your hook is well baited!

Putting it all together

When you have all the parts – the appeal, the fact base and the design – you're ready to put your brochure together. The appeal, with its enticing headline and compelling copy and visual, goes on the front of the brochure – or the outside when you fold it for mailing, or the central panel out of three if you fold a sheet twice. The subheads that structure the main copy respond to objections and highlight strengths on the inside pages. You then organise the fact base, for reference use, in the copy and illustrations beneath these subheads.

Although you can design a brochure in many ways, we often prefer the format (along with dimensions for text blocks or illustrations) in Figure 4-1. This format is simple and inexpensive because you print the brochure on a single sheet of 490mm × 210mm paper that you then fold three times. The brochure fits in a standard DL (110mm × 220mm) envelope or you can tape it together along the open fold and mail it on its own. This layout allows for some detail, but not enough to get you into any real trouble. (Larger formats and multipage pieces tend to fill up with the worst, wordiest copy, and nobody ever reads those pieces.)

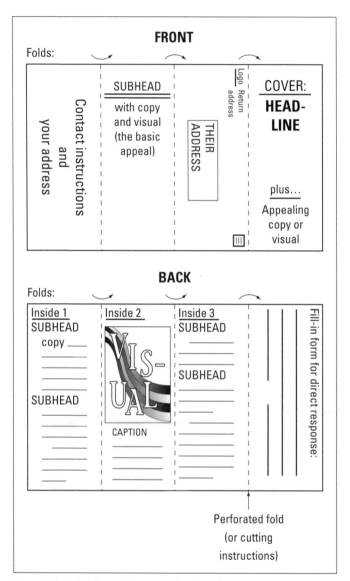

Figure 4-1: A simple, multi-purpose brochure layout.

You can use the design shown in Figure 4-1 for direct mailings to generate sales leads and you can also hand the brochure out or use it for reference in direct-selling situations. You can produce this brochure, using any popular desktop publishing software and you can even print and fold it at the local copy shop (if you don't need the thousands of copies that make off-set printing cost-effective). To convert this design to an even simpler, cheaper format, use A4 paper and eliminate the *return mailer* (the left-hand page on the front, the right-hand on the back, which can be returned with the blanks filled in to request information or accept a special offer). If you do remove the return mailer, however, be sure to include follow-up instructions and contact information on one of the inside pages!

Remember: the bigger the ad, the bigger the impact. But also consider the fact that the percentage of readers noticing your ad doesn't go up

Introducing the Essential Sign

Signs are displays with brand or company names on them and sometimes a short marketing message or useful information for the customer, too. In our experience, every marketer needs to make good use of signs.

Signs are all over the place; if you're in an office right now, look out of the nearest window and you can probably see a handful with ease. Signs are undeniably important. Even if they serve only to locate a shop or office, signs do a job that marketers need done. If your customers can't find you, you're out of business. So why do marketers – those marketing experts who write the books tend to ignore signs so completely?

The Outdoor Advertising Association (www.oaa.org.uk) provides information on how to buy outdoor advertising space, relevant regulations and standard sizes. While the Outdoor Advertising Association can help with some general guidance, when evaluating signs, we can't send you to the experts as easily as we can with radio, TV, print or other outdoor media. You'll probably end up working with a local sign manufacturer, and you and your designer will have to specify size, materials, copy and art. Fortunately, you're not all on your own; you can find some guidance and help. You need to remember a few things:

Appreciating what your sign can do

Signs have limited ability to accomplish marketing goals but perhaps not as limited as you think. As well as displaying the name of your business, you can include a phone number, website address or e-mail contact details so that, even when your premises are closed, potential customers know how to get in touch with you. And you can say what your business does –a butcher doesn't have to be just a 'butcher', he can be a 'family-owned, free-range butcher'. With signs, as with all marketing communications, the way you say it is what counts!

Writing good signs

As a marketer, you need to master the strange art of writing for signs. Too often, the language marketers use on signs is ambiguous. The sign doesn't say anything with enough precision to make its point clear. Keep in mind the suggestions outlined in the following sections.

Make sure your sign says what you want it to

One of our favourite stories about how to easily turn a bad sign into a good one comes from the marketing consultant Doug Hall. A friend of his put up a sign that read 'Seasons in Thyme – Epicurean Food & Wine'. Do you have any idea what that company does? Doug changed his friend's sign to 'Seasons in Thyme RESTAURANT. Casual, Elegant, Island Dining'. For the first time in all his years in business, the owner received some customers who said they came in because they'd seen the sign.

Use a header to catch your customer's eye

Marketers design some signs to convey substantial information – directions, for example, or details of a shop's merchandise mix. Information-heavy signs are often too brief or too lengthy. Divide the copy and design into two sections, each with a separate purpose, as follows:

 ✔ **Have a header.** The first section resembles the header in a print ad and you design it to catch attention from afar and draw people to the sign. Given this purpose, brevity is key – and don't forget the essential large, catchy type and/or visuals.

✔ **Communicate essential information.** The second section of the sign needs to communicate the essential information accurately and in full. If the first section does its job, viewers walk right up to the sign to read the part with all the important information, so you don't need to make that type as large and catchy. The consumer should be able to easily read and interpret the wording and type used for the information, and this section needs to answer all likely viewer questions.

Most signs don't have these two distinct sections, and so they fail to accomplish either purpose very well – they neither attract people very strongly nor inform them fully. Unfortunately, most sign-makers have a strong urge to make all the copy the same size. When pressed, the sign-makers sometimes make the header twice as big as the rest of the copy, but going further than that seems to upset them. Well, to get a good sign, you may have to upset some people. As in many aspects of marketing, if you want above-average performance, you have to swim against the current.

Be creative!

Another problem is that marketers write the copy on most signs in the most tired and obvious manner. Tradition says that a sign, unlike any other marketing communication, must simply state the facts in a direct, unimaginative way. One reason for this lack of creativity is that most marketers assume people *read* signs. The conventional wisdom is that your customers and prospects automatically find and read your signs.

Try walking down an average high street and later listing all the signs you remember seeing. Some stand out, but most go unseen. And we bet you can't re-create the text of the majority of those signs your eye bothered to linger on long enough to read. To avoid having yours being lost in this sea of similar signs, you have to make it stand out!

Here are some of the many variations in form that you can take advantage of when designing a creative sign:

- ✔ Vinyl graphics and lettering (quick and inexpensive but accurate to your design)

- ✔ Hand-painted (personal look and feel)

- ✔ Wood (traditional look; routing or hand carving enhances the appeal)

- ✔ Metal (durable and accurate depictions of art and copy, but not very pretty)

- ✔ Window lettering (hand-painted or with vinyl letters/graphics)

- ✔ Light boxes (in which lettering is back-lit; highly visible at night)

- ✔ Neon signs (high impact)

- ✔ Magnetic signs (for your vehicles)

- ✔ Electronic displays (also known as *electronic message repeaters*; movement and longer messages, plus a high-tech feel, make these displays appropriate in some situations)

- ✔ Flat-panel TV screens (with shifting sign content and images or video; the price of these TVs has been coming down in recent years)

- ✔ Pavement projection (a unit in the shop window moves and spins a logo or message at the feet of passers-by at night)

Putting up Posters: Why Size Matters

If you're planning to use posters to advertise, one of the first things to think about is how much time customers will have to read your ad and how far away they'll be. This information will help you decide how much you can say in your ad and how to say it.

Deciding on outdoor ad formats

The Outdoor Advertising Association (www.oaa.org.uk) describes three different sectors in the outdoor market – roadside, transport and retail/point-of-sale/leisure:

- ✔ **Roadside.** You can choose anything from phone booths to 96-sheet ads, which at 40-feet wide by 10-feet high are the largest of the standard poster formats.

- ✔ **Transport.** While it includes standard poster sites in stations, airports and on trains and tubes, transport is a wide-ranging outdoor sector that also covers (literally) bus-sides, taxis and trucks.

- ✔ **Retail/point-of-sale/leisure.** As well as poster sites at supermarkets, the retail sector includes shopping centres, cinemas, gyms and petrol stations, and can include ads on trolleys and screens.

- ✔ **Non-traditional formats and ambient** is also a sector, but no one's come up with a straightforward name for it, which just proves its diversity. Think petrol pump nozzles, takeaway lids, ticket backs, beer mats and floor stickers.

Chapter 5

Press, TV and Radio Ads

In This Chapter

▶ Recognising the elements of printed advertising

▶ Understanding design and layout issues

▶ Designing with type

▶ Designing ads for radio

▶ Creating great video ads for little cash

▶ Harnessing the emotional power of television

▶ Advertising online

*M*any marketers start with their printed marketing materials (such as ads, brochures or downloadable PDF product literature on their websites) and then work outward from there to incorporate the appeal and design concepts from their printed materials or ads into other forms of marketing. (A common look and feel should unite your print ads, brochures and website.)

In this chapter we talk about what forms of marketing there are, how they work best and how to take full advantage of them.

Dissecting printed materials

Before you can create great printed marketing materials, you need to dissect an ad and identify its parts. Inside most printed marketing materials, you'll find parts and each part has a special name:

✔ **Headline:** The large-print words that first attract the eye, usually at the top of the page.

✔ **Subhead:** The optional addition to the headline to provide more detail, also in large (but not quite as large)
print.

✔ **Copy or body copy:** The main text, set in a readable size.

✔ **Visual:** An illustration that makes a visual statement.
This image may be the main focus of the ad, or it may be
secondary to the copy.

✔ **Caption:** Copy attached to the visual to explain or discuss that picture. You usually place a caption beneath
the visual, but you can put it on any side or even within
or on the image.

✔ **Logo:** A unique design that represents the brand or company (like Nike's swoosh). Register logos as trademarks.

✔ **Slogan:** A short phrase evoking the spirit or personality
of the brand. For example, when you think of sportswear
company Nike, you immediately conjure up its famous
slogan summing up the brand in three short words: 'Just
Do It.'

The shorter and snappier the slogan, the more likely it is to be
recalled by the consumer.

Figure 5-1 shows each of these elements in a rough design for
a print ad. We use generic terms in place of actual parts of an
ad ('headline' for the headline, for example) so that you can
easily see all the elements in action.

Putting the parts together: Design and layout

Design refers to the look, feel and style of your ad. Design is
an aesthetic concept and, thus, putting it into precise terms
is difficult. But design is vitally important: it has to take the
basic appeal of your product and make that appeal work
visually on paper Specifically, the design needs to overcome
the marketer's constant problem: nobody cares about your
advertising. So the design must somehow reach out to readers, grab their attention, hold it long enough to communicate
the appeal of the product you're advertising and attach that
appeal to the brand name in the readers' memories.

Figure 5-1: The elements of a print ad.

A memorable photograph is often the easiest way to grab attention. Depending on your brand or product, you could choose options such as an interesting face, a photo of a child or a beautiful scene, as long as you can make the image relevant in some way to your product; pretty much anything that grabs attention goes.

Great advertising has to rise off the page, reach out and grab you by the eyeballs. In the cluttered world of modern print-based marketing, this design goal is the only one that really works. So we want you to tape up a selection of ads from the same publication(s) that yours will go in (or use samples of competitor brochures or catalogue sheets or whatever exactly it is you'll be designing in print). Put a draft of your design up along with these benchmarks. Step back – a long way back. Now, does your ad grab the eye more than all the others? If not . . . back to the drawing board!

Understanding the stages in design

Designers often experiment with numerous layouts for their print ads or other printed materials before selecting one for formal development. We strongly recommend that you do the same or insist that your designer or agency does the same. The more layouts you look at, the more likely you are to get an original idea that has eye-grabbing power. But whether you design your own print materials or have experts do the work for you, you want to be familiar with the design stages.

- ✔ **Step 1. Thumbnails:** The rough sketches designers use to describe layout concepts are called *thumbnails*. They're usually small, quick sketches in pen or pencil. You can also use professional design and layout packages like Quark XPress or InDesign to create thumbnails.

- ✔ **Step 2. Roughs:** Designers then develop thumbnails with promise into *roughs* – full-size sketches with headlines and subheads drawn carefully enough to give the feel of a particular font and *style* (the appearance of the printed letters). Roughs also have sketches for the illustrations. The designers suggest body copy using lines (or nonsense characters, if the designer does the rough using a computer).

- ✔ **Step 3. Comprehensive layout:** Designers then develop chosen roughs into a *comp* (short for *comprehensive layout*). A comp should look pretty much like a final version of the design, although designers produce a comp on a one-time basis, so the comp may use paste-ups in place of the intended photos, colour photocopies, typeset copy and headlines. Designers used to assemble comps by hand, but now most designers and agencies do their comps on computer. A high-end PC and colour printer can produce something that looks almost like the final printed version of a four-colour ad or other printed marketing material. Designers refer to a computer-made comp as a *full-colour proof*.

✔ **Step 4. Dummy:** A *dummy* is a form of comp that simulates the feel – as well as the look – of the final design. (Every design should have a feel or personality of its own, just as products should have a personality. Often you can create the best personality for your ad simply by carrying over the brand identity you've created for the product. Consistency helps.) Dummies are especially important for brochures or special inserts to magazines, where the designer often specifies special paper and folds. By doing a dummy comp, you can evaluate the feel of the design while you're evaluating its appearance.

Designing and submitting your ads

If you're quick and able on a computer and like to work in design and layout programs (such as Adobe InDesign or Quark XPress), you can do the same kind of creative rough designing simply by searching for images on the web. (To find an image, try specifying an image search in Google, but remember not to use copyrighted images in your final design without permission or payment. Plenty of royalty-free image websites are available, or consider budding photographers who won't charge too much for using their pictures.) Copy the chosen images onto your computer and you can click and drag them into different programs and pages.

Invest a bit of time and effort in honing these computer-based design techniques. Look up the latest *For Dummies* books on how to use Quark Xpress, Adobe InDesign or any other design and layout program of your choice, or just work in Microsoft Word, which is pretty impressive in its latest incarnations as a basic design program itself. Also, take a look at the growing number of great-looking ad templates you can purchase online and then adapt them in any of the common graphic design programs. As an example, see many options at www.stocklayouts.com or www.mycreativeshop.com.

When your preliminary design is ready for the printer, you can send the design over the web using desktop publishing software. You can even do the colour separations for four-colour work on your PC and send those colour separations too. (Ask the printer for instructions to make sure that you submit the design in a format that their system can use.) The printer then makes plates for printing the design straight from the file that you've e-mailed to them. (*Plates* are metal or plastic sheets with your design on them – the printer applies the ink to the plates when the printing press does its thing.)

Until recently, electronic submission to printing firms generally had to be done from a professional software package like Quark XPress, but increasingly, printers are accepting Word files or PDF files generated by Acrobat (lots of people prefer this route because it reduces the chances of incompatibility problems). And if you're designing in a recent version of Word, you'll find that creating a PDF file can be done from your program because Acrobat is now built in.

Finding your font

A *font* is a particular design's attributes for the *characters* (letters, numbers and symbols) used in printing your design. *Typeface* refers only to the distinctive design of the letters (Times New Roman, for example). Font, on the other hand, actually refers to one particular size and style of a typeface design (such as 10-point, bold, Times New Roman).

The right font for any job is the one that makes your text easily readable and harmonises with the overall design most effectively. For a headline, the font also needs to grab the reader's attention. The body copy doesn't have to grab attention in the same way – in fact, if it does, the copy often loses readability. For example, a *reverse font* (light or white type on dark paper) may be just the thing for a bold headline, but if you use it in the body copy, too, nobody reads your copy because doing so's just too hard on the eye.

Choosing a typeface

What sort of typeface do you want? You have an amazing number of choices because designers have been developing typefaces for as long as printing presses have existed. (Just click on the font toolbar in Microsoft Word to see an assortment of the more popular typefaces.)

A clean, sparse design, with a lot of white space on the page and stark contrasts in the artwork, deserves the clean lines of a *sans serif typeface* – meaning one that doesn't have any decorative *serifs* (those little bars or flourishes at the ends of the main lines in a character). The most popular body-copy fonts without serifs are Helvetica, Arial, Univers and Avant Garde. Figure 5-2 shows some fonts with and without serifs.

Figure 5-2: Fonts with and without serifs.

A richly decorative, old-fashioned sort of design, in contrast, needs a more decorative and traditional serif typeface, such as Century or Times New Roman. The most popular body-copy fonts with serifs include Garamond, Melior, Century, Times New Roman and Caledonia.

Table 5-1 shows an assortment of typeface choices, in which you can compare the clean lines of Helvetica, Avant Garde and Arial with the more decorative designs of Century, Garamond and Times New Roman.

Table 5-1	Popular Fonts for Ads
Sans Serif	*Serif*
Helvetica	Century
Arial	Garamond
Univers	Melior
Avant Garde	Times New Roman

In tests, Helvetica and Century generally top the lists as most readable, so start with one of these typefaces for your body copy; only change the font if it doesn't seem to work. Also, research shows that people read lowercase letters about 13 per cent faster than uppercase letters, so avoid long stretches of copy set in all capital letters. People also read most easily when letters are dark and contrast strongly with their background. Thus, black 14-point Helvetica on white is probably the most readable font specification for the body copy of an ad (or other printed marketing materials), even if the combination does seem dull to a sophisticated designer.

Generalising about the best kind of headline typeface is no easy task because designers play around with headlines to a greater extent than they do with body copy. But, as a general rule, you can use Helvetica for the headline when you use Century for the body, and the other way round. Or you can just use a bolder, larger version of the body copy font for your headline. You can also reverse a larger, bold version of your type onto a black background for the headline. Use anything to make the headline grab the reader's attention, stand out from the body copy and ultimately lead their vision and curiosity into the body copy's text. (Remember to keep the headline readable – nothing too fancy, please.)

Making style choices within the typeface

Any typeface gives the user many choices and so selecting the typeface is just the beginning of the project when you design your print. Other questions include: how big should the characters be? Do you want to use the standard version of the typeface, a lighter version, a **bold** (or darker) version or an *italic* version (one that leans to the right)? The process is easier than it sounds. Just look at samples of some standard point sizes (12- and 14-point text for the body copy, for example, with

24-, 36- and 48-point for the headlines). Many designers make their choice by eye, looking for an easy-to-read size that isn't so large that it causes the words or sentences to break up into too many fragments across the page – but not so small that it gives the reader too many words per line. Keep readability in mind as the goal.

Figure 5-3 shows a variety of size and style choices for the Helvetica typeface. As you can see, you have access to a wonderful range of options, even within this one popular design.

Helvetica Light 14 point

Helvetica Italic 14 point

Helvetica Bold 14 point

Helvetica Regular 14 point

Helvetica Regular 24 point

Helvetica Regular Condensed 14 point

Helvetica Bold Outline 24 point

Figure 5-3: Some of the many choices that the Helvetica typeface offers designers.

Keep in mind that you can change just about any aspect of type. You can alter the distance between lines – called the *leading* – or you can squeeze characters together or stretch them apart to make a word fit a space. Assume that anything is possible. Ask your printer or consult the manual of your desktop publishing or word-processing software to find out how to make a change.

Choosing a point size

When designers and printers talk about *point sizes*, they're referring to a traditional measure of the height of the letters (based on the highest and lowest parts of the biggest letters). One *point* equals about $\frac{1}{72}$ of an inch, so a 10-point type is $\frac{10}{72}$ of an inch high, at the most.

Personally, we don't really care – we've never measured a character with a ruler. We just know that if the letters seem too small for easy reading, then we need to bump the typeface up a couple of points. Ten-point type is too small for most body copy but you may want to use that size if you have to squeeze several words into a small space. (But why do that? You're usually better off editing your body copy and then bumping up the font size to make it more readable!) Your eye can't distinguish easily between fonts that are only one or two sizes apart, so specify a larger jump than that to distinguish between body copy and subhead or between subhead and headline.

Radio and TV Advertising

Radio and television are well-established, extremely power-ful marketing media, while video (especially if shot in digital format) is a hot new item for streaming-video messages on your website. Video can also offer marketing messages on television screens and computers on your stand at a trade show.

The problem with radio and TV is that the costs associated with producing and broadcasting ads have traditionally been quite high, making these media too expensive for smaller mar-keters. We want to encourage you to be open-minded about radio, video and TV because new and easier ways to produce in these media are emerging all the time, along with a growing number of low-cost ways to broadcast your ads. Every year brings more radio and television stations, including those appearing online, on mobile phones, and on cable and satel-lite TV channels. Digital radio is also available that you can listen to through a digital set, digital TV or your PC.

Even if you don't use these commercial media, you can pos-sibly find more modest ways in which to share your ads with prospects. In fact, increasingly marketers use CDs or websites that communicate using digital video, PowerPoint or radio-style voice-overs. Modern technology is making these media more flexible and affordable for all marketers.

Creating Ads for Radio

Conventional wisdom says you have only three elements to work with when you design for radio: words, sound effects and music. In a literal sense that wisdom's true, but you can't create a great radio ad unless you remember that you want to use those elements to generate *mental images* for the listener. And that means you can often perform the same basic plot on radio as on TV. Radio isn't really as limited as people think but is now rarely used to its full advantage. Society's love affair with radio has been eclipsed by its love of TV and films.

When creating radio ads, favour direct action goals over indirect ones. . Sometimes you may want to use radio just to create brand awareness *(indirect-action advertising)*, but in general, the most effective radio ads call for direct action. Give out a web address (if the listener can remember that address easily) or a freefone number in the ad.

 Put your brand name into your radio ad early and often, regardless of the story line. If you fail to generate the desired direct action, at least you build awareness and interest for the brand, which supports other points of contact in your marketing campaign. Radio is a great support medium and not enough marketers use it that way. You may as well fill the vacuum with *your* marketing message!

 Here's a simple rule that can help you avoid confusion in your radio ad: ensure that your script identifies all sound effects. Sound effects are wonderful and evocative, but in truth, many sound very similar. Without context, rain on the roof can sound like bacon sizzling in a pan, a blowtorch cutting through the metal door of a bank vault or even an alien space-ship starting up. So the script must identify that sound, either through direct reference or through context. You can provide context with the script, the plot or simply by other sound effects. The sounds of eggs cracking and hitting a hot pan, coffee percolating and someone yawning, all help to identify that sizzle as the breakfast bacon, rather than rain on the roof or a blowtorch.

Buying airtime on radio

We often find ourselves urging marketers to try radio in place of their standard media choices. Why? Because, although local retailers frequently use radio to pull people into stores for sales or special offer periods, many other marketers overlook radio as a viable medium. Those advertisers don't realise how powerful radio can be and may not be aware of its incredible reach. In the UK, around 45.1 million people (74 per cent of the population) tune into digital and non-digital radio every week. We bet your target audience is in there somewhere! (Also consider radio not just for advertising but for editorial publicity. Many radio talk shows will be willing to invite you on as a guest if you pitch your expertise well and have a unique angle to discuss.)

RAJAR (Radio Joint Audience Research) is the UK's audience measurement system for commercial radio stations and the BBC. Every quarter, RAJAR releases detailed listening figures for all the UK's national and local radio stations, which you can access for free at www.rajar.co.uk. You can also get in touch with the Radio Advertising Bureau (RAB), which does a good job of promoting radio as an advertising medium and is a great source of campaign data and ideas for creative radio advertising (www.rab.co.uk).

Radio airtime is cheaper and more cost-effective than TV airtime, but the biggest advertisers can reach a larger total audience by using TV, so this medium's not ideal for everyone. For some younger audiences, web advertising may be even more suitable. But some radio bodies claim that studies have shown that radio airtime is a seventh of the price of TV and that radio offers three-fifths of the advertising awareness effect of TV. If you divide effectiveness by cost, you can see that radio is around four times as cost-effective as TV.

Targeting advertising via radio

We like the fact that radio stations make a real effort to target specific audiences – after all, most advertisers try to do the same thing. You can get good data, both demographic and lifestyle- or attitude-orientated information, on radio audiences. And you can often find radio stations (or specific programmes on those stations) that reach a well-defined audience, rich in those people you want to target, making radio an even better buy.

You can get details of radio station formats and audience characteristics for all UK commercial radio stations from the communications regulator Ofcom, just by going to the Radio Broadcast Licensing section of its website, at www.ofcom. org.uk.

If you're planning to make radio a big part of your marketing plan, we can recommend a book dedicated to telling you how to do it better – *An Advertiser's Guide to Better Radio Advertising*, by Andrew Ingram and Mark Barber from the RAB, also published by Wiley.

Finding Cheaper Ways to Use the Power of Video

If you're thinking of skipping this section, consider this: video can cost £1000 per minute to produce – or even £10,000 if you're making a sophisticated national TV ad – setting aside the cost of the airtime to actually air the ad! But video can also cost £50 a minute or even less.

Do you have access to a high-quality, handheld digital video camera? Well, that camera (when combined with a good microphone) is actually capable of producing effective video for your marketing, especially for use on the web, where low-resolution video files are usually used, making camera quality less important. Just think of all those videos getting millions of viewers on YouTube; the quality isn't great but people keep watching because they're interested in the content.

Many marketers don't realise that the limiting factor in inexpensive or homemade video is usually the sound quality, not the picture quality. So as long as you plug in a remote microphone and put it near anyone who's speaking, you can probably make usable video yourself.

Here are some tips if you decide to shoot video yourself:

✔ Write a simple, clear script and time it before you bother to shoot any video.

✔ Clean up the background. Most amateur efforts to shoot video presentations or ads for marketing are plagued by stuff that shows up in the background. Eliminate rubbish bins, competitors' signs and anything else unsightly.

✔ Use enough light and try to have multiple light sources. A digital video camera is just a fancy camera and it needs light to work. Normal indoor lighting is too dim for quality video. Instead, add more lights, including bright floodlights and open windows. And make sure light shines from both sides so that you fill the shadows. (Shadowed areas get darker in the video.)

✔ Shoot everything more than once. Editing is easy (well, easier) as a result of the many software programs you can use on your own computer to edit video. But editing is much easier if you have lots of footage to select from. Always repeat each short section several times, then, in editing, choose the version that came out best. That approach is how they make films stars look good and it can work well for you, too! If you have more than one camera, you could even edit shots from different angles.

✔ You can produce radio ads or sound-only messages for your website using the same digital recording and editing capabilities as you use to do home-made digital video. The key is a quiet environment and a good microphone for recording. Or you can go into a production studio's sound booth and let the technicians there worry about the technical aspects.

✔ If you want actors, consider recruiting them locally and even asking people to volunteer. We hate to promote this idea, but if you're still a small organisation, avoiding paying Equity rates for your actors makes things considerably cheaper. Paying union rates and residuals is appropriate for major or national campaigns but can be prohibitive for small marketers. However, employees can make great brand ambassadors too, just look at the popularity of Howard in the Halifax adverts!

For information on editing and production, check out the many *For Dummies* books that can help you better understand what's involved or hire a media production firm that can do high-quality work at moderate rates. With plenty of smaller production firms around, try interviewing some in your area and getting samples of their work plus price quotes – you may find that by the time you master the software and come up to speed, you're spending as much doing your own work!

Designing Ads for TV

Television is much like theatre. TV combines visual and verbal channels in real-time action, making it a remarkably rich medium. Yes, you have to make the writing as tight and compelling as good print copy, but the words must also sound good and flow with the visuals to create drama or comedy.

TV ads must use great drama (whether funny or serious), condensed to a few seconds of memorable action. These few seconds of drama must etch themselves into the memory of anyone who watches your ad.

You can't reduce a great film to a formula. You must have a good script with just the right touch of just the right emotion. Great acting. Consistent camera work and an appropriate set. The suspense of a developing relationship between two interesting characters. Achieving this level of artistry isn't necessary to make a good TV ad, but to stand out yours certainly needs to be higher than average, and if you can create truly great TV, your ad pays off in gold.

TV looks simple when you see it, but don't be fooled – it's not simple at all. Hire an experienced production company to help you do the ad or do what many marketers do and hire a big ad agency (at big ad agency prices) to design and supervise its production. This choice costs you, but at least you get quality work. Just remember that *you* ultimately decide whether the script has that star potential or is just another forgettable ad. Don't let the production company shoot until they have something as memorable as a classic film (or at least close).

If you work for a smaller business and are used to shoestring marketing budgets, you may be shaking your head at our advice. You think you can do it yourself. But why waste even a little money on ads that don't work? If you're going to do TV, do it right. Either become expert yourself or hire an expert. Without high-quality production, even the best design doesn't work. Why? Because people watch so much TV that they know the difference between good and bad ads and they don't bother to watch anything but the best.

If you're on a shoestring budget and can't afford to hire an expert or don't have the time to become one yourself, consider the following bits of advice:

✔ **Forgo TV ads and put your video to work in more forgiving venues.** Simple video can look great in other contexts, like your website or a stand at a trade show, even if it would look out of place on television.

✔ **Consider doing a self-made *spoof ad*.** Make fun of one of the silly TV ad genres, such as the one where a man dressed in black scales mountain peaks and jumps over waterfalls to deliver a box of chocolates to a beautiful woman. Because the whole point is to make a campy spoof, you don't want high production values. You can follow this strategy on your own pretty easily, but you still need help from someone with experience in setting up shots and handling cameras and lights.

✔ **Find a film student at a nearby college who's eager to help you produce your ad.** To budding film-makers, your video is an opportunity to show they can do professional work. For you, using a student may be an opportunity to get near-professional work at a very low price. But make sure the terms are clear upfront. Both the student and their tutor need to clarify (in writing) that you'll own the resulting work and use it in your marketing.

Getting emotional

TV differs from other media in the obvious way – by combining action, audio and video – but these features make TV different in less obvious ways as well. Evoking emotions in TV and video is especially easy, just like in traditional theatre. When planning to use TV as your marketing tool, always think about what emotion you want your audience to feel.

Select an emotional state that fits best with your appeal and the creative concept behind your ad. Then use the power of imagery to evoke that emotion. This strategy works whether your appeal is emotional or rational. Always use the emotional power of TV to prepare your audience to receive that appeal. Surprise, excitement, empathy, anxiety, scepticism, thirst, hunger or the protective instincts of the parent – you can create all of these emotional states and more in your audience with a few seconds of TV. A good ad creates the right emotion for your appeal. The classic Hamlet cigar ad, which no longer appears on TV, always aimed for a strictly emotional appeal ('Happiness is a cigar called Hamlet'). Even though that ad hasn't been on the box for years, we bet you can still hear the music as you read that line.

Some marketers measure their TV ads based on warmth. Research firms generally define warmth as the good feelings generated from thinking about love, family or friendship. Although you may not need to go into the details of how researchers measure warmth, noting *why* people measure it can help you. Emotions, especially positive ones, make TV ad messages far more memorable. Many marketers don't realise the strength of this emotional effect because you can't pick it up in the standard measures of ad recall. In day-after recall tests, viewers recall emotional-appeal TV ads about as easily as rational-appeal ads. But in-depth studies of the effectiveness of each kind of ad tend to show that the more emotionally charged ads do a better job of etching the message and branding identity in viewers' minds.

So when you think TV advertising, think emotion. Evoking emotion is what TV can do – often better than any other media, because it can showcase the expressiveness of actors and faces – and emotion makes for highly effective advertising.

Showing your message

Be sure to take full advantage of TV's other great strength: its ability to show. You can demonstrate a product feature, show a product in use and do a thousand other things just with your visuals.

Actually, in any ad medium, you want to show as well as tell. (Even in radio, you can create mental images to show the audience what you want them to see.)The visual and verbal modes reinforce each other. And some people in your audience think visually while others favour a verbal message, so you have to cover both bases by using words and images in your advertising. But in TV, you have to adapt this rule: the

TV ad should *show* and tell (note the emphasis on showing). Compare this scenario with radio, where you show by telling; or print, where the two modes balance each other out, so the rule becomes simply to show and tell.

Considering style

You can use a great variety of styles in TV advertising. A celebrity can endorse the product. Fruit modelled from clay (claymation) can sing and dance about it. Animated animals can chase a user through the jungle in a fanciful exaggeration of a real-life situation. Imagination and videotape know no limits, especially with the growing availability of high-quality computerised animation and special effects at a reasonable cost. But some of the common styles work better – on average – than others in tests of ad effectiveness. Table 5-2 shows styles that are more and less effective.

Table 5-2	It Don't Mean a Thing If It Ain't Got That Swing
More Effective Styles	*Less Effective Styles*
Humorous commercials	Candid-camera style testimonials
Celebrity spokespeople	Expert endorsements
Commercials with children	Song/dance and musical themes
Real-life scenarios	Product demonstrations
Brand comparisons	

Most studies show that the humour and celebrity endorsement styles work best. So try to find ways to use these styles to communicate your message. On the other hand, making ads that are the exception to the rule may give you an edge, so don't give up hope on other styles.

For a great example of exceptions to the rule, consider the Cadbury's ad featuring a drumming gorilla. On the face of it, this scenario doesn't have a great deal to do with chocolate. However, this ad has great standout value, uses music (retro Phil Collins) and imagery (gorilla and purple background) together in a very powerful way and is easily one of the most memorable ads of the past few years.

Buying airtime on TV

Which television stations work best for your ad? Should you advertise on a national (*terrestrial*) channel or on a digital channel? Should the ad run in prime time, evening or late night-time slots? What programmes provide the best audience for your ad?

The UK's main provider of TV audience measurement is BARB (Broadcasters' Audience Research Board; www.barb. co.uk). BARB is a not-for-profit organisation owned jointly by the BBC, ITV, Channel 4, Five, BskyB and the Institute of Practitioners in Advertising (IPA). It keeps track of how many people are watching which channel (and TV programme) by installing homes around the country with a little black box that sits on top of the TV. Although BARB is not for profit, you can't get this data for free. An annual subscription will cost you upwards of £5910, so consider whether you really need that depth of data. For instance, if you're trying to sell gardening products to amateur gardeners and know that you're only interested in home-improvement TV programmes, the channels themselves can give you the viewing figures you need.

Some of BARB's biggest customers are the ad and media-buying agencies, so if you're using an agency to buy your airtime or create your ad, asking them for media data before getting out your own credit card is worthwhile.

Working out the cost of a TV ad

Several different factors affect how much you'll pay for a TV advertising campaign.

The first, and most important, bit of jargon you need to know is *TVRs*, which means television ratings. Audience delivery is measured in TVRs, which can be confusing but has the merit of giving you an idea of how many people in a particular target audience will see your ad. Knowledge of target audiences is important to avoid wasting money advertising to people who're unlikely to buy your product. A TVR is defined as the percentage of a particular audience that has seen a piece of TV content (although they may have spent an ad break talking to their partner or making the tea, so this figure is always an approximation). So, for example, if *Coronation Street* achieved a Housewives TVR of 20 in Yorkshire, this means that 20 per cent of all housewives in the Yorkshire region watched the soap opera.

You can actually get a TVR for your ad that's higher than 100 per cent, which means that a viewer may see your ad more than once and this is counted separately each time. The actual number of times viewers are exposed to a commercial break is called *impacts*. If you think that repeat viewing is important to your campaign, these can be useful programmes or times of the day to target.

Identifying your target audience

You can choose any of the target audiences, shown in the following list, that are commonly sold by broadcasters. Heavy TV viewers such as housewives or general audiences are usually cheaper to buy because they're easier to reach than audiences such as upmarket men.

> Adults
>
> 16- to 34-year-old adults
>
> ABC1 (upmarket) adults
>
> Men
>
> 16- to 34-year-old men
>
> ABC1 men
>
> Women
>
> 16- to 34-year-old women
>
> ABC1 women
>
> Housewives
>
> Housewives and children
>
> ABC1 housewives
>
> Children

Timing your broadcast

The size and type of audience likely to see your ad is governed by the time of day it appears – so that factor will also affect how much you pay. Broadcasters call these *dayparts*, and they're timed as follows:

Daytime 6am–5.29pm

Early peak 5.30–7.29pm

Late peak 7.30–11pm

Night-time 11.01pm–5.59am

Some broadcasters may break down these dayparts even further, adding in such elements as 'breakfast time' during the day. The highest price you'll usually pay is for the highest audience – in peak time, between 5.30pm and 11pm, although again this timing can vary.

Remembering other factors

You also need to factor in a few other variables to the cost of your ad:

- ✔ **The length of your commercial.** Airtime is sold in multiples of 10 seconds, with 30 seconds being the most common ad length.

- ✔ **What time of year you need to advertise.** If you're in the business of selling Christmas gifts, you'll pay considerably more for airtime than if you can advertise in the cheaper months of January, February, March and August.

- ✔ **Size of the region you advertise in.** Prices also vary by *macro region*, which reflects the size of the local population and relative demand. The highest advertiser demand is for London, which makes it the most expensive. If you operate outside London, however, targeting the precise areas where you're based, such as Yorkshire or Tyne-Tees, may be more cost-effective. Some TV macro regions can even be split into *micro regions*. So if your business is in the East Anglia area, for instance, you can buy just that small part of the larger Anglia macro region, giving you tighter targeting and better value for money. You can find a good explanation of how the regions are broken down on the website of TV marketing body, Thinkbox (`www.thinkbox.tv`). Look under 'Planning', then 'Targeting', then 'Regional TV'.

 Because of the complexity of some of these calculations, think hard about using a media agency to plan and buy the airtime. You can let a media agency know what you're trying to achieve with your ad and what type of people you need to target and then let their experts do the rest. Many of these agencies buy up chunks of airtime in advance, so you benefit from an agency-wide deal and don't have to negotiate individually with the TV sales houses. Media agencies can also advise you on TV opportunities you may not have previously considered.

Making your own TV (or radio) programme

A lot of TV and radio ads exist out there and yours is in constant danger of becoming just one of the many that people are exposed to and increasingly, trying to avoid. You don't want your ad to be the one that makes the viewer leave the room to make the tea. The following sections give you a few alternative strategies to consider.

Using advertiser-funded programming (AFP)

The experts have come up with a new term, *branded content*, to describe something that is not quite an ad but which can be used to communicate a commercial message. In TV and radio, branded content means creating your own show (or at least, segment of a show) – the official term for which is *advertiser-funded programming* or *AFP*. This type of communication is becoming increasingly frequent, although many restrictions are still in place about what you can or cannot say about your product. But asking your agency, or the radio stations and channels themselves, about these opportunities is worthwhile because they allow your message to stand out from the clutter of all the other ads.

Vodafone TBA and *Transmission With T-Mobile* are just two examples of AFP. Both of these shows have been screened on Channel 4. *Vodafone TBA* involves the telecoms company organising 'secret' gigs by stars, including rapper Kanye West. The gigs are then shown on TV. *Transmission With T-Mobile* is a Friday night TV music show, which includes street gigs hosted by the mobile phone company. This type of communication is generating a lot of excitement because it allows advertisers to give viewers something they want (entertainment) rather than something many of them don't (ads).

Now look at those programme names again. The real benefit of AFP is that you can give viewers *relevant content* or information that's close to your product or service. Vodafone and T-Mobile use these shows to promote their growing music services. Don't get too close, though. Heinz nearly got fined by the TV regulators for showing recipes that used baked beans and spaghetti hoops when it ran a show called *Dinner Doctors* on Five in 2003. This area is still in development, but AFP will become a popular route for advertisers and you need to look out for likely opportunities.

The social networks, are also creating programme placement and branded content opportunities for brands. As yet, the regulations relating to brands and content online aren't as restrictive as those for TV. Online soap operas such as *Sofia's Diary*, which showed on Bebo in 2008, attracted millions of young viewers. *Sofia's Diary* gathered 5 million viewers in its first month and featured Unilever's Sure deodorant brand and Pearl Drops toothpaste as part of the storyline. As a result of its popularity, this soap opera later went on to appear on a digital channel, Fiver, moving from the computer screen to the TV screen.

Sponsoring a TV or radio programme

If AFP is still waiting in the wings, then sponsorship must be centre stage. Alright, you don't quite get your own TV or radio programme, but if you find a show that's a good fit with your product, this route's almost as good (and a lot less risky).

TV and radio sponsorship is growing fast in the UK as advertisers try to avoid the dual issues of ad clutter and digital personal video recorders (PVRs) such as Sky+, BT Vision and TiVo, which allow viewers to skip through the ad break. You don't need us to tell you that TV and radio sponsorship is growing – you'll have seen it for yourself. TV sponsorship was worth around £190 million last year; *Loose Women* and Maltesers, *Wrigley's* and Hollyoaks and Bombadier English Bitter and *Al Murray's Happy Hour* are all good examples of current sponsorship deals because you can see how the brands are relevant to the programmes.

You don't need to pay anything like the £10 million that Cadbury paid to sponsor *Coronation Street* for three years. You can find relevant programmes at less popular times of the day, or on digital channels, for a sponsorship price of around £150,000.

Video Advertising online

Television is no longer confined to the box in the corner of the living room; it also appears on your computer. You may think the computer is a relatively small market but nearly a third of all Internet users watched video clips and webcasts in 2007, according to a report by the UK communications regulator, Ofcom. This figure is 50 per cent higher than the previous year.

Multiple TV streaming and download channels are now available for all the main broadcasters on terrestrial television, and also web-only channels such as Babelgum and Joost. As these are still relatively new media channels, you may find opportunities to get involved with sponsorship or advertising at a lower cost than with normal TV. And if you're targeting young people who use the web a lot, this medium may be the best place to promote your products or services.

Even if you don't have the budget or know how to appear on an online TV channel, why not consider using video site YouTube? You can post a version of your ad on the site, create a little trailer to promote your product or even just come up with a humorous spot to generate interest. If your product needs some explaining or assembling, why not create a 'how-to' video? You may be surprised by how many people find a demonstration useful and how offering one may bring publicity to your company through sites such as YouTube and www.videojug.com.

Even huge brands use YouTube to generate interest in their products and marketing. The American Super Bowl, during which the biggest and most expensive ads are shown each year, even has its own branded channel on YouTube! People can see the ads, post their own spoofs and leave comments. YouTube offers a tool for research, feedback and promotion all in one. Just make sure that you monitor any responses to your promotional work carefully!

Part III
Powerful Alternatives to Traditional Advertising

'In your marketing plan, you said you wouldn't
spend unnecessarily. I thought that only
applied to your business!'

In this part . . .

In marketing, the goals never really change. This year's
crop of marketers are no more nor less eager to find
new customers and grow our revenues than were last
year's or last decade's marketers.

But the means of achieving these goals can and do change.
You should always look for alternatives and fresh
approaches. You especially have to stay on top of your game
in today's advertising because entirely new ways of communicating with customers and prospects have emerged in the
last couple of decades. Marketers no longer need to feel confined to traditional advertising. Corporate websites, social
networks, e-mail, paid listings on search engines and many
more innovations are transforming marketing.

In addition, we highly recommend that you explore the
power of publicity and of events in your marketing area.
Sometimes, these approaches can be more effective than
anything else in the entire field of marketing, yet marketers traditionally give them little thought and funding in
most companies.

You can, in fact, design an effective marketing programme
for any business that completely skips conventional
advertising and substitutes one or more of the many alternative media instead.

Chapter 6

Digital Marketing

. . . .

In This Chapter

▶ Choosing a web address that has maximum impact

▶ Creating a compelling website

▶ Designing and placing banner ads

▶ Utilising affiliate marketing

▶ Getting to grips with how search engines workUnderstanding Search Engine Optimisation (SEO)

▶ Integrating paid search with other channels

. . . .

*W*hat does digital marketing make you think of? Websites and the Internet, yes. But digital or e-marketing includes online advertising, e-mail and also using text, pictures or even video to reach customers through their mobile phones. It also includes search marketing and social network marketing. These digital tools have opened up lots of new ways to help you sell your products or services. Even better, a lot of these tools are cheaper and certainly more cost-effective than traditional advertising using press or TV.

Nearly every month it seems a new way to communicate with customers using digital media emerges. The market is indeed rapidly evolving but for most marketers, waiting a while before jumping in to the newest techniques is safest, as they can be untried and possibly aggravating to the very people you're trying to win over if you don't execute them well. However, if used properly, many of these new techniques can provide immensely valuable.

According to the communications regulator Ofcom, more than half of UK homes are now online using broadband (58 per cent), and 12.5 million 3G (or Internet-capable) mobile phone connections exist, representing 17 per cent of total mobile connections in the UK. These figures mean that, however much or little you spend on e-marketing, you have to find a space for it in your marketing budget. For that reason, this chapter covers just what you need to know to begin your digital adventures.

Reaching Out with a Website

E-marketing changes fast and often and changing with it is essential. To be a part of the revolution, you need to create a website for your business.

Consider this fact: people spend more time using the Internet than they do any other media apart from TV. In fact, a recent report from the European Interactive Advertising Association found that 16–24 year olds are now accessing the Internet more frequently than they're watching TV – 82 per cent of this younger demographic use the Internet between five and seven days each week, while just 77 per cent watch TV as regularly. Advertising online is something you can afford to do. In fact, you can't afford not to!

Gaining a web presence is relatively easy. Sometimes doing so can be as simple as getting a listing on an online business directory covering your area, so that when consumers key in your company name or look for the type of services you offer using a search engine such as Google, they can find your address and phone number. We strongly believe that every business – including yours – needs a website, even if all it does is provide your contact details and opening hours. Think of your website as a shop window, where potential customers from all over the world can look at the products or services you offer. You can even turn this site into an actual shop. Having a transactional website can be one of the lowest-cost ways to expand geographically without having to move out of your neighbourhood (it's not called the World Wide Web for nothing, you know!).

A good website can bring in customers who would never find your product or service were it not for the Internet. So spending some time and money creating a decent website to attract them is worthwhile.

You need a unique and memorable website address and an easy to use and appealing design (doubly so, if you intend creating a *transactional site* where customers can buy products or services using a credit or debit card).

Choosing a web address

First you need to find and register a web address (also known as a *domain name* or *URL*). Unless you're starting a business from scratch, you probably already have a web address in mind that you want to use. Your web address should be as close as you can possibly get to the name of your business or product. You may think this detail sounds obvious, but we see too many web addresses falling into the trap of having little to do with the parent business (usually because the most obvious name is being used by someone else).

As you search for potential web addresses, keep the following points in mind to ensure you end up with the best name for your site:

- ✔ **A good address relates to your business or product.** The web address www.streetspavedwithgold.com is available to register, along with all of the other main name extensions. The address is catchy and amusing. Should you rush off and register it? Not if it fails this first test: does the name relate to your product or service? Remember, being relevant is better than being clever.

- ✔ **A good name is memorable.** Customers should be able to remember your web address easily. That doesn't mean you have to register anything stunningly cool or clever – and besides, if the web address is obscure, people are less likely to remember it. Using your company name makes the site memorable to anyone who knows the name of your business. You can easily remember that IKEA's global web address is www.ikea.com and for the UK is www.ikea.co.uk. But you can just as easily combine two or three easy words and make a string into a memorable address. An online competitor to IKEA in the UK is the very simply named www.thisisfurniture.com.

- ✔ **A good name isn't easily confused with other addresses.** If consumers can easily mix up your site with similar addresses, some will go to the wrong site by accident. If your company name is a common word or is similar to others, add an extra term or word to your web address to distinguish it. For example, Triumph is a brand name that the lingerie maker and the motorcycle manufacturer have equal claim to. Although customers are unlikely to mistake one brand for the other, they could easily find themselves on the wrong website. As a result, the motorbike brand trades from www. triumphmotorcycles.com while Triumph International uses www.triumph.com.

✓ **A good name doesn't violate trademarks.** You don't want to bump into someone's trademark by accident. Legal rights now favour the trademark holder rather than the domain-name holder – putting an end to the ugly practice of 'cyber-squatting' that existed a few years ago. To be sure that you don't inadvertently step on someone else's toes, check any web address against a database of trademarks. The Intellectual Property Office provides a searchable database at www.ipo.gov.uk but if you think you may run into a problem, ask a lawyer to do a more detailed analysis.

Checking your name's availability

Picking a name is the easy part. The tricky part is finding out whether that name's available and then getting creative if you find out it's not.

First check a domain name's availability by typing it into the web browser to seeing if someone already has it.

Any good provider of web services will have its own site that allows you to check on the availability of a web address. One such provider is www.networksolutions.com, the administrator of the .com domain name extension, but you can just type in 'domain names' and pick any of the companies that offer registration services. The service you need will be on the homepage of any of these sites; just remember to check your preferred address against all of the main *extensions* – .com, .co.uk, .net or .org are among the most desirable, as people remember them first.

Interestingly, www.networksolutions.com/whois/index. jsp gives you information on who owns a domain name, so if a URL fits your business perfectly, you could always offer that person some money to hand it over!

In the best of all possible worlds, your web name search will reveal that your name is free. If that's the case, thank your lucky stars, jump up and down and make a few happy noises. Then register your name.

If someone has registered the name you want with one or most of the main extensions, but left the more obscure `.biz`, `.org.uk` or even `.me.uk` extensions, seeking another name is wisest because customers could forget your extension and go to someone else's site instead. If the other businesses using the extensions are selling similar products to yours, in the same country, people may be confused, so choosing another name is crucial.

When the web's an important sales route for your business, aim to own most or all of the possible extensions and versions of your web address.

If the person who owns the rights to your web address isn't willing to sell it, consider going back to the drawing board and finding another name that isn't being held hostage. Many online operators are looking to make easy money by buying up web addresses for the purpose of selling them at a profit.

Other routes can help you secure the name you want. Many sites that were registered in the frenzy of the dotcom boom eventually come back on to the open market because they were never used or because the original registrar forgot to re-register. When this happens, the web address becomes *detagged*. Alternatively, if you believe you have a stronger or more legitimate claim to a web address than someone else, you can use a disputes resolution service, or even legal action, to make them give the name up. For information on detagging and disputes, visit Nominet at `www.nominet.org.uk`, which is officially recognised as the `.uk` name registry by the industry and government.

If consumers may get confused by alternate spellings or mis-spellings of your domain name, register them too. Registering a name is cheap, so don't lose a prospective customer just because they can't spell your name. You can always redirect them from a mis-spelt URL to your website – if you don't, your competitors may view this mistake as an easy way to steal potential customers from you.

Creating a Compelling Website

Designing good web pages is a key marketing skill, because your website is at the centre of all you do to market online. If you're a consumer-orientated marketer, you want your website to be friendly and easily navigated, as well as to do the following:

- ✔ Engage existing customers, giving them reasons to feel good about their past purchases and connect with your company and other consumers (at least to connect emotionally, if not in actual fact).

- ✔ Share interesting and frequently updated information about your products or services, industry and organisation on the site, so the consumer can gain useful knowledge by visiting it.

- ✔ Maintain a section of the site or a dedicated site for business-to-business (B2B) relationships that matter to your marketing (such as distributors, stores and sales reps). Almost all consumer marketers also work as B2B marketers so bear this in mind.

Finding resources to help with design

You can easily create a basic website – one that includes your contact details plus a few pages showing what your business does – on your own. If your needs are more advanced and you want customers to be able to buy direct from your site, for example, skip down to the section on 'Hiring a professional designer'. This section doesn't cover how to use authoring languages or do any of the programming. That information would fill an entire book, not a chapter, let alone a section. If you decide to create a sophisticated website yourself, you can find excellent books that do go into all the details.

If you want to create your own web pages, we recommend, in particular, *Creating Web Pages All-in-One Desk Reference For Dummies* by Richard Mansfield and Richard Wagner (Wiley). It goes a bit deeper than the also good *Creating Web Pages For Dummies* by Bud E. Smith and Arthur Bebak (also by Wiley). These two titles cover the range in both price and detail, so take your pick.

Consider using your domain name and provider to create your own e-mail addresses, too. An example is `jane@jane smithflowers.com` if your website is `www.janesmith flowers.com`. Having your e-mail reflecting your own website URL looks so much more professional than going through a public domain does. An email like `jane@jane smithflowers.com` looks much better than using `janesmithflowers@yahoo.co.uk`.

Hiring a professional designer

If you aren't a do-it-yourself type, a very easy way to create good web pages is available: find an expert who can do it for you under contract.

Good website design is harder than it looks and going to a reputable design firm and asking them to do it for you is probably best. We recommend a business relationship (spelled out on paper in advance) that specifies that you, not they, own all content at the end (so that you can switch to another vendor if it doesn't work out or they go bust) and also specifies an hourly rate along with an estimate of the site's size and complexity with a cap on the number of billable hours needed to design it.

You can expect to pay anything from £750 for a basic brochure-style website of ten pages to upwards of £10,000 for a Flash-animated fully transactional (or e-commerce) one. That's quite a range, even for custom-designed pages, so here's a basic list of what you can expect to get, and for what price:

- ✔ If you have no budget at all – not even £25 – you can always use a free blog site service such as Wordpress or Blogger to make a very basic updatable site. This option allows you to post stories and makes your contact details available for Internet users. But bear in mind that this site will look very homemade and amateur, so is probably only an option if you really have no other alternatives and are prepared to update it regularly.

✔ You can get a simple template-style website for as little as £50 from some of the web providers that register domain names and host websites, or with web authoring software programs like FrontPage and Dreamweaver. Some programs are quite good, but people often recognise these one-size-fits-all designs, which may lower their opinion of your site design.

✔ For a basic, custom-designed site (around five to ten pages), where the client provides a company logo, images and copy, plan to spend around £750 to £1500. A dedicated *Content Management System* (*CMS*) costs around £2000 to £2500. You can get a web designer to arrange web hosting set up, too. A basic hosting plan costs around £50 to £100 per year, which includes domain name registration.

✔ A more advanced site of up to 20 pages with a custom look built around your logo, and which contains navigation suited to the service or product that you're offering, costs between £1500 and £3500 (although here the price starts climbing depending on what bells and whistles you want to add on). The customised graphics and stock photography necessary for these sites can also drive up your costs, but if your online presence needs this unique, professional look to set you apart from your competitors, then the money may well be worth it.

Beyond the cost of the site, you also need to be aware of additional costs that you may incur – or that you should budget for – in order to enhance the professional appearance and functionality of your website:

✔ Consider an online shopping trolley, for an extra £300 to £500 on top of your bespoke site design. Many basic hosting plans include a shopping trolley, so you can implement this feature fairly easily by using theirs (but you lose out on the custom-look website). Assume that you'll be adding products over time, so select a shopping trolley that gives you room to grow.

✔ Consider streaming video, animation and database management. You can use these technologies as important delivery methods, like showing a speaker in action, demonstrating a new product or providing services, and supporting the consumer online.

✔ Build some room for stock photography into your budget because sites with relevant images – especially of real people – are graphically more appealing and hold the visitor's attention longer. Use pictures optimised (or small enough) for web use so page loading doesn't take too long.

✔ Get your contractor to update your site monthly (web designers charge around $70 per hour) because these updates give customers good reasons to keep coming back to the site. Special promotions or some other monthly feature will add to this evolving appeal.

✔ Plan to spend more for search engine submission, a service which automatically submits your website to all the major search engines so that traffic goes up. This service costs around $100 per year for monthly submissions.

Developing a registration service

Many sites used to have a registration system for consumers to complete to gain access to the website. But beware of creating a site that needs the user to register to gain access to basic information – after all, you want to sell something to them, so why stop them from looking at the produce? We know that creating a free registration hurdle in order to collect their information for future marketing purposes is tempting, but in the long run, this tactic is the wrong way to go about getting hold of this valuable information.

Instead, a handy trick is to offer some extra content – the latest product updates, exclusive content or behind-the-scenes photos – in order to get your customers to sign up with their details.

Driving traffic with content

Most websites are really just huge, interactive advertisements or sales promotions. After a while, even the most cleverly designed ad gets boring. To increase the length of time users spend with your materials and to ensure high involvement and return visits, you need to think like a publisher and not just an advertiser. For this reason, we consider web content to be the hidden factor for increasing site traffic. Unless you have valuable and appealing content, you may have difficulty building up traffic on your site.

Make sure you offer information and entertainment. People like to use the web for research. Often, that research relates to a purchase decision. To be part of that research and purchase process, put useful, non-commercial information on your site. B&Q, the home improvement retailer, strikes a nice balance between online sales and DIY advisor. Its site, at www. diy.com, lists all its major product lines as you'd expect, but also offers a useful 'Knowledge Centre' area that provides step-by-step instructions on everything from building a barbeque to tiling a wall.

Tracking Your Site's Traffic

The web offers an unmatched ability to evaluate how effectively your online marketing is working and to capture information on the people who are visiting your site.

Interpreting click statistics

You may find click-through statistics a useful and easy-to-get indicator of how well an ad or search-engine placement is performing. If you get a lot of people clicking through to your site from an ad or placement, that ad is clearly doing its job of attracting traffic for you. So, all else being equal, more clicks are better. However, all else isn't equal all the time. Here are a few wrinkles to keep in mind when interpreting click rates:

- When a pop-up ad appears, the companies you buy the ad space from usually report it as a click. But don't believe the numbers because you have no indication that someone actually read or acted on that pop-up – they may have just closed it without looking. Dig deeper into the statistics.

✔ Some ads have multiple elements that load in sequence, creating a countable click with each loading, so that one ad may generate several click-through counts. This counting method may lead you to think that the more complex ad is better, but the higher number can be an artifact of the way those who sell ad space on the web count the clicks. (Ask your provider if it can sell web ad space to you, or visit a really popular site and look for the section offering ad space to advertisers.)

✔ Quality is more important than quantity. Who are these people who clicked to your site? Evaluate the quality of those clicks. See the following section 'Paying attention to your site's visitors' for details on how to find out who's visiting your site.

✔ If you're generating poor quality traffic, experiment with putting ads in other places or redesign your ads to specifically focus on your desired target. Keep working on it until you achieve the best click through rates, regardless of numbers.

Paying attention to your site's visitors

Each time someone visits your website, they're exhibiting interest in you and your products. And someone exhibiting interest makes them interesting to you. So whatever you do, however you go about setting up a site, make sure that you capture information about your visitors in a useful form that gets sent to you regularly.

Ask your web provider what kinds of reports they can offer you – probably more than you imagined possible. With these reports in hand, you can track traffic to your site. You probably notice that you, unlike the giants of the web, don't have as much traffic as you may want. Sure, millions of people use Google to do searches or go to eBay to bid on auctioned products. But the average website only has a few dozen visitors a day. For an effective site, you need to build up this traffic at least into thousands of visitors per day. How? By making sure it gets noticed in search engines (see later in this chapter).

Designing and Placing a Banner Ad

A lot has changed in just a few years in Internet advertising. You can see how quickly things have moved on just by looking at what's happened to the most common form of online advertising – the *banner ad*. A banner used to be the only format for online advertising. That traditional format still exists, but for many marketers 'banner' has become a generic term for a whole host of different online ad formats.

We've jumped from one-size-fits-all banners, through as many different types of ad formats as you could wish for, and have come out at the other end with a selection of standard sizes that fit the needs of most advertisers (see Figure 6-1). The *Universal Advertising Package* (*UAP*), as its creators at the Internet Advertising Bureau (IAB) call it, comprises a banner (running across the top of a web page), skyscraper, large rectangle and regular rectangle. You can find out all about the technical specifications for UAP formats at the IAB's website (www.iabuk.net).

UAP formats make the whole process of buying online advertising much more cost-effective. You should pay less for the production of an online campaign if you don't have to re-create your ad for each website you advertise on, and you can compare costs of online ad space more easily if you're comparing like with like – rather than apples with oranges, as was the case before.

Hiring a web media service

Companies providing *web media services* (meaning web page design) can also design and place banner ads and pop-up ads for you. Searching for agencies or individuals to do this work for you can be a long and random process, however. If you're lucky enough to know a competent web designer or programmer, seriously consider using their services – they can create custom banners to your specification quite easily because they're such a small ad format.

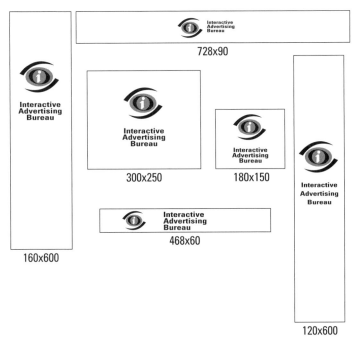

Figure 6-1: UAP formats.

If you have more ambitious plans for rich media online ads, however, you'll need to study the extensive field. We recommend you go straight to the Internet Advertising Bureau website (www.iabuk.net) and visit the membership directory section.

Creating your own banner ad

Not surprisingly, the web is a good starting point for finding templates for banner ads. Because the format is now so common, a lot of sites allow you to use their standard designs for free. One of the best known is AdDesigner.com (you can guess the web address), which makes designing a professional looking animated banner ad within minutes easy.

Focusing on a simple design

The best design for starters is a banner that flashes a simple one-line offer or headline statement, shows an image of your logo or product and then switches to a couple more lines of text explaining what to do and why to do it ('Click here to take advantage of our introductory offer for small business owners and get 20% off your first order of . . . ').

Being positively creative with your ad

Online advertising, done well, can do many more tasks for you than a TV ad, press ad or poster. An online ad can be tactical, by alerting customers to a special offer, or it can help with brand-building, by raising awareness of your product or service without a clear call to action. Unlike TV or press ads, you (or the size of your budget) control how intrusive your ad becomes.

Avoid any ad that totally obscures a page someone's trying to view, that chases their cursor around the screen, and basically forces them either to pay attention or close it. That technology runs contrary to every other trend in the advertiser–customer relationship, which is why this tactic has fallen out of favour in recent years. Instead, create some eye-catching online ad designs that integrate with the web page they appear on and don't irritate potential customers.

Placing your banner ads

Designing the banner is just the beginning because you then have to buy space to display it from publishers. If you poke around on large sites like Google, you can find sections devoted to advertisers like you, where you can explore ad buying options and rates and ask for help from a salesperson. Alternatively, you can go to an online media-buying agency and hire them to do the placement. These agencies take a small commission but probably more than make up for this loss by knowing where to place the ads to target your core customer base, negotiating better rates and avoiding some of the inflation of exposure numbers that can happen when you have to rely on the publisher's accounting.

Placing a banner ad typically costs between £1 and £5 per thousand viewers, depending on where it's placed– not bad if you have an ad that actually generates some responses. But watch the banner ad closely and pull or modify it, or try running it elsewhere, if the click rate is too low to justify the cost. You may have to try a few versions to get it right.

Getting Others to do the Work: Affiliate Marketing

Affiliate marketing is another term for 'finder's fees' or 'lead fees'.

Affiliate marketing programmes work by rewarding websites that deliver users to other websites. Affiliate programmes are usually used by online retailers who pay the referring website a fee for every consumer that completes a certain function, such as purchasing or signing up for something. Although early affiliate deals rewarded on a click basis, so that every click that went through to the destination was paid for, this system has changed in recent years and nearly always uses a performance-based remuneration model – so, as an advertiser, you only pay if you make money. Brilliant!

Carried out correctly, affiliate marketing can be a remarkably effective method for advertisers to get people to their site to buy things. Its payment by results nature also means that you needn't be afraid to get involved.

Getting started

Unless you're a big company with lots of time and resources to spare to develop your own programme, seek to join an existing affiliate network.

To begin with, here's a list – in no particular order – of the bigger networks active in the UK today:

www.affiliatefuture.co.uk

www.dgmaffiliates.com

www.affiliatewindow.com

www.buy.at

www.paidonresults.com

www.webgains.com

www.linkshare.com/uk

Choosing a network

Picking your way through the different affiliate network offerings can be a bit of a minefield, but when you're engaging any agency for outsourced work, try to get as much information about them as possible.

Use the checklist below to help you select an affiliate partner:

- ✔ Ask the network about their expertise in your chosen sector and ask them to back it up with examples and case studies, if possible.

- ✔ Get them to show you a client list and any testimonials that they have.

- ✔ Ask them about the size and breadth of their network. Is it only UK based? What are the demographics?

- ✔ Check out the top ranking affiliate networks from a search engine results page, using the search term 'affiliate marketing'. Search is a key part of affiliate marketing and the result may say a lot about the network.

- ✔ Have an immediate conversation about pricing and costs. You're better off knowing what you're dealing with at the outset.

- ✔ Come into the process with your eyes wide open. These people want to sell you the affiliate marketing dream, so don't get carried away with the hype. If their claims sound too good to be true, they may well be.

- ✔ Ask them what support and services they offer to advertisers.

- ✔ Find out which networks your competitors use. Being in the same network as a competitor can drive up the price of your affiliate marketing as your rival may offer a better commission deal to publishers than you do. Publishers will then try harder on behalf of your competition than for you and force you into a bidding war.

- ✔ Find out what measurement technology the network uses to track clicks to your site.

- ✔ Discover the publishers' payment basis.

Going through this checklist means you've applied due diligence to the process and will thus know less chance exists of anything going wrong when you begin using affiliate marketing.

Using E-mail for Marketing

E-mail is a powerful digital marketing tool. This medium may seem a bit old hat in a world of Facebook and MySpace, but you can create yourself, or hire a designer to create, a professional e-mail that looks like a well-designed web page, with animation and clickable buttons linking to your site. Now, all you have to do is blast out your message to millions of e-mail addresses and surely you can make millions overnight!

Not so fast! Okay, so you have this great marketing message or sales pitch, and you want to send it to everyone in the world who has an e-mail address. You can actually do that, but we don't advise doing so. The more specific and narrow your use of e-mail for marketing, the better. In fact, since the introduction of legislation in the UK, Europe and the US, marketers must be careful to avoid violating all sorts of restrictions on *spam*, or junk e-mails. We help you stay on the sunny side of the law in this section.

Sending only good e-mails

The best e-mail is a personal communication with a customer you know (and who wants to hear from you), sent individually from you with an accurate e-mail return address as well as your name, title, company name, full mailing address and phone number. The e-mail may read as follows:

Dear So-and-so

I wanted to follow up after your purchase of (your product) on (date) to see how it's working out for you and to thank you for your continuing business. If you have any concerns or questions, please let me know by return e-mail, or feel free to call me directly on 0123 123 1234.

Best wishes

Your Name

Use e-mail as much as you can for legitimate, helpful, one-to-one contact and support of customers or prospects. Sometimes you can offer services or content online that requires a registration. As part of that registration process, consider asking your customers if they want to receive more information on any of your products. If they opt-in, you can be sure that they'll value your follow-up e-mails.

Sending out an e-mail to a list rather than an individual is also possible, but ensure that you have a clear purpose that benefits those people on the list. Also make sure that your list only includes people who've indicated they're happy to be communicated with so you stay within the law and don't anger people. Never attempt to contact people who've opted-out of contact with you.

Understanding e-mail etiquette

Goodwill is a valuable asset, so don't destroy it with your e-mails! The following list provides some additional rules for good mass e-mailing. Our inspiration for these rules comes from the Direct Marketing Association's guidelines for responsible use of e-mail. We also bear the legal restrictions in mind.

✓ **Send e-mails only to those people who ask for them.** Your bulk e-mails should go only to those people who give you permission to contact them. The law (the Privacy and Electronic Communications Regulations) requires that no e-mails are sent without prior consent. What does that mean? It means that everyone you send an e-mail to should have 'opted in' to receive e-mails from you, and each time you contact them, you must give them an option to reply and be taken off the list.

If you have a 'prior relationship' with that contact (such as them being a previous customer or requesting information from you) the rules are slightly softer. Consider asking visitors to your website to register for extra information; you can then get these requests by creating a useful e-newsletter and advertising it on the web as a free subscription. Those people who sign up really want it, and they're happy to see the next issue arrive.

✓ **Remove addresses from your list immediately when people ask for them to be removed.** Remember that refusing to allow people to opt out is illegal. Also, people have such widespread distrust of web marketers that you may consider writing the person a brief, individual e-mail from you (identify yourself and your title for credibility), letting them know that you have eliminated them from the list and are sorry if you've inconvenienced them. You shouldn't say any more in the e-mail. Don't try to make a sale – you just irritate the person even more. You generally make a positive impression by being so responsive to the person's complaint, so don't be surprised if your special attention to their request leads them to initiate a sale later on.

- ✔ **If you insist on buying e-mail lists, test them before using them.** We're assuming that the list you buy in is legal (check first that the people on it have agreed to being contacted by third-party advertisers, like yourself). Then try sending a very simple, short, non-irritating message to people on the list, such as an offer to send them a catalogue or free sample, and ask for a few pieces of qualifying information in return. See what happens. Cull all the many bounce-backs and irritated people from the list. Now your list is a bit better quality than the raw original. Save those replies in a separate list – they're significantly better and more qualified and deserve a more elaborate e-mail, mailing or (if the numbers aren't too high) personal contact.

- ✔ **Respect privacy.** People don't want to feel like someone's spying on them. Never send to a list if you'd be embarrassed to admit where you got the names from. You can develop an e-mail list in plenty of legitimate ways (from customer data, from web ads, from enquiries at trade shows, from return postcards included in mailings, and so on), so don't do anything that your neighbours would consider irritating or sleazy.

- ✔ **Send out your bulk e-mails just like you send an individual one.** Use a real, live, reply-able e-mail address. We hate it when we can't reply to an e-mail – it makes us angry!

- ✔ **Make sure that the subject line isn't deceptive.** Good practice and good sense dictate that you make the subject line straightforward. In marketing, you want to know straight away if someone isn't a good prospect, instead of wasting your time or theirs when they have no interest in your offer. A whole other book could be written about creating snappy lines that ensure e-mails get opened, but just consider what makes you do so. Opening with a deception such as 'Free money for you!' just looks like spam and will be deleted.

✔ **Keep your e-mail address lists up to date.** When you get a *hard bounce-back* (notice that a message was undeliverable) from an address, remove it immediately and update your e-mail list for the next mailing.

A *soft bounce-back* is an undeliverable message resulting from some kind of temporary problem. Track it to see if the e-mail eventually goes through. If not, eliminate this address from your list, too.

People change their e-mail addresses and switch servers. You can have bounce-backs on your list who may still be good customers or prospects. At least once a year, check these inactive names and try to contact them by phone or mail to update their e-mail addresses. Some of these people are still interested and don't need to be cut from your list; they just need their e-mail addresses updated.

If you're e-mailing to an in-house list of people who've bought from you, gone to your seminar or asked for information in the past, remind them of your relationship in the e-mail – they may have forgotten.

We hate *spam* – junk e-mails that clog up our mailboxes. We bet you feel the same way. So don't let your web marketing make you part of this problem. Use good quality lists, be polite and respectful, and integrate e-mail into your broader web strategy so that you don't have to rely too heavily on e-mail. Real people live at the end of those e-mail addresses. Treat them as such!

Getting Mobile with Your Marketing

A staggering 6.5 billion text messages were sent in the UK during May 2008. According to the Mobile Data Association, 16.43 million mobile Internet (WAP) users were evident in the UK in the same month, and the latest Ofcom Communications

Market Report showed that 12.5 million 3G (the fastest mobile speed) connections existed in the UK in August 2008.

Mobile marketing is held up as being one of the most important mediums of the future but, as you can see from the numbers, the possibilities for now aren't half bad either. We emphasise that things are constantly changing in mobile marketing, so the technologies of today will certainly be superceded some time soon.

The most basic, and therefore most developed, method of mobile marketing is by Short Message Service, or SMS – which most people simply call texting. You can send a personal, targeted message by text in the same way as you send an e-mail (and subject to the same laws on privacy; see 'Understanding e-mail etiquette' earlier in this section), and you can reach your customers 24 hours a day.

Of course, you can also use a mobile phone as the launch-pad for a whole host of marketing wonderment. MMS, WAP, Bluetooth, 3G – the terminology is almost as impenetrable as the average marketer's ability to take advantage of it. For the time being we suggest that, if you're interested in trying out mobile marketing, stick to the tried and tested methods (or at least as tried and tested as a less than ten-year-old method can be). The following list gives some pointers and ideas on how to use mobile marketing:

- **Keep it short and to the point.** An SMS message can only be 160 characters long – so your message has to be quick and clear. That's enough, however, to provide customers with a money-off message or coupon, for example.

- **Know who's using the mobile.** People of all ages use mobile phones, so try to fit the message to your knowledge of who owns the number.

- **Be prepared for a good response.** If you do plan to offer a mobile token or other giveaway, be aware that response rates can be as much as 15 per cent higher than direct marketing – and a large chunk of that response will be immediate.

- **Respect privacy at all times.** Mobile marketing is subject to the same laws as e-mail marketing, covered earlier in this section. You must have the permission of the person you are texting. Respecting the principles of permission-based marketing makes good sense.

✔ **Get help (you'll need it).** You can build your own data-base of mobile numbers and send messages directly to them, but doing so is time consuming and, for all but the smallest databases, uneconomical. Consider buying in a list of numbers from a database company and then get-ting an SMS broadcast provider to send the messages for you. Like a mailing house or call centre, these companies can give you feedback on the campaign and manage the customer response.

For now, we suggest leaving the development of Apple iPhone applications or Google Phone services to the larger brands, as new advertising eco-systems like these have multiple pitfalls. Letting someone else discover them before you take on this type of sophisticated mobile advertising is probably best.

Entering the Blogosphere

You have your website, an email programme and also maybe an affliate programme; now you're ready to enter the Blogosphere! We don't mean outer space but the online world of blogs.

At its most basic, blogging is a way of recording thoughts, col-lecting links and sharing ideas with other people via a very simple website. In effect, blogs are online journals for indi-viduals or organisations. A blogging craze is currently sweep-ing the world, with millions of people writing them on a daily basis.

Some blogs have also turned their authors into mini-celebrities. 'Perez Hilton' is the world's most famous celebrity blogger, reporting on the underbelly of Hollywood, and is now a media mogul in his own right with everything from a clothing range to a TV show.

 If you want people to keep coming back to look at your blog you need to keep it up to date, interesting and relevant. Boring blogs are a turn-off!

Blogger and Wordpress are free blogging tools but many others charge you a monthly or annual subscription. Moving your blog from one tool to another isn't easy, so make your decision carefully.

A number of the biggest companies, such as Guinness, Honda and BT, are now using blogs to communicate with their customers with varying degrees of success. These are known as corporate blogs and yours will fall into this category (albeit on a smaller scale). The Guinness blog (www.guinnessblog.com) is perhaps the most engaging of the corporate offerings as the black stuff's marketing team write it and it gives Guinness fans a behind the scenes look into how the drink's produced and how the company goes about making its ads.

✔ Be open and honest. Hiding the truth on the Internet is impossible and if you try to mislead consumers via your blog you'll get burnt (or 'flamed' in blog jargon).

✔ Keep your blog up to date, relevant and interesting. No-one wants to read a blog from two years ago; it looks like your company gives up on things when they become too much trouble.

✔ Be clear about the aims of your blog from the outset and stick to them.

✔ Do let bloggers comment on what you write and make sure you don't over-react if or when they post anything negative about your company. If you really want a conversation with customers, be prepared for people to tell you their truth, not just yours.

✔ If negative posts do appear, react in an open and honest way. Blogs are a very useful way of developing your product or service to better meet the needs of your customers.

✔ Avoid 'corporate speak'. Blogs are about presenting a side to the business not encompassed in the official website, so don't weigh them down with jargon.

✔ Don't try to sell to your audience. That's a job for an official website; if you make your blog a sales pitch, people simply won't visit it.

> ✔ Make sure that if more than one person is blogging on
> behalf of the company, everyone is clear on what are
> acceptable topics for discussion and the right tone
> and style so it remains consistent rather than appearing
> confused.

Bloggers hate being sold to and react badly to companies that
try to do so. Using subversive means is particularly frowned
upon.

Search Engine Marketing

Search engine marketing can be one of the most effective
tools in a marketer's armoury and is vital to success if you're
running an online business. Paid search advertising accounts
for 60 per cent of all online advertising spend in the UK, with
the vast majority going on those services offered by Internet
giant Google. We thus use examples of how to use Google to
get the best from your search efforts in this chapter – but
remember, Yahoo! and Microsoft also offer paid search advertising and having your eggs in more than one basket is always
wise. After finishing reading this chapter you should be well
armed to tackle your own paid and natural (the 'normal' part
of search engine results) search advertising.

This chapter explains the basics of search marketing, both
paid advertising and search engine optimisation (SEO) – otherwise known as how to build your website so people can find
it in search engines.

Getting to Grips with How
Search Engines Work

Search engines are now *the* way to find information. The
Internet carries so much data that these engines are indis-
pensable for sifting through it and, as such, can make the difference between your website succeeding or failing. Consider
booking a three-star hotel in London. In the past, you'd have
flicked through guides in the bookshop; now, you just type
'three-star hotel, London' into Google.

Building and maintaining a website that features high in the listings on a search engine results page isn't an exact science but you can follow guidelines to ensure that you do get listed towards the top of the results when someone searches using terms relevant to your business. If you want to know even more about this area and digital marketing in general, you can find more detail in *Digital Marketing For Dummies* (Wiley) by Greg Brooks and Ben Carter.

The term Search Engine Optimisation (SEO) covers a vast amount of different techniques tha can be used in order to ensure that your website is found and indexed by a search engine, so that when consumers type in your name or the name of your products, they will be able to find you.

To understand how to fully optimise your website so that it features as high as possible in the rankings of search engines, you need to understand how search engines work.

Search engines such as Google use software agents known as *crawlers* or *spiders* that are sent out onto the web and automatically 'read' a site. They pick up not only the words on the pages, but also the special *metadata* information that web page creators encode in the page but can't be seen by the final viewer. This metadata contains information that describes the content of the page and it is what the 'spiders' look at when deciding how to list the web page in the search engine's index. For example, if your web page is all about cookery, and specifically Italian cookery, the metadata will contain relevant terms to this such as 'pasta', 'lasagne', 'Italy', 'pizza' and so on. This is the information used to match the request someone types into the search engine to your web page. The spiders then follow the links from that site, and links to the site from other web pages, before returning the information to the central database, where the data is stored and then interrogated every time a search is made. These spiders return to pages every now and again to see if any of the 'metadata' information has changed.

A page ranking in the search engines listings is determined by the relevance of the 'metadata' and visible web page text to the request and also by the quality and number of links that link to that page. Every search engine has a slightly different algorithm it uses to determine its page ranking, so SEO can become a very complicated art. You can gain a good ranking on one engine but it won't guarantee you the same result on another.

If you haven't already built your website, you can build accessibility into it to improve the number of users that visit you online and, in turn, raise your search ranking. The 'Understanding SEO' section covers accessibility.

Finally, you can also use online public relations as part of your SEO campaign. If these stories are published online and linked to your site, you'll gain traffic. The stories can also be talked about by people who read them, who may then comment on them and also link to your website – all increasing your relevancy in the eyes of the search engines.

However you choose to approach SEO, you need to have a firm understanding of the necessary skills, whether you undertake it yourself or bring in a specialist to help you.

Understanding SEO

Good SEO should begin before you even build your website. Planning out your site so that you make it as relevant and accessible as possible will help you to maintain a good ranking in search engine results pages. As soon as you decide that you require a website, you need to ensure that the way that you design and then build your site makes it as accessible as possible. The World Wide Web Consortium (www.w3.org/WAI/guid-tech) carries a list of guidelines to follow to make your website is accessible as possible.

Obviously, a badly designed site will be hard for people to navigate and the same will be true for the search engine spiders that collect information and rank your site.

To see if your site is already well designed – or if you haven't built yours yet and want to see what works – look at competitors' sites to see how well theirs work. Note things such as the speed of page loading, the ease of navigation, whether links point to relevant information and what details they give on their home pages.

Creating an eye-catching website with the latest Flash technology and whizzy graphics is all very well, but search engine spiders can't appreciate these details. They're cold, calculating little creatures that simply apply their logic to your site to give it a ranking and then move on to the next. So, when designing a site, focus on your customers, but also keep one eye on the spiders.

Dos and Don'ts of SEO

SEO can be a dangerous world; fortunately, guidelines and rules are widely available online to help you navigate the minefield.

You need to use SEO to:

✔ Pull in as many customers to your website as possible

✔ Get as many links to your site as possible

✔ Design the best possible experience for both visitors and spiders alike

✔ Ultimately get a good search engine ranking in the results under relevant keyword search terms

Crucially, though, using SEO doesn't mean undertaking practices that trick users or spiders into thinking that your website is something that it isn't just to get them through the door or improve your ranking. Doing so – definitely result in you being de-listed from the index of a search engine. Being de-listed is the SEO equivalent of football's red card and incurs a nasty stigma, as we explain below.

Good and bad SEO practices are known as White Hat and Black Hat practices, respectively. To further complicate matters, a continual argument rages between the two groups as to what constitutes unethical SEO. The aim of SEO is to try to rise up the rankings and Black Hatters argue that any means of doing so are justified since all SEO is an attempt to manipulate the rankings. You can see their point – it's the law of the wild – but we strongly advise you to avoid Black Hat practices. Search engines frown upon them, and if you're found out you'll be kicked off the index and be out in the cold.

The following sections give you the low-down on White Hat and Black Hat practices.

White Hat practices

To make sure you stick to White Hat practices:

✔ **Make searching the page easy:** On each page, use a unique and relevant title and name and do the same in metadata so spiders can easily read the page and its content.

✔ **Keep the content as relevant as possible:** When spiders read the page, the terminology they find should be relevant to the subject of the page. Make the content what a user expects to find after searching on specific keywords.

✔ **Add content:** Content is king in SEO, so add as much content as possible to your site, but don't *scrape* it from elsewhere as doing so is frowned on. (Content scraping is when you copy wholesale content from another site.) Create your own unique content.

✔ **Make your metadata relevant:** Make sure that your metadata is relevant to your site and specific page content, but avoid the use of excessive repetition of words and over the top punctuation such as exclamation marks. If you repeat keywords, a search engine may believe that you're attempting to fool it, and visitors too.

✔ **Avoid cookies:** Set up your site so that spiders can crawl through your pages without having to accept *cookies* – packages of text that get swapped between a site and its users – this allows them to do their job much faster and takes up less resource.

✔ Develop linking strategies to entice links from other websites. Sometimes called 'link bait' strategies, in essence, you create your own interesting content, as sites with useful or entertaining information tend to get linked to more than those without. This linking increases your ranking.

✔ Join a *web ring* that is relevant to your business. A web ring is a group of sites that have all linked to each other to form a ring. When someone visits a site in the ring, they are offered links to relevant content from others within it.

✔ Increase your online PR through writing interesting articles that can be offered to other sites in exchange for a link back to your own site alongside the article.

These are just a few basic principles of White Hat practice. You need to take a whole host of other things into consideration, too, which is why getting guidance from professionals or at least doing a lot of research before setting up your website is so useful.

If you want an exhaustive look at White Hat practices, try these links for the major engines' suggestions:

```
www.google.com/support/webmasters/bin/
answer.py?answer=35769
```

```
help.yahoo.com/l/us/yahoo/search/websearch
```

Black Hat practices

Spamdexing is the big no-no in SEO. *Spamdexing*, a mixture of spamming and indexing, falls into two categories, either content or link spam. We explain these terms below.

Content spam

This type of Black Hat practice is designed to alter the search engine spider's view of the website so that it is different from what the user will encounter when they click through on the search results. All of the techniques aim to boost the sites ranking in the results lists.

✔ **Keyword Stuffing:** Hidden, random text on a webpage to fool the spiders into thinking there are more keywords on the page than there really are in the content.

✔ **Gateway or doorway pages (also know as cloaking):** Particularly sneaky, these are low quality hastily built web pages that are stuffed with very similar keywords.

These pages will then rank highly in the search results and will then have a link on them to the destination site.

✔ **Hidden or invisible text:** This is the act of disguising keywords and phrases by making them the same colour as the background, using a tiny font size or hiding them somewhere else on the page or in the HTML (metadata). This makes the site seem more relevant to the search engine spider, when in fact it will be less relevant to the user.

✔ **Content Scraping:** Programmes designed to 'scrape' content from search engine results pages and websites, dumping it on a site that will then probably be filled with unrelated adverts. The content is designed to fool the spiders and attract users who see and also may click on the ads meaning the site owner can generate income from advertising.

✔ **Meta tag stuffing:** This is the act of 'stuffing' keywords in the meta tags, which the spiders use to decide what the page is about, repeating them over and over and often using unrelated words to the content of the Web page to fool the spiders.

Link spam

Linking to other websites can help boost your page ranking. But link spam is specifically targeted at search engines' web-page ranking systems that are partly based on the quality and quantity of links from other similar quality websites to the destination site.

✔ **Hidden links:** The act of hiding links where they will not be found by Web surfers, but where they will be found by spiders, in order to increase the Web page ranking.

✔ **Link Farms:** These farms are created by designing a group of Web pages that all link to each other over and over and over. This practice is also carried out with blogs.

✔ **Spam in blogs:** Since blogs became popular they have been targeted by Black Hatters who place links in any comment sections of the blog, linking back to a specific site. This practice has even become automated with computers posting links all over the Internet.

✔ **Google Bombing:** This happens when a large number of sites combine to link to one site and drive it to the top of the search listings. It works due to the nature of Google's search algorithm, but is usually only used for malicious non-commercial purposes such as the famous use of a Google Bomb to promote a joke 'File Not Found' page that was returned top of the list when searching for the phrase 'Weapons of Mass Destruction' on Google.

If you follow the rules given out by the search engines and the White Hat rules that we have outlined, you should have no problem creating a site that is visible to search engines and useful for visitors too.

Choosing between In-House or Outsourcing

We think that by now you have realised that SEO is not a very simple process and that you may need to have quite a bit of experience in dealing with its subtle nuances. Luckily, help is at hand. . A huge number of SEO agencies have sprung up all over the UK to feed the growing market for specialist search skills and most reputable Web design agencies offer these services as part of their build fee.

One thing to take into account is that it is often beneficial to hire an agency that can handle both your SEO and also your paid search – often called SEM – needs. There are a number of agencies that will offer you this dual service. The bigger media agencies that will offer paid search services will most likely offer SEO services as well, but it won't be them carrying out the work – they will then use their own SEO partner to do the work. It's not a big issue but obviously any degree of separation is less desirable than none at all, so do your homework and make sure that you find a partner that meets your needs.

So do you need to hire an SEO agency? Well if you feel comfortable with everything that we have talked about so far, then you are probably well equipped and educated enough in the market to go it alone. But for the majority of people, an agency or at least some individual expertise, will be required to implement an SEO strategy.

Agency Checklist

- ✓ The first and most obvious place to start is to use the major search engines like Google and search under the terms 'Search Engine Optimisation' and SEO. The agencies that come up top have obviously got their act together and should be worth a look.

- ✓ As well as checking out potential agencies' rankings on the search engines, check out their Web site for work they have done, which clients they work for and any case studies and customer recommendations Any decent agency worth their salt will carry information on work they have done and you could even ask for recommendations based on the agency's client list.

- ✓ You should be able to request a site review from any decent agency free of charge. This will show you how well they operate and it will be an interesting gauge if you get a few of them to compare.

- ✓ Remember that in this instance, we are talking about SEO, not paid search, so if agencies spend a lot of time talking about paid services, they may not have the expertise that you want in SEO.

- ✓ Set your price. It is your money, so whichever agency you choose, insist on a set price for the work and set some targets to achieve as well. You can even see if you can set up a 'payment on results' business model.

- ✓ Ask questions about the White Hat / Black Hat practices that we outlined earlier in this chapter to ensure that you are not going to be working with an unethical company.

- ✓ Make sure that the agency explains to you exactly what work needs doing. Don't let them bamboozle you – you are paying them, so make sure they explain things satisfactorily to you.

- ✓ Beware of anyone that will offer to get you to number one in the Google rankings or other wild promises; they won't be true, certainly not by any White Hat practices and without massive investment.

- ✓ It is a good idea to protect yourself legally by getting the agency to sign up to a money-back guarantee or getting the agency to sign a document indemnifying your brand from damage.

✔ Ask the agency how it will work with your other marketing efforts. Any decent agency will want to know the whole marketing picture and really understand your company so it can achieve the best results.

Following these rules should ensure that you don't end up with the John Wayne of the SEO world. You don't have to get pedantic, but it is sometimes worth going down to the level of asking for meetings in the agency's office – just to make sure they actually have one. It may sound a bit drastic, and we do not want to put anyone off from carrying out SEO, which can be massively beneficial to your digital marketing efforts, but you must be aware of all the pitfalls as well.

What Is Paid Search?

Put simply, paid search is the service that is offered by search engines such as Google, Yahoo and MSN that allows a business to advertise next to search results that have been requested by a user. For example, you are searching for an Apple iPod. The search listings may bring up Apple's own website but the paid results down the side of the page show adverts from retailers stocking the iPod, such as Amazon.

The system works on an auction basis using keyword bidding, meaning that a business can bid on relevant keywords that are entered into the search engine by users. The keywords that someone uses determine what results they are shown. If you can find out what your potential customers are searching for, you can make sure that you are prominent in the paid listings by bidding on those keywords.

Paid listings are found on the right hand side of search results pages (and at the top) and are marked out separately from the 'natural' results which make up the main bulk of the page. The paid results comprise of a link to your site and small ad blurb underneath that can describe what a company offers or highlight a special promotion. Writing these ads in this small amount of space can be a skill in itself!

The difference between paid listings and natural listings is that you cannot buy your way to the top of the natural listings; this can only be achieved by building a good Web site, generating lots of links and most probably, employing a reputable Search Engine Optimisation (SEO) agency (which we cover earlier in this chapter).

One of the benefits of paid listings is that you can jump the queue and go to the head of the class by by outbidding competitors on your chosen keywords. This can be very useful if you want to get some instant traffic to your Web site; for example, if you are running a specific campaign or special offer but do not have the time to undergo extensive SEO, which will take much longer. When a Web site visitor sees your ad and clicks the link, they are then delivered to your home page or a specific page you have chosen for the campaign.

Another benefit of paid search is that if you have chosen your keywords wisely – we will help you with this later in the chapter – you will be advertising to consumers that are already interested in the product or service that you offer as they have made the effort to look for information on your chosen keywords using the search engine. This is one reason why in the first half of 2008 the UK paid search industry was worth £981m (60 per cent of the total online ad market) and was yet to break the £2bn a year mark for the whole year (at time of writing).

Google, Yahoo! and Microsoft

Once you have made the decision to carry out paid search marketing, the next thing you have to do is make a decision about how many search engines you will use. In the UK the big three are Google, Yahoo! and Microsoft.

Google has an almost unassailable lead in the search market in the UK at present, so if you are going to carry out any search marketing, you must use Google's service AdWords or you will miss out on almost the entire market.

The other big search players Yahoo! and Microsoft each have their own systems that you can use to conduct paid search marketing. Yahoo!'s offering is called Yahoo! Search Marketing and Microsoft's is accessed through the Microsoft adCenter, which allows you to advertise across all of Microsoft's Web businesses, including the search service.

Although the array of services looks daunting at first, each company offers in depth tutorials into paid search marketing and how their particular tools can be used.

For a brief introduction to each engine visit these sites:

- ✔ **Yahoo! Search Marketing**: `searchmarketing.yahoo.com/en_GB/srch/index.php`

- ✔ **Microsoft adCenter**: `advertising.msn.co.uk/MSNKeyWords/default.aspx?pageid=902`

- ✔ **Google AdWords**: `adwords.google.com/select/Login`

Discovering How to Bid on Keywords

With paid search, the devil is in the detail; in this case, the detail is keyword bidding. Each search engine has its own services that will guide you through the bidding process, but before you get to this stage, you must first of all decide what keywords are best suited to your business.

A few basic rules exist when it comes to choosing your keywords for your paid search marketing. The main rule is to ensure that the words that you decide upon match the product or services that you offer. This may sound obvious, but if you trick users into clicking through to your site from an ad and when they get there the products you sell are not relevant to the advert, you are losing money as they will only be disappointed when they get there. Keep it simple and truthful.

For example, if you sell books, you may find that some people search for 'books' but they also choose 'good reads' or 'stories' or particular authors.

It is at this point that you might discover that although a certain word is most relevant to your Web site, it is also the most relevant word to thousands of other sites. Under the auction system that search engines use, this means that unless you have deep marketing pockets, you may want to shy away from these popular keywords.

A good tip if you are using Google is to use the keyword matching options (`http://adwords.google.com/support/bin/answer.py?answer=6100`), which can improve results and lower potential costs. Using the service you can 'broadmatch' your keyword phrases, meaning that if you use the phrase 'running shoes' your ads will appear when someone's query contains 'running' and 'shoes', in any order and even if other terms appear. You can also enter your keyword in quotation marks, as in "running shoes" and your ad will appear when a user searches on the exact phrase 'running shoes', in this order, and possibly with other terms in the query, but not when the words are out of order. You can even use a negative keyword match which means that if your keyword is 'running shoes', you can add a negative keyword such as 'blue' so your ad will not appear when a user searches for blue running shoes.

Once you have found your main keywords, you can get help from sources online that will give you more keywords on the periphery, but linked to your own.

Try out these for a start:

- `www.wordtracker.com`
- `adwords.google.com/select/KeywordToolExternal`

Now that you have decided to carry out paid search marketing, selected your search engines to use and chosen your keywords, you are ready to get started.

For ease of use, we will explain the Google AdWords sign-up process as it covers the most of the UK market at time of writing.

1. **Go to `www.google.co.uk/ads`.** Click on the AdWords link on the top left of the page. The next page will give you a description of the AdWords service, how it works, the costs involved and some case studies to look through. Once you are satisfied that it is right for you, click the *Sign Up Now* link at the bottom of the page.

2. **Sign up for either the Starter or the Standard Edition.** If you are new to paid search then it is best

to choose the Starter edition until you are more confident. Don't worry, you can upgrade at any time. Check the Starter edition box and click *continue*.

3. **Create your ad.** First enter in the details of where your customers are located – are they just in the UK? This will help to target your advertising. Also pick the language you would like your ad displayed in.

- Enter your website URL in the box provided in order to create the link from your advert to the site where you want people to go when they click on it.

- Next you will be asked to enter the text of your ad. At this point, there is also information available to help you to create this including *Top Five Keys to Powerful Ads* and *Editorial Guidelines.* It is worth reading both of these.

- Once you have read the information you should enter the headline and text of your ad in the box provided. text in the box provided, a sample of your ad will show up on the left so you can see what it looks like.

- The next step is to enter your keywords in the box provided. Again, tips are provided at this step to help you out and they are worth a read.

- You can then choose the currency in which you would like to pay for your ads.

- The next step is vital. Setting your budget. This is important as once you do this you now know you cannot spend more than this amount initially on your ad.

- When you have done all of this you can choose whether or not to receive information in the future from Google and click the *continue* button to get to the next stage.

4. **Set up an account with Google**. If you already use Google services, such as Google Mail, you will already have an account and you simply tick the corresponding box and fill in your details. If not you will have to sign up before proceeding. Once you have signed up click the *continue* button.

5. **Sign in:** You should now see a congratulations page and should be asked to sign in to your AdWords account to provide billing information and to activate the account. The account info section is self explanatory. Simply select your location, choose your form of payment – you can pay by Bank Transfer or by Credit Card, agree to the terms and conditions and provide your billing information.

Congratulations, you are now a paid search advertiser!

Deciding Between In-House or Agency

One of the biggest decisions you will have to make is whether to carry out your paid search in-house or whether to outsource to a specialist search marketing agency.

There are pros and cons on both sides of this argument: carrying it out in-house, you have more control over what is happening, but you may not necessarily have expert skills. Employing a specialist agency may cost you more money than handling it in-house, but the agency may make your marketing budget work harder for you and save you money in the long run. Dealing with it in-house means that you will have to build relationships with the search engines over time but the agency will already have these in place.

If you have made the decision to handle it in-house, then you must get at least a couple of people up to speed with the ins and outs of paid search marketing. Unlike many other marketing disciplines that you may have undertaken, paid search is a fast moving and constantly changing medium. Unless you are on the ball, you will lose out to the competition.

As soon as you have a couple of people in place to handle search marketing, they should then liaise with your other marketing people to ensure that they know exactly what activity is taking place so they can change the paid search strategy accordingly.

This is important as people's searches are often impacted by other marketing channels. For example, if someone sees a TV, press or billboard ad for a detergent, they may not remember anything more than the name or the tagline of the ad. One of the first places they will look for more information is through a search engine. If your paid search team knows that ads are out carrying these taglines, they can spend more on those search terms and catch customers who have seen the ads when they search.

If you are going for an agency, however, the most important things to be looking for are:

- ✓ **Dedication to your account:** Make sure that your business will be high on the priority list of the agency.

- ✓ **Client list and case studies:** Check out what the agency has done in the past and how it is regarded.

- ✓ **Memberships of associations:** This will ensure that the agency has a good working relationship with the key search players.

- ✓ **Press cuttings:** Look at the cuttings the agency has on its site and also check out its profile online. Try a few searches on the Google News site and see what comes up.

Once you have checked out the basics, you can move on with your shortlist and chat to your chosen agencies about what they can offer you and how they will work with you to get the most out of your paid search.

Integrating Paid Search with other Channels

Once your paid search campaign is up and running and you have got to grips with optimisation, you can go to the next level by integrating your paid search campaigns with other marketing channels.

Here is an example: You sell cars and a consumer is interested in buying a car. They have done some research online; possibly they have even seen an ad of yours in the paid or natural listings. Then they are sitting in a cinema waiting for a movie to start and they see your ad for your latest model. They like the look of it, but can't do anything about it as they are sitting in the dark at that moment. So they watch the film. Later when they are driving home, they hear a radio ad for the car, but don't catch much of it, just the tagline 'the faster the better'. When they get home, they want to find out more information about the car, but can't remember the name of it; all they have got stuck in their head is 'the faster the better' in an irritating jingle.

So they go online, type in 'the faster the better' into a search engine and if you have integrated your paid search into the rest of your marketing, hey presto! Your bidding on that keyword means your ad comes out top of the paid listings. The consumer can now get the information they wanted and possibly even buy the car or arrange a test drive. Without integrating the paid search into the rest of your marketing, you would have lost that potential lead – the consumer would have had nowhere to go for the information or could have ended up at a more Web-savvy competitor's site.

That is just a simple example of how easy it is to integrate paid search into your wider marketing mix. In order to make this work, you must ensure that your paid search team or agency is fully up to date with your marketing department so everything can work together rather than sending consumers to rivals' businesses.

This shows that in order for a paid search marketing strategy to be successful, it has to be integrated into the wider marketing mix. If it isn't, then you will never realise its full potential.

Social Network Marketing

The Internet isn't just a business tool. You're probably already using it to boost your own life by searching for things that interest you or staying in touch with friends and family.

If this is the case then you can't have failed to have noticed the rise of social networks online and we would make a bet that you are a member of at least one social network, be it Facebook, LinkedIn or any of the other hundreds of networks online. Known collectively as 'social media', these communication and interactive tools and services are not only great fun but also powerful marketing tools. This area, also often referred to as 'Web 2.0' is one of the most exciting and important areas of the Internet for a modern web marketer to get to grips with and in the following pages we try to help you do just that.

Understanding 'Web 2.0'

The term *Web 2.0* is often banded around by Internet marketing professionals but what does it actually mean? Well, in simple terms, this term refers to the evolution of the Internet and what people do on it.

Web 2.0 has three key factors that you need to understand. They explain how people are now using the Internet – community, communication and content:

- ✔ **Community.** Refers to using the web to manage your friendships and social and professional networks, and expressing your likes and dislikes via websites. Millions of people do this on Facebook and other social networks around the world every day.

- ✔ **Communication.** People have been using the Internet to communicate since the very early days of the web – in chatrooms for example – but now, thanks to the widespread use of broadband, it's enabling more advanced participation. For example, people can make calls over the Internet on services like Skype. Or they can share video and photos through photo service Flickr and networking websites like Facebook. The increased communication between friends, people with similar interests: family members, lovers, business colleagues and so on is leading to a world where everyone likes to feel constantly connected to their friends and those things that matter to them.

- ✔ **Content.** This term covers pretty much everything that's fun, interesting or informative online. A TV show, photo or song is a piece of content. While content isn't new to the web, more services than ever are now allowing users to create and share their own content online. YouTube has sought to harness user-generated content (UGC) by asking people to send in videos of themselves doing some funny (and some not-so-funny) things, which people then invite others to view in their thousands – and sometimes millions! People also regularly share their favourite TV or film clips with friends – often whether it breaks copyright laws or not.

This chapter explains how, as a business, you can get involved in this new Web 2.0 world and gives you a few pointers to get your feet on the bottom rung of the social ladder.

Introducing Social Networks: Facebook and LinkedIn

A 'social network' is just a fancy name for a very simple idea. They're websites that combine lots of services that allow people to stay in touch with each other, swap messages and photos, play games and lots more.

One social network dominates in the UK: Facebook. Numerous specific social networks exist out there, too. If you're operating in the automotive industry, for example, you may want to visit CarSpace. But the biggest player in the professional or business-to-business social networking world is LinkedIn; here, you can meet other people in your sector, make referrals, search for employees and generally do business.

Marketing with Pull not Push Strategies

Social media marketing represents a difference from advertising as people usually perceive it. A lot of the usual forms of advertising on other media, such as radio, TV and outdoors, can be summed up as 'push' advertising. The marketer pushes (or shouts) out the message to people and they passively accept (or ignore) the communication.

This method doesn't work very well online. The social space is about building conversations with people, and allowing your message to be 'pulled' by the consumer and becoming a useful part of their online experience.

You can best approach or understand any sort of social marketing by first considering how your message would work in a traditional social setting. Imagine you're at a dinner party at a friend's house. He's in the building business and you meet one of his business partners for the first time. What would you think of his partner if, before even shaking your hand, he said:

'My business is better than any of my competitors. It is better quality, better value and better for the environment. I've won loads of awards and been recognised by the industry I work in as one of its leading practitioners. In fact, you'd be mad to hire anyone else but me.'

We suspect that, like us, you'd try your best to get as far away from him as possible and making a beeline for the opposite end of the table!

Now, what would your impression of this man be if, instead, he said:

'Welcome, can I get you a drink?'

You'd say 'thanks very much' and then proceed to have a nice chat with him and probably ask him what he does for a living.

These two approaches sum up the difference between most offline advertising and online social media advertising. Facebook is used by consumers as part of their daily lives; people aren't there to be sold to in a 'shouty' way. Companies need to pull off the trick of making themselves useful to people in a social context and, if possible, starting a mutually interesting conversation.

Setting Up Your Own Brand or Professional Profile

To take your first steps into social advertising, you can create your own social network profile page for your company. But don't expect people to flock to this page as soon as you publish it; if only the process was that simple! A profile page for your business is the bottom rung of the social ladder, but it does establish your organisation in the social world online and gives you a spot to send people looking for information on your business and a place where you can interact with customers.

Each of the social networks has their own systems for signing up, as described in the following sections.

Signing up to Facebook

Before you begin your social journey, creating your own personal page and using the service for a while is sensible, so you get the hang of how people use Facebook and discover what they find important. Always read the terms and conditions of social networking sites so you know what you are and aren't allowed to do. Surf the site and find out what you like and what you don't – doing so will help you to decide what should go on your own profile page.

1. **Click the 'Advertising' tag at the bottom of your profile page**. This will take you to the commercial area of Facebook. Ignore the majority of this page to begin with. For now, click the 'Pages' tab at the top of the screen. You will now be on the start page for creating your new business profile page.

2. **Choose the 'Create Facebook Page' button:** You can then choose to define what you do by choosing either local business; Brand or Product; or Artist, Band or Public Figure. Choose the type that is relevant to you and make a further choice from the drop-down menu to refine this choice. In the last box, add the name of your product or business that you are creating the page for.

3. **Create your page:** Click, 'create page'. You're now looking at the template of your business profile page. From here, you can start to create the look and feel of your business profile.

4. **Add content:** You can choose to add photos, logos, videos, reviews, business information, event information and pretty much anything else that you think best represents your organisation. At this point your initial surfing will come in handy. Did you like pages that had lots of videos to watch? Is the product you sell best explained by a video – does it need lots of explaining in text otherwise? Depending on your company or product, each business profile will be slightly different. Simply follow the easy to use guides to add different aspects of the page. Simply follow the easy to use guides to add different aspects of the page.

Signing up to LinkedIn

LinkedIn is different from Facebook and MySpace as it focuses purely on the professional sector. LinkedIn isn't the site to advertise on if you want to sell products – unless you're selling Ferraris and Rolex watches and want to target very wealthy individuals. Instead, join LinkedIn so that you can connect with professionals in your own industry, look for jobs and network with other business people that can be helpful to you in the future. Signing up for LinkedIn is just as easy as signing up for other social networks.

1. **Go to `www.linkedin.com` and read the 'user agreement' at the bottom of the page.** This tells you what you can and can't do on the site. Once you're happy, you can return to the home page.

2. **Fill in your information in the boxes provided.** First Name, Last Name and Email. Next, click 'continue'. You're now on a fuller registration page that prompts you to add your personal information.

3. **Fill in your personal information:** As this is a professional network, it doesn't askfor your favourite football team or what type of food you enjoy most. It asks what company you work for, what position you hold and what industry you work in. Once you've filled in this information, click 'join LinkedIn' at the bottom of the page.

4. **Tell the site what sort of user you want to be.** You're now on a page that asks you to tell the social network a little about how you want to use the site. This page is split into two sections. The first, 'To Find', section will be used by the social network to determine what kind of user you are and why you're using its service (in order to show relevant advertising to you). Options include: finding a job, searching for consulting or contracting positions, hiring employees or contractors, and so on. Simply tick the box next to those statements that best fit your desires.

   The second, 'To Be Found', section will be used by the social network to determine what people can contact you about. Options include: messages from friends or colleagues trying to reconnect with you, requests to provide a reference for a past or present colleague, deal proposals for your company, contract or consulting offers, and so on. Again, simply tick those options that you'd like to receive information about. Once you've chosen your options, click 'save settings' at the bottom of the screen.

You're now a member of the LinkedIn community. On your home page, you can search for and connect with former colleagues and classmates, create a presentation about yourself and your company, join relevant groups and flesh out your profile and work history. The beauty of LinkedIn is that people are eager to connect with you because the site becomes more useful the more you use it, so you don't have to worry about making friends. Used properly, LinkedIn can gradually build into a powerful marketing tool for you and your business.

Since the global recession took hold, at the end of 2008 and start of 2009, the usage of LinkedIn has rocketed. This has been driven by users needing to leverage their contacts much harder in order to continually generate business, keep their jobs, ensure that more orders for products and services are in the pipeline and generally stay active in what is a very tricky market. So now it's even more important for you to know about LinkedIn and understand what it does – even if you're not ready to use it yet.

Attracting Visitors to Your Page

The whole point of being active in the social space for an organisation is for you to continue a conversation with your existing and potential customers in an environment that's comfortable for them. 'Push' advertising by getting in people's faces is totally inappropriate on networking sites, but you can do some things that will grab attention - as long as you're offering people something in return for their time.

First, remember to tell people about your social networking efforts. You wouldn't set up a website and then not tell anyone the web address, would you? Nor would you create a new product and put it on the shelves without letting anyone know what it does. The same needs to apply to your social media efforts. You can't expect consumers to be instantly excited by the fact that you've created a social network page for your business without telling them that it exists.

When you're creating your social network profile, put something up there that's worth visiting and won't just disappoint people. If they visit your page on a website that is primarily about them having a good time with friends and family, you need to make it worth their while.

If you don't sell products online, satisfying visitors can be tricky, which is why many brands have started to create their own content and applications. But for examples of what you can do on Facebook, check out these pages via the website's search function:

- ✔ **'Coca-Cola Store':** A shop in Fort Worth, Texas, that sells all things Coca-Cola related. The Facebook page contains product information but also an interesting and amusing video showing how plastic bottles are being recycled by Coca-Cola to create new items.

- ✔ **'Royal Opera House':** Not necessarily the first organisation that you'd expect to see on Facebook, but the ROH is posting behind-the-scenes footage, photos and trailers of upcoming performances on its Facebook page. The ROH has also held specific nights for fans of its Facebook Page.

- ✔ **'Social Media for Small Business – Powered by Dell':** Dell sells computers, but it has created a series of tutorials for small businesses to help them get the most out of social media – one of these is titled 'Harness the power of Facebook' and is well worth a read.

Advertising Your Presence

Once you've created something useful for your potential customers to visit, you need to alert people to the fact that you're in their social world.

Social networks operate by keeping friends up-to-date with each other's lives. So if someone likes your Facebook Page and becomes a 'fan' of it, this fact will show up on their home page in the 'news feed' that catalogues what everyone they know is up to. Their fan status will also be highlighted to their network of friends, who, upon seeing this situation, may want to check out what all the fuss is about. If you have something interesting on your page, the effect can snowball and you could potentially quickly find yourself with literally millions of fans. (Although most brands will probably have a few hundred to a thousand 'fans' rather than unmanageable millions.)

The simplest way to start attracting fans is to highlight your Facebook Page's existence on your existing marketing material; doing so will drive users to your Facebook efforts and start the ball rolling in terms of virally distributing your efforts through the social network. You can speed up this process by using Facebook's proprietary advertising system Facebook Ads.

Signing up to Facebook Ads, through the 'advertising' tab at the bottom of your homepage, allows your ads to be displayed to social network users who might have an interest in your product or service. The social stories, such as a friend becoming a fan of your Facebook page, make your ad both more interesting and more relevant. Facebook Ads are placed in highly visible parts of the site without interrupting the user's experience on Facebook.

Follow these steps to utilise Facebook Ads:

1. **Click on the 'Advertising' button on the bottom of the homepage on www.facebook.com. You'll be taken to the advertising homepage.**

2. **Click on the 'Create an Ad' tab in the middle of the top of the page under the banner 'Facebook Ads'.** Next, you will get the chance to design your ad by creating a headline, body copy and also add ay photos you want to use on the advert. You will also be asked to add a URL that you want to drive your respondents to. It is very important that you think carefully about what you want to achieve with your Facebook advert before you enter this URL. (we assume that'll be to your organisation's website homepage).

3. **Review Facebook's 'list of suggested best practices' and 'list of common reasons for rejection'.** This helps you to avoid having to redo the ad if you break any rules.

4. **Create your ad.** Facebook Ads are very simple and text based, so as not to be intrusive on the social network user's experience. In the boxes provided, insert the headline of your ad, and the body copy of the ad

itself. As you do so, a sample of the ad will appear to the right, so you can see how it will look.

You can now add a photo to your ad, if you so wish. If you do want to add a photo, select this option from the drop-down menu and browse on your computer for your chosen image. When you're ready, click 'continue'.

5. **Now choose whom to direct your advertising at.** If you only sell products and services inside the UK, choose the UK option. However, if you want to use Facebook to stretch your wings, you can choose any of the countries that are offered – but remember to use the appropriate language in your ad!

   You can also choose to target your ad at a specific gender or age group. The final box allows you to target the ad against certain keywords, so that it will be shown to people to whom it is relevant. For example, if you're advertising football boots, relevant keywords are probably 'football', 'goal', 'sports' and 'Premiership'.

   As you choose your targeting options, keep an eye on the last section of the page. Every time you refine an option by gender, age or keyword, it changes the number of people that your ad could reach. You need to make your ad as targeted as possible but not so specific that only three people in the whole of the UK can see it – you won't bring in much business that way!

   When you're happy with your ad's look and targeting, click the 'continue' button.

6. **Decide how much you're willing to pay for your advertising.** You have two options: you can choose to pay for each click (CPC) – each time a user clicks on your ad to go to your site; or for the cost of 1000 (CPM) – meaning for each thousand times your ad is shown to a user, whether they click on it or not.

   You set either the maximum amount per click that you're willing to pay or the maximum amount per 1000 impressions. You also set a daily limit on how much you're willing to spend per day, an amount that will never be exceeded. This limit is helpful, as it stops things getting out of hand if you're too successful.

The automated service will offer you a suggested bid range that corresponds to what other advertisers in your sector are currently paying, to give you a ballpark figure.

We cannot advise you which is the better option for your organisation. Your decision depends on your business objectives but by playing around with the service you should soon find which option works best for you. When you've set your CPC or CPM amount and daily spend cap, you can also decide when you want your ad to run – either straight away and continually running until you stop it or between set dates. Again, this choice depends on your personal objectives.

When you've set your run times, click 'continue'. You end up on the last page and get the opportunity to review your ad to make sure you're happy with it. Your ad strategy – targeting, payment model (cost-per-click or cost-per-thousand) and timing (continuous or between set dates) – is also laid out for review.

7. **Complete the ad ordering process.** Read the terms and conditions, fill in the payment information – credit card only – and press the 'place order' button. Congratulations – you're now running social advertising across Facebook.

Unleashing the Power of Applications in Online Advertising

Possibly, you're already a member of a social network and a good chance exists that you're already using applications. Have you added a 'Super Wall' to your profile? A 'Gift' service? Have you indulged in any Zombie or Vampire making or Poking yet? If you have, you're one of the 23 per cent of social network users globally who've downloaded an application.

While social media is a fairly new phenomenon (Facebook was only founded in 2004), the last 12–18 months have seen a massive growth in the use of applications inside social networks. But just what are these applications?

Essentially, applications are the little tools, services and games that are created by third parties that can be downloaded and sit on your Facebook profile. In Facebook, you can access them through the 'Applications' tab on your homepage.

However, applications can also be added to blogs, homepages, desktops or any other place on the web where people control the content. Applications are also called widgets or gadgets, depending on where they're found online or on mobile phones such as the iPhone or the G1 Google Phone. Don't let this language confuse you. Generally, these applications all do pretty much the same thing – they provide the consumer with a specific service or content inside another platform or Web page. (Technically, a slight difference exists between them, but we'll leave that to the techies to worry about. For our purposes, we refer to these applications as one group.)

iLike is an example of a successful application. This service lets users of Facebook choose music and videos that they like from the Apple iTunes library and add a special 'box' to their profile page to show off the choices. For example, if someone likes Bob Marley, they could choose a clip from his hit song 'Exodus' and display it in the box to illustrate their musical taste. The secret of iLike's success is that, not only can you choose songs or videos to display for yourself, you can also dedicate tracks and videos to others with accompanying messages. If you dedicate a track to someone without iLike, they may well download the application so they can show off their dedication to their friends. This results in more people seeing the iLike box on profile pages and signing up to it themselves. iLike's use continually drives its uptake.

But how do people developing applications know what to create? You may have a great idea for an application that would appeal to your target audience (an interactive race calendar if you're a betting shop owner, for example), but how do you know if enough of your target audience would use it? Well, Facebook's two-way dialogue works in your favour here. Facebook's become such a popular place to host applications because it's able to give developers access to information about its users. As a result, developers can create engaging applications that are more useful to people at relatively low cost.

Applications can achieve two distinctly different things depending on how you use them. First, if you create your own applications, you'll be able to create content or services that mean consumers spend time with your brand. Doing so will generate a positive feeling about your company with the users of the application, which will help you to market to them and hopefully sell them products or services.

Second, you can use other people's applications to advertise your services or products. Application/widget advertising networks have sprung up everywhere in the last couple of years. It is a young but growing market. Application advertising networks are regarded as great places to advertise because research show that Internet users spend a lot of time using these applications and are very engaged when they do so. This situation means they'll hopefully spend longer looking at one of your ads.

You can, of course, create an application yourself and then allow others to advertise through your efforts, generating yourself some additional revenue. However, think about whether you want to have other brands occupying a space in which you're trying to develop a deeper relationship with your customers. Most applications are developed either by a brand and take no advertising or are created by a third party with the express purpose of attracting advertising. Decide which approach suits you best.

If you're interested in finding out more about advertising inside applications, take a look at these companies' websites: www.adknowledge.com, www.clearspring.com and www.slide.com/advertise for some useful advice.

Creating Your Own Applications

If you decide that the best route for you is to create your own application to spend a little more time with your customers, you'll probably need to hire an agency to help you create it. You can have a go yourself if you're very technically savvy, but at the end of the day, the application space is competitive and creating an engaging application is harder than you think. Getting expert help is probably best.

All social networks that use applications have released tools to help people create services that use the best parts of their social network platforms. However, these *software development toolkits* (*SDKs*) don't really help you if you have no experience in writing code for the Internet. If you have no in-house capability to write code, you need to employ an agency to do it for you.

We can't recommend an agency to you – hundreds, if not thousands, operate in the UK, ranging from one-person outfits to big international players, and singling any one out would be unfair. We can, however, help you to get the selection process underway.

Step 1

First, you need to decide on a brief. Essentially, what is it that you want to achieve? Do you want to give your customers something fun to play with – a game; or a useful tool – a tracking application for deliveries; or simply a window into your inventory so they can buy products through the application?

Step 2

When you've decided roughly what you want to offer, create an RFP – a Request for Pitch – document. An *RFP* is an outline (no more than two sides of A4) of what you want to achieve that you can send out to a number of selected agencies. Agencies will use the RFP to come up with ideas to meet your needs. The RFP needs to outline who you are, what your business is, whom your target audience is and what you want to achieve. It might also be useful at this stage to indicate the size of your project, so nobody's time is wasted if it is too big or too small for a particular agency to handle.

Step 3

Start choosing and contacting a few agencies. We recommend contacting somewhere between five and ten to begin with. You can select your agencies to contact in a number of ways:

✔ Ask your industry contacts to recommend some agencies – this is particularly easy to do through LinkedIn.

✔ Go through the list of member agencies at organisations such as the Internet Advertising Bureau (IAB), the UK's interactive advertising trade body (www.iabuk.net).

✔ Look for agencies via your local business organisations and in local directories.

✔ Discover which companies made your favourite applications.

✔ Use a search engine to look for digital agencies in your area.

Step 4

Now undertake the selection process. When you've contacted agencies and those that are interested have indicated a desire to talk further, you should be able to decide on the five that you'd like to invite to a beauty parade. Choose five agencies to come to your office and present their ideas to you.

Don't invite more than five agencies as making them put in a lot of effort if they have to compete against ten others for the business is unfair. If less competition is encountered, they may put more effort into meeting your brief requirements too as they'll feel they have more of a chance to win the business. After you've met all five (we recommend you avoid letting them meet each other in the process, to keep things above board), then select the two you like best for whatever reason (price/chemistry/locality) and invite them back for a second round to iron out any last issues that you have. At the end of this process, you should be able to make a decision on the right agency for you.

Maintaining Your Conversations and Adding Value

Chances are that some kind of community already exists inside a social network or using social media elsewhere online that you can tap into. They could be talking directly about your products and services or be interested in content that is related to what you do.

By entering the social space and offering these people something, you've made the first step in becoming part of that community and added a bit of value to their discussion.

The worst thing you can do, but something that we see happen all too often, is to start a conversation with customers only to stop it when the 'campaign' comes to an end. Customers are still customers after a campaign has ended and you've sold them something. So why would you stop offering them value and listening to them? If you act in this way, you're not reaping the full benefits of the marketing you've done so far and you're not setting yourself up to be someone who they'll talk to in the future.

To be a successful social media advertiser, you need to continually add value to people's experiences and this means throwing away your 'campaign' short-term marketing mentality and entering into social media with a long-term commitment to helping your customers.

You can maintain the conversation with your customers in several ways and none of them need to be prohibitively expensive:

- ✔ If you have existing assets such as articles, photos, or anything else that's generated in the course of your business, allow your customers to access and use it in a useful way. Anything that is not sensitive to your business can be useful to the consumer. Your openness will make you look like a more trustworthy and interesting company. (For example, if your company's a building firm and you take photos and videos of your new developments as they're created – for health and safety purposes – why not let the online audiences play with them? Providing them online costs you very little as you're taking these photos anyway, and you'll create some interest around your company.)

- ✔ Once you've created an environment in which people can interact with your company – either by posting comments online or any other method – continue to respond to them. Nothing is more frustrating for a customer than finding nobody at the end of an email or blog post.

✔ If you start a blog or social network profile page, keep it up. An out-of-date profile page that only has one or two postings is shoddy. It looks exactly what it is – a half-hearted effort – and people will form that impression of your company

✔ If you decide to reinvent yourself in some way, remove any earlier social media efforts so that people don't find them and start interacting with your company in the wrong place. This advice sounds obvious, but leaving incorrect or misleading information online can cause real business problems

Another way to continue your conversations is to employ online PR (public relations) to create a buzz around events at your company such as product launches or anniversaries. Find out more about PR later in this book.

Chapter 7

Direct Marketing and Telemarketing

· ·

In This Chapter

▶ Boosting response rates and sales with direct marketing

▶ Using telemarketing

▶ Understanding direct marketing and the law

· ·

Direct marketing is easy to do, but difficult to do well. You have to master direct marketing to the degree that you can beat the odds and obtain higher-than-average response rates. We share multiple ways to achieve this goal in this chapter as we help you review the varied problems and practices of direct marketing. This chapter focuses on conventional media – print ads, conventional mail and the telephone.

Beating the Odds with Your Direct Marketing

Direct marketing, relationship marketing, one-to-one marketing: they're all the same thing at heart, so we don't care what term you use. To us, direct marketing occurs whenever you, the marketer, take it upon yourself to create and manage customer transactions through one or more media.

The odds of success in direct marketing aren't particularly good. The average direct appeal to consumers or businesses goes unanswered. Yet if you can up the response rate even a little bit over the average, you can make some serious money by direct marketing.

Developing benchmarks for your campaign

Because your goal is to stimulate consumers to respond to you, your direct marketing has a fairly difficult task to accomplish. You need to understand that most of the interactions between your ad and your prospects fail to stimulate the response you want. Failure is the most common outcome of direct marketing! So your real goal is to minimise failure. Look at the statistics if you don't believe us:

- ✔ A direct-mail letter, individually addressed, typically gets a response from 6.7 per cent of the names you mailed to. So you can expect, at most, 67 responses per thousand from an average letter.

- ✔ The average response from a direct-mail campaign to consumers (as opposed to a *business-to-business* (B2B) campaign) is 7.1 per cent. For business campaigns you can expect a 6.2 per cent response rate.

- ✔ A *door drop*, where your message is delivered to home addresses but is not individually addressed, has an even lower hit rate – typically 5.0 per cent.

- ✔ Of all direct mail, 40 per cent goes into customers' bins unopened. Of the 60 per cent that does get opened, a further 20 per cent doesn't get read.

- ✔ A telemarketing call centre making *outbound* calls to a qualified list can typically achieve responses from up to 5 per cent of the households called for a consumer product, but can get as high as 10 per cent for some B2B sales efforts. However, telemarketing generates far more failures than successes and its cost per thousand is often higher than direct mail because it's more labour intensive.

In short, direct marketing doesn't generate very high response rates, and you have to make realistic projections before deciding to embark on any activity. However, before you despair, know that good direct-marketing campaigns beat these odds and can be highly profitable – campaigns with more than 50 per cent response rates aren't unknown. So don't be discouraged; just be dedicated to doing direct marketing better than average.

Boosting sales from your offers

Here are a few starting tips to help you get focused on the goal of generating high responses to your direct marketing:

- ✔ Send out a letter, special announcement or brochure by first-class post once in a while to find out how well your customer list responds. The Royal Mail will return undeliverable items of mail so you can remove or update addresses.

- ✔ Regularly update your mailing list. Not only will doing so keep your postage costs down, it is also your legal responsibility since the introduction of the Data Protection Act (see the 'Keeping It Legal (and Decent)' section later in this chapter). The Royal Mail's Postcode Address File, or PAF, is the most accurate and up-to-date address database in the UK. It lists more than 28 million addresses. You can license it direct for prices starting at £85 or go through one of the many licensed resellers and *list brokers.*

- ✔ Run a very small display ad because they're the least expensive. Limit yourself to 15 words or less. Describe in a simple headline and one or two brief phrases what you have to sell and then ask people to contact you by post or phone for more information. (Include a simple black-and-white photo of the product to eliminate the need for wordy description.)

- ✔ Replace your existing advertising copy (your words) with *testimonials* (quotes praising your product or firm) from happy customers or with quotes from news coverage of your firm or product. These comments attract more buyers because they seem more believable than positive things you say about yourself.

- ✔ Give away a simple, useful or fun gift in exchange for placing an order. People love to receive gifts!

- ✔ Swap customer lists with another business to boost your list size for free. Before you do so, make sure you're trading contact addresses for people who've given their consent to be contacted. See the 'Data Protection Act' section later in this chapter.

And remember that behind every effective direct-marketing campaign stands a well-managed database of customer and prospect names.

Delivering Direct Mail

Direct mail is the classic form of direct marketing – in fact, the whole field used to be called direct mail until the experts changed the term. *Direct mail* is the use of personalised sales letters, and it has a long tradition of its own. Direct mail is really no more nor less than a form of print advertising. So before you design, or hire someone to design, a direct-mail piece, think about it in the context of being an ad.

Actually, a direct-mail piece isn't like a print ad – it resembles two print ads:

✔ **The first ad is the one the target sees when the mail arrives.** An envelope, usually. And that ad has to accomplish a difficult action goal: getting the viewer to open the envelope rather than recycling it. Most direct mail ends up in the recycling pile or the bin, without ever getting opened or read! Keep this fact in mind. Devote extra care to making your envelope:

   • Stand out – it needs to be noticeable and different.

   • Give readers a reason to open it (sell the benefits or engage their curiosity or, even better, promise a reward!).

   Or send a colour brochure with a stunning front and back cover readers can't resist. Make sure the recipient can see the brochure's exterior by using a clear plastic wrap – don't hide it under a dull envelope.

✔ **The second ad goes to work only if the first succeeds.** The second ad is what's inside, and it needs to get the reader to respond with a purchase or enquiry. In that respect, this ad is much the same as any other direct-response ad. The same rules of persuasive communication apply – plus a few unique ones that we discuss in the following section.

Getting your letter mailed

How to send your letter is the first question to resolve. As direct mail is such a big revenue earner for Royal Mail, it offers many different mailing systems and services for businesses of all sizes (such as mailmedia, where you can pay an upfront discounted price for outgoing mail and a certain level of postage-free response).

One little detail often puzzles first-time direct mailers – how to actually get your mailing printed, folded, stuffed and mailed. If you don't know, you should probably hire someone who does. Your local telephone directory and Google list some companies that do this kind of work under 'mailing' or 'marketing' and commercial printers often do this type of work as well. Printers can often handle anything from a small envelope to a major full-colour catalogue. Talk to various printers to get an idea of the range of services and prices.

Purchasing mailing lists

When you don't have a database of your own, or you want to expand the one you do have quickly, you can use purchased lists to prospect for leads. Don't expect the purchased lists to work very well – response rates can be low, and you may get high returns or undeliverables. But that situation's okay because you're using these purchased lists just to build up your own higher-quality in-house list of purchasers. So, plan to send out relatively inexpensive mailings with easy-to-say-yes-to offers and then focus on the replies. If you get any calls, e-mails or postcards from these purchased lists, qualify them as leads or customers, and move them to your own list.

We recommend buying one-time rights to mailing lists, with phone numbers (plus e-mail addresses, if they're offered) to make replying to a response easier for you. One-time use means that you don't own the list, just rent it. But you do own the replies. As soon as someone contacts you from that mailing and you begin to interact with and gather information about them, you can add that person to your own list.

You can buy lists from list owners (those who first developed the list and rent it out), list managers (who manage it on an owner's behalf), list compilers (whose business it is to create bespoke lists from a wide range of sources) or list brokers (who can point you in the direction of the right list for your purposes and advise you how best to use them). You can find hundreds of list brokers through the List & Insert Manager on the Direct Marketing Association (DMA) website, at www. dma.org.uk.

Tuning in to Telemarketing

In the UK, a company with an 0800 freefone number will generate around three times as many calls as a business without one. With a free, or at least very cheap, phone number you're inviting customers to call you rather than giving them a reason not to. Telemarketing has gained a poor reputation in recent years, as many people think it just means unsolicited sales calls by companies they don't want to hear from. Those people don't think of the calls they make to companies as telemarketing, but it is. In fact, *inbound telemarketing* – where the customer is invited to call the business – can be one of the most effective sales channels, as you're not wasting resources on people who don't want to do business with you and are simply making yourself available to those who do.

Inbound telemarketing

Although telemarketing requires nothing but a telephone, combining it with free, or at least low-cost, inbound calling usually makes it most effective. You can offer free calling to your customers and prospects with all 0800 or 0808 numbers. You, the marketer, get to pick up the cost of the customer's telephone call so that you can remove a possible objection to calling. By using an 0800/0808 number, you can provide customers and prospects with a single, memorable and free (93 per cent of customers know about 0800 numbers) route to contact you. These numbers also mean you can direct all calls to a centralised call centre, which is why many marketers prefer *freefone* to other types of numbers.

Other types of phone numbers exist that keep down the cost of calling for customers and also allow you to route all calls through a single call centre. The following freefone or low-cost numbers are useful in *inbound telemarketing*, in which customers call you in response to direct-response advertising:

- ✔ **0800/0808:** Freefone is a zero-cost way to encourage customers to call. At its most basic, freefone can route all calls to a specific telephone line or can be linked to a call management monitoring programme to improve the way your business handles calls.

- ✔ **0845:** Lo-call allows customers to contact you from anywhere in the country, but they pay only the cost of the local call while you pick up the difference in price. The advantage is a single number for customers to remember and a single call-routing system for you.

- ✔ **0870:** NationalCall means customers pay a single national-rate call from anywhere in the country. While your customers pay a 'fair' price for the call, this type of number can actually be a revenue-earner. The advantage of a single, memorable number for your business still applies.

- ✔ **09xx:** ValueCall is a premium-rate phone number, charged at various rates to your customers, depending on the service being offered. While it is a single business number, customers associate 09xx numbers with higher-cost calls, so they're best used for competitions or advice lines.

Outbound telemarketing

Outbound telemarketing involves salespeople making calls to get prospects on the phone – and then pitching to them to make a sale. You can do a little bit of outbound telemarketing informally as part of a broader routine of contacting customers and following up on leads, or you may have a full-blown outbound telemarketing campaign set up in a call centre that you either run yourself or contract with (the bureaus are the same as for inbound telemarketing).

One way or the other, though, every marketer makes some calls to customers and prospects and must be prepared for the reality that outbound telemarketing yields plenty of rejections. In fact, we don't generally recommend outbound telemarketing for *cold call* lists, or lists of strangers who've never done business with you before. You can buy such lists from *list brokers* easily, but expect lower response rates than from lists you build yourself.

You can improve the success rate of outbound telemarketing dramatically by developing a good list before you start calling. Preferably, this list is of people who've had some contact with you before (they've purchased, returned an enquiry card, tried a sample or responded to a print ad or web banner ad). With a good list, you can afford to put competent salespeople on the phones so that your company puts its best face forward. We don't know why most telemarketers haven't worked out that the first contact between their company and a prospective customer shouldn't be in the hands of a temp worker who can't even pronounce the name of the product correctly. To avoid such problems, you need to develop lists and a calling style that give your callers at least a 15 per cent success rate – more than ten times the average for typical unfiltered consumer telemarketing operations.

Keeping it Legal (and Decent)

A host of new laws have recently been introduced to protect consumers and any data about them – and that affects a lot of what marketers do day to day. Whether you're storing or using customer data, mailing, e-mailing or phoning customers (new or old), these laws make a difference to how you should be doing it. And abiding by the law isn't your only concern. Industry codes of practice and preference services (which allow people to opt out of receiving many communications) also need to be borne in mind – they're not legally binding, but we explain later why adhering to them makes good sense.

The following sections cover the basics on new laws and codes that restrict what you can do when trying to contact your customers. We urge you not to treat these restrictions as the enemy – in many cases, making sure you're only using *clean* data and aren't trying to contact consumers who don't want to hear from any businesses (not just yours) makes sense and will actually save you money in the long term.

Observing the Data Protection Act

Before you can do anything with the data you hold, you need to formally notify the Information Commissioner's Office of who you are and what you're planning to do. This notification costs £35 per year. The Information Commissioner (www. informationcommissioner.gov.uk) is the office responsible for administering the DPA, and as well as registering there, you can find more detailed guidance on the Act.

The DPA is based on eight principles (actually they're enforceable but this term makes them sound nicer) of good information handling practice. They state that data must be:

- Fairly and lawfully processed
- Processed for limited purposes
- Adequate, relevant and not excessive
- Accurate and up to date
- Not kept longer than necessary
- Processed in accordance with the individual's rights
- Secure
- Not transferred to other countries without adequate protection for the individual

The good news is that, while the DPA may look like a legal minefield, you can easily navigate it if you're only using the data for advertising and marketing purposes and if you've obtained the consent of the customers you plan to contact.

The 'fair and lawfully processed' principle in the DPA is the one that most relates to you and your direct marketing, because here is where you must be able to prove 'prior informed consent' before contacting customers. 'Prior' means that you've obtained consent before you begin mailing or calling them, and 'informed' means you haven't buried the consent clause somewhere in the small print.

As long as you're clear in your communications, you can give customers the chance to *opt out* of or *opt in* to your information –

worded properly, both count as informed consent. You have to give customers this choice every time you communicate with them. You'll have seen tick boxes, of the opt in or opt out variety, on a lot of the mailings and e-mails you get from companies – and similar, easily understood devices should be on all materials you send out to your customers (for e-mail, you must make sure the tick box actually works or you're in breach of the DPA).

We suggest that you always use opt in boxes when designing new forms or web pages. While opt out boxes have always been popular with marketers because they mean people have to actively choose not to receive ads or promotional material, this approach is a pretty poor idea. Having people signed up who are genuinely interested in receiving your messages is better, so always choose opt in boxes to ensure this happens.

While it's early days for the DPA, you can be sued if you're in breach of it. That means that you need to make sure you've got consent to contact your customers, but also that your suppliers have, too. If you're buying or renting a list, use a reputable source such as the Direct Marketing Association (their site, at www.dma.org.uk, has a searchable List & Insert Manager of list suppliers), or make sure you have legal cover to indemnify you against bought-in data.

Chapter 8

Public Relations, Word of Mouth and Live Marketing

*W*hen people bump into reminders of your company name, brand, product or service, they're more likely to buy. And if those exposures to your identity create a strongly positive impression, they can have a big impact on sales. So far, so simple.

But while advertising does work, most people who are affected by it don't like to admit to it. Plenty of people will deny ever having bought anything as a result of seeing an ad for it. However, we'll bet you've never come across anyone who says the same about a magazine article or something a relative or friend recommends to them.

Independent endorsements for your product or service can be so much more powerful than 'pure' advertising, for the simple reason that consumers are more sceptical about a message that's been paid for and is self-serving.

In this chapter, we discuss the two key ways of gaining independent endorsement for your business: *public relations* (when exposure to or mention of your company, service or product becomes part of the news or an editorial feature) and *word of mouth* (what people say about you to others). Each endorsement can make a positive impression in a low-key, polite manner and can do so – if managed well – for surprisingly low cost.

Using Publicity to Your Advantage

Publicity is coverage of your product or business in the editorial portion of any news medium. Why would journalists cover a product as a story? One reason is that the product is better or worse than expected. If, for example, *Which?* magazine runs an article praising your product as best in a particular category, that's publicity. Good publicity. If, in contrast, the evening television news programmes run a story saying that experts suspect your product caused numerous accidents, that's publicity, too. Bad publicity.

Tackling public relations

Public relations (PR) is the active pursuit of publicity for marketing purposes. You use PR to generate good publicity and try to minimise bad publicity. Generally, marketers have the responsibility of generating good publicity. If marketers create good stories and communicate them to the media effectively (see the following two sections), the media pick them up and turn them into news or entertainment content. Good publicity.

If you need help writing a good press release and placing the story, enlisting professional help is worthwhile – you may not get any coverage without it.

PR consultancies vary in size from international groups employing thousands to single owner-operator PR professionals. You can also find specialists, who have expertise in industry sectors such as IT or healthcare. Around 3000 PR consultancies operate in the UK, so you'll need help narrowing down your search. If you're serious about hiring one, the

Public Relations Consultants Association offers a free online service called PReview (`www.prca.org.uk`), which matches your needs with the member consultancies that most closely match them.

Creating a good story

To a journalist, a *good story* is anything that has enough public interest to attract readers, viewers or listeners and hold their attention. For example, a good story for a journalist covering the plastics industry must hold the attention of people in that industry.

Finding the hook

The *hook* is what it sounds like: the compelling bit of information that snags your reader's interest and draws him or her to the story.

Here's a simple exercise to help you understand how hooks work. Scan today's newspaper (whichever one you like to read) and rank the top five stories based on your interest in them. Now analyse each one in turn to identify the one thing that made that story interesting enough to hold your attention. The hooks, the things that made each story interesting to you, differ. But every story has a hook, and all hooks have certain elements in common:

- ✔ Hooks often give you new information (information you didn't know or weren't sure of).

- ✔ Hooks make that new information relevant to your activities or interests.

- ✔ Hooks catch your attention, often by surprising you with something you hadn't expected.

- ✔ Hooks promise some benefit to you – although the benefit may be indirect – by helping you understand your world better, avoid something undesirable or simply enjoy yourself as you read the paper.

Combining the hook with your marketing message

You need to design hooks to make your marketing message into stories that appeal to journalists. Your hooks need to be just like the ones that attracted your attention to those newspaper stories, with one exception: *you need to somehow tie them to your marketing information.* You have to make sure that at least a thin line exists connecting the hook to your brand identity, the news that you've just introduced a new product or whatever else you want the public to know. That way, when journalists use your hook in their own work, they end up including some of your marketing information in their stories as an almost accidental side effect.

Communicating your story to the media: Press releases

For communicating a news story the most basic format is the press release. Unfortunately, journalists don't like press releases. We know this because we are journalists. We get hundreds of press releases e-mailed and posted to us every day. Most of them are rubbish, which is exactly where they end up. At the head of every magazine, covering every imaginable professional or consumer interest, is the equivalent of us – a stressed-out editor with the next deadline looming. So look on your challenge as getting past us, or at least the equivalent of us.

When we say that journalists don't like press releases, what we mean that we don't like admitting to being influenced by them – a bit like consumers with advertising, really. Now we're not going to attempt to hold back the tide of press releases that flood into our inbox, but we shall give some insider advice about how to get on the right side of journalists by giving them what they need and not troubling them with what they don't.

A list of dos

Here's a list of ways that you can get a positive response from the journalists you contact:

- ✔ **Do offer exclusives.** An exclusive means that the journalist you're dealing with gets the story before it appears anywhere else, the story gets a more prominent position in the newspaper or magazine and the journalist scores points with their editor. Everybody's happy.

- ✔ **Do make it relevant and timely.** Target the right media and contacts. The food critic doesn't need a release about a new robotics manufacturing facility. And the business correspondent doesn't either, if the facility opened two months ago, because now that story's old news.

✔ **Do build up a list of media contacts.** You need to create an accurate database of journalists, with all contact details so you can get in touch with them quickly. E-mailing your release can be sensible because journalists work on tight deadlines, so include fields for e-mail addresses in your database. You can get commercial lists and information on journalists from PR directories and list-sellers. You can find these through any search engine or PR agency.

✔ **Do think creatively.** Journalists need stories; you need some positive PR – so think up a story idea that serves both needs. A common but effective PR tactic is to carry out a piece of consumer research that's relevant to your business and let a newspaper publish the results. For example, a DVD rental company might research a list of people's favourite films.

✔ **Do offer yourself as an expert commentator on industry-related matters, in case they need a quote for another article.** A journalist may just include one sentence from you, but if they mention your company name, you just got some good publicity. For example, an article on how to shop for a used car in the Sunday magazine of a newspaper may quote the owner of a large car dealership as saying, 'If you don't have an independent mechanic evaluate a used car before buying it, I guarantee you'll be in for some unpleasant surprises.' The article may also mention that this dealership's repair department does free evaluations for car buyers. The combination of a quote and a bit of information about the free service is going to attract many new customers, some of whom will become steady users of the dealership's repair service, and some of whom will become buyers of new or used cars from the dealership.

✔ **Do keep it brief.** Journalists are quick on the uptake and work fast, so let them call or e-mail if they need more information.

✔ **Do post your press releases on your website.** Even if you've given your story as an 'exclusive', your press releases can do double duty on the web, providing information for journalists to follow up once the exclusive story becomes public. Remember to provide a phone number too in case reporters want more information on a story.

✔ **Do send releases to every local editor in your area, no matter how small their publication or station.** You can get local coverage more easily than regional or national coverage and that local coverage can be surprisingly helpful.

And a few don'ts

The dos must be balanced by a few helpful don'ts that will help your information stand out from the junk that flies into every journalist's inbox:

✔ **Don't make a nuisance of yourself.** One of the worst pieces of advice that is seemingly given to every aspiring PR practitioner is to make a follow-up call. If your media contacts database is accurate, the journalist will have received your press release: if it's a good story they'll use it; if not, they won't. You can't do anything to change your press release after the event, so make sure that what you send is as carefully crafted as it can be.

✔ **Don't ask for clippings.** Journalists don't want to send you clippings of the articles they write, so don't bother asking. Nor do they care to discuss with you why they didn't run a story, or why they cut off part of a quote when they did run a story. They're busy with the next story. Forget about it. You should focus on the next story too. If you want a clipping, most publications keep an online database of all their published stories.

✔ **Don't make any errors.** Typos throw the facts into question. Don't include any inaccurate facts, either. You want the journalist to have trust in the information you're providing. Prove that you're worthy of that confidence.

✔ **Don't forget that journalists work on a faster clock than you do.** When a journalist calls about your release, return the call (or make sure that somebody else does) in minutes or hours, not days. If you handle media requests slowly, a journalist will just find another source or write another story by the time you've returned the call.

prnewswire.co.uk and businesswire.co.uk

For easy access to a cheap way of distributing releases, check out www. prnewswire.co.uk, where you can click on 'Our Services' and then 'Small Business Toolkit' to access information on prices charged for distributing press releases. At time of writing, the site offers to create and send a release to all the media in the UK, plus consumer and trade publications, thousands of news-orientated websites, and online services and databases for prices from £220. Not bad, but we recommend using this service alongside making key journalistic contacts because you can't beat the personal touch. A similar service is offered at www. businesswire.co.uk.

Being interviewed for TV and radio

So now you've got a hook or a reputation for expertise within your sector, the requests for interviews will come flooding in. Okay, usually the process isn't that simple; you need to be prepared for when a broadcast interview does come your way. A few people are naturally confident and gifted when speaking publicly or on radio or TV – but they're not normal! You will feel nervous the first time you're in an unusual interview situation. Professional media training is available, where you'll be put into mock interviews in front of real cameras and microphones and put through your paces by professional journalists. Or you can prepare yourself by simply following these basic (and much cheaper) tips:

- ✔ **Give no more than three key messages.** If you're tempted to blurt out everything you know about your subject, your main messages will get lost and people won't remember anything. Prepare in advance what you want to say and then say it.

- ✔ **Know your audience.** Find out as much as you can about the interview, the programme and its audience. Is it live or pre-recorded? Light-hearted chat or serious comment? For business experts or housewives?

✔ **Be positive.** State your main messages in positive terms, and provide examples rather than go on the defensive. Whatever you do, don't say 'no comment' – the interviewer and audience will assume you've got something to hide. Watch how politicians manage this scenario when they're being interviewed. They repeat their key message and studiously ignore the question.

✔ **What not to wear.** Avoid patterns when on TV, as sometimes the cameras can't cope and viewers get a disturbing strobe effect. Small checks and herringbone are obviously out, but also avoid bold patterns as they'll detract attention from what you're trying to say. Keep your attire simple and light – dark clothes can drain colour from your face.

✔ **Speak like a normal human being.** After all, normal people are watching or listening, so thinking about what they may or may not know about the subject and tailoring your message to them pays. Imagine you're speaking to someone who's bright, but knows nothing about the topic. Don't patronise, but definitely don't overwhelm them with jargon and abbreviations.

Making the Most of Word of Mouth

Word of mouth (WOM) gives a consumer (or a marketer) the most credible source of information about products, aside from actual personal experience with those products. What consumers tell each other about your products has a huge impact on your efforts to recruit new customers. WOM also has a secondary, but still significant, impact on your efforts to retain old customers.

If you survey customers to identify the source of positive attitudes toward new products, you generally find that answers such as 'my friend told me about it' outnumber answers like 'I saw an ad' by ten to one. WOM communications about your product don't actually outnumber advertising messages; but when customers talk, other customers listen.

How can you control what people say about your product? You can't very effectively encourage customers to say nice things about and prevent them from criticising your product. But you can influence WOM – and you have to try. Making your product special is the most obvious way to influence WOM. A product that surprises people because of its unexpectedly good quality or service is special enough to talk about. A good product or a well-delivered service wins fans and turns your customers into your sales force. Other tactics for managing WOM about your business or product may not be so obvious. Fortunately, we discuss them in the following sections.

Spicing up your sales promotions

A 20p-off coupon isn't worth talking about. But a competition in which the winners get to spend a day with the celebrity of their choice can get consumers excited – and can be cheaper, too. You can generate positive PR and a lot of word of mouth with such a premium.

You can use special offers and competitions to get people to recommend a friend. For example, the mobile phone company T-Mobile has run offers giving subscribers £20 credit if they recommend the service to a friend who then signs up. The friend also gets £20 credit. Everyone wins and even those people who don't want to sign up immediately may remember this 'generosity' when considering a new mobile deal later on. You see, you can influence word of mouth.

Identifying and cultivating decision influencers

In many markets, some people's opinions matter a lot more than others. These people are *decision influencers,* and if you (hypothetically) trace back the flow of opinions in your industry, you may find that many of them originate with these people. In business-to-business (B2B) marketing, the decision influencers are often obvious. A handful of prominent executives, a few editors working for trade magazines and some of the staff at trade associations probably exert a strong influence over everybody else's opinions. You can find identifiable decision influencers in consumer markets, as well. Just think about chat show host Oprah Winfrey, in the US. If she recommends a book on her TV show, the author sees an immediate spike in sales. She's so important to the publishing market that now any titles that Oprah picks for her special 'book club' are often marketed more heavily on that detail than their plot or author. The same has happened in the UK with Richard and Judy''s Book Club and sales of certain products named by celebrity chefs – such as the 10 per cent lift in egg sales after Delia Smith's *How to Cook* TV series was aired in 1998.

To take advantage of decision influencers, develop a list of who falls into that category for your product or service and then make a plan for cultivating them. Match these people with appropriate managers or salespeople who can take them to events or out to lunch, just for fun. You just need to make sure that people associated with your business are in the personal networks of these decision influencers. Consider developing a series of giveaways and mailshots to send to these decision influencers. If we wanted to sell a football boot to youth players, we'd send free samples of a new shoe to youth coaches. When you know who's talking and who's listening, you can easily focus your efforts on influencing the talkers.

Seizing control of the Internet

Okay, you can't actually take over the Internet, but you need to be aware of what people are saying about your product or service online. Weblogs, or blogs as they're commonly known, are one of the latest phenomena of the Internet age. What are blogs? The term *blogs* refers to personal web publishing based on a topic or topics that attract a like-minded community of online participants. In other words, blogging is word of mouth on the web. Blogs exist dedicated to pretty much every subject you can imagine, from cars to politics to chocolate. You need to know about blogs because you can use them to your advantage in two key ways:

   ✔ **Get in on the discussion.** If a website dedicated to your market exists, try to get your product mentioned or even establish a link between your site and the blog (blogs make extensive use of links to other sites). A survey among more than 600 blog publishers found that two-thirds would be happy to consider a direct public relations approach. Microsoft has sent out new laptop models to key bloggers before they become available to the public in order to generate some buzz about them.

✔ **Create your own blog.** Blogs are cheap and easy to set up, which is why they're blossoming on the web. You can use free blog sites such as www.wordpress.com or www.blogger.com and start publishing within the day. You can use your blog to promote your products and services and elicit feedback (bad as well as good) from potential and existing customers. Make sure you can moderate any feedback before it goes live to avoid libellous information but don't be tempted to ditch any negative comments – people won't use your service to give their views if they think you ignore anything but good news.

Not all blogs or their users are business friendly, and you need to remember this when making approaches or setting up your own blog. Blogs are run by enthusiasts and are usually independent of corporate ties: that's their point, as well as their appeal. While Microsoft attracted a lot of attention for its laptops by sending them to bloggers, it also received criticism as some people considered it too close to paying for publicity.

Controlling what people say about you on blogs is also difficult. You can't and you shouldn't try to. If a comment about your product or service is incorrect, identifying yourself and responding is the best approach. Or just leave it be: you need to accept that not everyone will like what you do but that situation's alright.

Regulations now exist to control corporate blogging. These regulations ensure that consumers aren't fooled into thinking that corporate remarks are those made by ordinary people.

In 2005, people working on behalf of household cleaner Cillit Bang made the mistake of commenting on some blogs in the guise of the brand's fictional spokesperson Barry Scott. This deceit was uncovered by a blogger and the clumsy marketing attempt made online headlines around the world.

Now posting on blogs on behalf of businesses without revealing your identity as representing that organisation is banned. The Consumer Protection from Unfair Trading 2008 regulation aims to stamp out this practice. Read up on this regulation if you plan to comment on other people's blogs or start your own. Visit the Office of Fair Trading's website (www.oft.gov.uk), where you can find the relevant information under 'Advice for Businesses' in the 'Competing Fairly' section.

Harnessing the Power of Face-to-Face Marketing

Face-to-face marketing has to have considerable drawing power. Think of this approach as theatre – a performance that entertains or stimulates people in a satisfying way (and sometimes includes people as participants, not just as an audience). At an exhibition or trade show, you may need to add interactive activities to your stand or invite a team of massage therapists to do their thing at specified hours to attract your target audience. In a store, appealing to your audience can mean bringing in an expert to give a weekend workshop. For a consulting firm, it may mean offering a special one-hour seminar led by your directors, accessible to all clients and prospects over the web.

Face-to-face marketing is a great example of the real-world marketing principle that you should give away as much as you can. Facing stiff competition, you often have to give potential customers an interesting performance to win their attention. Here are more ideas for face-to-face marketing that you may want to promote:

- ✔ A client-appreciation event (what used to be called a party).

- ✔ A musical performance.

- ✔ A weekend at a golf resort for your top customers, along with prizes for the winning golfers – and everyone else, too.

- ✔ A fundraising dinner for an important charity.

- ✔ A community event, such as a fair or children's workshop.

> ✔ An exhibit or hospitality suite at a major trade show for people in your industry.

> ✔ A workshop in which you share your expertise or solve problems for participants.

Endless and varied possibilities exist. But they all attract people and hold their attention. And you need that attention to communicate and persuade as a marketer.

Using Business and Industry Opportunities

Turn first to your professional groups and industry trade associations for appropriate business-to-business (B2B) marketing. These venues differ for each industry but have the benefit of collecting your prospective customers altogether in one place in common. Attend conferences and trade shows if your budget is small and do plenty of informal networking. If you can afford to, also rent display space at trade shows, present at conferences and sponsor industry events. The more visible you are at your own industry events, the more customer attention and credibility you can generate.

Trade shows are great because they draw people who are wearing their business hats, ready to make purchase decisions for their companies. You can also put on special events for your own customers or employees. (In fact, employee events often provide that extra motivating power that you need to get your people fully behind your marketing plan.)

Sponsoring a Special Event

Some people assume that special events are only useful in special circumstances, when you can justify a major effort and expense. Not so. Staging small-scale events or (as we discuss in this section) riding on the coat-tails of somebody else's event can work, too. (You should also think of this strategy as piggybacking on others' investments in events, a helpful term in visualising the benefits.)

After all, why create your own event when so many wonderful events already exist? But if you're becoming involved with someone else's event, make sure you get a clear, detailed agreement in writing about where, how and how often it identifies your brand name. That identification is the return on your sponsorship investment. Too often, sponsors end up complaining that they didn't get as much good exposure as they expected, so make sure you and the event directors understand the exposure level up front.

You can find local organisations by following the events notices in local papers and on regional radio stations. A number of web-based companies now help you locate possible events to sponsor. For example, check out www.sports match.co.uk or www.uksponsorship.com for hundreds of possibilities in everything from sports to the arts. You can find an exciting new event sponsorship out there that fits both your budget and customers.

Evaluating the Options for Sponsorship

If you're considering event sponsorship, you're in good company. The UK sport sponsorship market alone is predicted to reach $15.8 billion in 2012, up from $10.2 billion in 2007, according to PricewaterhouseCoopers. But sports aren't the only option for sponsorship – consider arts initiatives or even TV and radio programmes.

To decide on the best approach for your company, use the three-step selection process discussed in the following sections.

Step 1: Explore the options

You can find sponsorship opportunities all over the place, so take time to explore all the available options – and, as you do with any other aspect of your marketing, employ a little creativity. Websites such as www.sportsmatch.co.uk can put you in touch with teams and events looking for business backing. Or visit Business in the Community's site at www.bitc.org.uk for examples of what other companies are doing with charities in their local areas.

Step 2: Run the numbers

Carefully analyse the marketing impact of each candidate for sponsorship. Cut any from your list if their audiences aren't a good match with your target market. Chop out any that may be controversial and likely to generate negative as well as positive publicity. Ditch any that don't seem to present strong, positive images – sponsoring something that your customers don't feel passionate about is pointless. Now compare the remaining options by calculating your cost per thousand exposures for each one.

Don't be afraid to negotiate. If a sponsorship opportunity appeals to you but is priced too high, show the team there your comparative numbers and ask if they can cut you a deal!

Step 3: Screen for relevance

Relevance is how closely the event relates to your product and its usage by customers, and, oddly, is the most important, but least considered, factor.

Putting on a Public Event

Sometimes, you have no alternative but to stage the event yourself. None of the sponsorship options fit your requirements. Or you really need the exclusivity of your own event – a forum in which no competitors' messages can interfere with your own.

Increasingly companies are staging their own events so they can tailor them to their own products and customers.

Starting your own event may seem like a great idea but if you don't have the expertise to run such experiences within your own business (why would a florist or a car dealer necessarily know how to organise an event?), leaving it to the experts is wiser.

Selling sponsorship rights

Finding other companies that want to help sponsor your event is a good way of making it pay for itself. Not your competitors, of course. Many companies may have an interest in the same event as you do, but for different reasons, and these firms make good co-sponsors. Basically, if the event is relevant, novel and likely to draw in their target audience, then you have a good pitch. Now you just need to go out and make sales calls to potential sponsors. Or consider hiring an event management firm that can sell sponsorships as well as help to organise and run events.

Getting help managing your event

Some people specialise in managing special events; they work on a consulting basis, from conception through completion, to make sure that everyone comes and everything goes just right. Many such specialists exist, from independent experts to major companies. We recommend bringing in a specialist of some sort to help you design and manage any event that involves a lot of people, shows, speeches or activities, meals, conference and hotel room reservations, security and transportation. To avoid disaster you must get these details right.

 You can find event management companies through the Association of Event Organisers (AEO) at www.aeo.org.uk. The AEO has a listing of all suppliers to trade and consumer exhibitions through its sister associations, the Event Supplier and Services Association and the Association of Event Venues.

Exhibiting at Shows and Exhibitions

Do you need to exhibit at trade shows? If you're in a business-to-business (B2B) selling situation, we assume that you do.

You can generate leads, find new customers and maintain or improve your current customers' perceptions of you at trade shows. You can also use them to introduce a new product or launch a new strategy. Trade shows also give you great opportunities to introduce back-office people (like the sales support staff or even the chairperson) to your customers face to face.

Use trade shows to network in your industry. You usually find the best manufacturers' representatives and salespeople by making connections at trade shows. If you're secretly hoping to find a better employer, a little mingling may yield an offer at the next big trade show. Also, be sure to talk with a lot of attendees and non-competitive exhibitors in order to find out about the newest trends and what your competitors are doing in the market. The information a good networker gleans from a trade show is often worth more than the price of attendance. Never mind selling – just get out there and chat.

Doing Demonstrations

Seeing is believing: if you think a demonstration is applicable to your goods or services, you should definitely consider giving one. A demonstration is often the most effective way to introduce a new product, or even to introduce an old product to new customers. This area of marketing falls under what the experts call *field marketing* or, even worse, *experiential marketing*. To you and us, this approach simply means getting your product in front of the people that might buy it, and giving them a reason to do just that.

A proper retail demo should be:

- ✔ **Realistic.** Show the product in a natural use context – and that includes normal portions of foods. (*Natural use* means how the customer would normally use it. If you eat a food product for dinner, find a way to demonstrate it on a table with real place settings, for example.)

- ✔ **Wonderful.** The event should be worthy of attention, with real entertainment value that adds excitement to the product. Try a cooking demonstration with a lot of action, not just a one-bite taste. What about getting a well-known chef to cook it for you? Or make the demonstration a taste test in which the product wins a contest and the tasters get the prizes. Imagine you're creating a skit for a TV show – that's the sort of entertainment people pay attention to.

✔ **A marketing priority.** Here's your chance to sell your product directly to customers. Think of a political candidate going out to shake hands (notice the candidate always wears his or her best suit and biggest smile). Too often, companies put poorly qualified temps in charge of demonstrations. Who do you really want out there selling on your behalf – someone who makes the product look good or someone who doesn't actually know anything about it?

When you follow these three rules, you create great demonstrations.

Part IV

Connecting With Your Customers

'And as they move so slowly, people can actually read the message.'

In this part . . .

1 f you can design a great product, give it an appropriate brand name, package it well and then turn it over to a good salesperson, you may be able to dispense with everything else discussed in this book. The combination of an appealing product or brand, plus good sales and service, can make a business successful, all on its own. And so it seems fitting to devote an entire part to these topics.

We have an interesting story to illustrate this. A consultant was hired to consult with the chief executive of a speciality chemicals company. They wanted him to evaluate the overall business plan and suggest ways of making the business grow. After poking around the premises for a few hours and interviewing a bunch of the people, he discovered a startling thing: the chemicals business apparently did no marketing at all. They had no marketing department, and the company had no brochures, no ads, no publicity, and no Web site. So, how had they gotten this far, and where in the world did their customers come from?

In this part, we explain the secrets of companies like this one. We show you how to maximise the impact of your product and its packaging, tell you how to price your products and services, keep you from underselling yourself by making common mistakes associated with distribution and pricing, and help you approach sales and service like an old pro.

Chapter 9

Branding, Managing and Packaging a Product

· ·

In This Chapter

▶ Designing and developing hot new products

▶ Fitting your products into product lines

▶ Finding the right name

▶ Creating strong identities under trademark law

▶ Packaging to boost sales

▶ Knowing when and how to improve or eliminate a product

· ·

*T*he product is the heart and soul of any marketing plan. If the product is good – if the target customer is really pleased with it – then that marketing plan has a decent chance of success. But if the product is nothing special in the customer's eyes, no marketing plan can make that product a winner in the long run. We call this the 'lipstick on the gorilla' effect.

Many people don't understand this point about quality. Something of real value has to be at the core of any marketing plan; it should be about emphasising a tangible benefit for the consumer, not pretending something without merit is worthwhile.

This chapter shows you how to develop winning products, how to manage them as part of a product line and how to select your products' names to amplify their natural strengths and communicate those strengths to the target customer.

 We use 'product' as an umbrella term that means a product, service or anything else your company wants to sell. A product can be a tin of beans, an insurance policy or a new piece of Internet software. If you're selling it, it's your product.

Finding Simple Ways to Leverage Your Product

Taking small steps to keep a product fresh and vital and to boost its visibility and appeal is one of the first and most important things you can do. Product management is a lot like gardening. You occasionally plant a whole new crop but you tend the existing plants routinely too.

Here's a list of simple and quick things you can do to build customer loyalty and grow sales by working on your product:

✔ **Update the appearance.** Many companies present good products to the world in poorly designed exteriors that don't dress for success. Look at the product itself (colours, attractiveness and visibility of any brand names). MP3 players exist that have more technical features than Apple's iPod but the latter outsells all its competitors because it has a distinct and desirable design.

✔ **Update the packaging.** A consumer product that sits on a shelf waiting for someone to pick it up should be highly visible and appealing (remember, in-store buying decisions are made in seconds or less).

✔ **Make sure the product is attractive and easy to use.** Your product should also feel nice – smooth, polished, soft or whatever texture is appropriate to the product's use. In some instances, the smell and sound of your product matters too. This doesn't just apply to food products; cars are deliberately given that special 'new leather' smell inside to help them sell. Many auto manufacturers also tune car doors to give a distinctive 'clunk'.

✔ **Improve any printed materials that come with the product.** Can you enhance their appearance? Dress them up? Make them clearer or more useful? Make sure they instill pride of ownership in the product.

✔ **Choose your product's best quality.** Coin a short phrase to communicate this best quality to the consumer and put that phrase on the product, its packaging and its literature in prominent places. Make up simple (but attractive) colour-printed stickers for this purpose – these are the quickest and cheapest way to add a marketing message.

✔ **Eliminate confusion about which product does what for whom.** Clarify the differences and uses of your products, if you have more than one, by pricing and naming them distinctly (to make them obviously different). Most product lines look confusing to the average buyer.

 You're only as good as your products, so try to update, upgrade or perhaps even replace your current line of products. Doing so's a long-term but vital activity that most marketing plans need to include, just as gardeners have to remember to plan the next planting session along with their more routine weeding and watering duties.

Identifying When and How to Introduce a New Product

We wish we could say that you don't need to worry about new product development very often. But if your market is like most, innovations give you a major source of competitive advantage. A rival's major new product introduction probably changes the face of your market – and upsets your sales projections and profit margins – at least once every few years. So you can't afford to ignore new product development, ever. You need to introduce new products as often as you can afford to develop them.

One product strategy or multiple strategies?

Do you sell into one market or more? How you answer this question determines whether you need to have one product line and one strategy or multiple lines and strategies. Many businesses sell into multiple markets. PepsiCo sells into the beverage and snack markets. Car manufacturers sell to consumers and to fleet buyers. Small companies use this strategy, too: a local cleaning service may have both homeowners and businesses as customers and the marketing (and specifically the product offering) needs to be different for each.

Coming up with the next great thing

Okay, you think you need a hot new product. But where do you get the idea? There are a host of brainstorming and idea-generating techniques that you can use.

Also consider two cheap but valuable sources of new product ideas: old ideas and other people's ideas.

Rediscovering old products

Old ideas are any product concepts that you or another company have previously abandoned. These concepts may have been considered but rejected without being marketed, or they could even be old products that have fallen out of use but could be revived with a new twist.

Old ideas may be a treasure trove, because technological or marketing developments may have made the original objections less serious than when marketers originally scrapped the idea. Technical advances or changing customer taste may make yesterday's wild ideas practical today. Even if you can't use any of the old ideas you find, they may lead you to fresh ways of thinking about the problem – perhaps they suggest a customer need that you hadn't considered before.

Also note that old products in one market may be new products in another. You may be able to turn your dead products into winners in other countries, if you can partner with local distributors.

Stealing – er, borrowing – ideas

You can often pursue the second source, other people's ideas, through licences. A private inventor may have a great new product concept and a patent for it, but may lack the marketing muscle and capital to introduce the product. You can provide that missing muscle and pay the inventor 5 or 10 per cent of your net revenues as reward for their inspiration.

Many companies generate inventions that fall outside of their marketing and sales focus. They don't want to take their eyes off their core activities. These companies are often willing to license to someone specialising in the target market.

Licensing is the official way to use other people's ideas; however, an unofficial way exists that's probably more common and certainly more important for most marketers. You simply steal ideas. Now, by steal, we don't mean to take anything that isn't yours – we're just being humorous. A *patent* protects a design, a *trademark* protects a name or logo and a *copyright* protects writing, artwork, performances and software. You must respect these legal rights that protect other people's expressions of their ideas. But legally protecting underlying ideas in many countries where you're likely to do business isn't possible.

If an idea makes it to your ears or eyes through a legitimate public channel of communication, you can use it. (Just don't bug your competitors' headquarters, go through their rubbish bins or get their engineers drunk – doing so may violate *trade secrecy laws* – ask your lawyer before planning any questionable research.)

In most markets, competitors (legally) steal ideas as a matter of routine. You can also look at other industries for inspirations that you can apply in your own. The good idea hunter has to be open-minded – you never know where you may find something worth stealing!

Note that you're less likely to violate these legal protections if you just take a public idea and develop it all on your own, but you may still want to have a lawyer (preferably one who specialises in intellectual property law) review what you've done before going public with it.

Picking your customers' brains

A final source of new product ideas is your customers – although often they don't know it. Ask a customer to describe a brilliant new product you should provide for them and you get a blank stare or worse. Yet frustrations with your existing products and all sorts of dissatisfactions, needs and wants lurk in the back of every customer's mind. And you may be able to help them with these gripes.

How do you mine this treasure trove of needs? Collecting the customers' words helps you gain insight into how they think – so talk to them and take notes or record their comments (with their permission). Get customers chatting, and let them wander a bit so that you have a chance to encounter the unexpected. Also watch customers as they buy and use your product. Observation may reveal wasted time and effort, inefficiencies or other problems that the customer takes for granted – issues that the customer may happily say good-bye to if you point them out and remove them.

Branding and Naming Your Product

Once you've got your product, everything you do to it and everything the customer sees, counts as *branding*. What do you call your new product? Should you launch it under a brand identity your business already owns or give it a new one? Should you attempt to add value (and raise the price) by promoting a positive brand identity, or should you save your marketing budget and just get the product out to point of purchase? You have to make all these difficult decisions. Let us show you how to make them well.

Designing a product line

A *product line* is any logical grouping of products offered to customers. (Remember, products can be goods, services, ideas or even people such as political candidates or celebrities.) You usually identify product lines by an umbrella brand name, with individual brand identities falling under that umbrella.

The Apple computer line includes many different products, called different things, from the MacBook to the iMac but they all bear the same brand logo (a trademarked asset of Apple Computer). The company has made each product distinct enough from each other that together they give the customer a wide range of choices but are recognisable as being related to one another. You can think of product lines like this one as families of products.

You need to consider two key issues when designing your product lines:

- ✔ **Depth.** How many alternatives should you give the customer within any single category? For example, should you make a single T-shirt design in a range of sizes? How about offering the design in a variety of colours? All these options increase depth because they give a customer more options. Depth gives you an advantage because it increases the likelihood of a good fit between an interested customer and your product. You don't want to miss a sale because somebody was too big to wear a size large.

- ✔ **Breadth.** This option allows you to generate new sales. For example, if you sell one popular T-shirt design, you can increase breadth by offering more T-shirt designs in your product line. When you add anything that the customer views as a separate choice, not a variant of the same choice, you're adding breadth to the product line.

Maintaining your product line: When to change

'Don't leave well enough alone' is the secret to good product management. But if you keep growing your lines, you can obviously bump into some practical limits after a while. How do you know when the pendulum is going to swing the other way – when you need to do some spring-cleaning?

You If your distribution channels can't display the full product line to customers you need to decrease your depth or breadth (or both). Often, distribution becomes a bottleneck, imposing practical limits on how big a product line you can bring to the customer's attention.

The household and personal products giant Unilever decided to cut back its 1600 brands to 400 as part of a five-year plan. Not all of the 1200 products it wanted to lose were failing; they just didn't fit with what Unilever was best at doing. Of the 400 chosen products left, the company then identified 40 *star brands* on which to focus its main marketing efforts. This focus didn't necessarily mean each line had fewer products within it; some, like Dove and Lynx, have since expanded into new and different areas.

But what Unilever wanted to do was concentrate its resources around fewer, well-thought-out product lines – making things easier for retailers and ultimately consumers. Too many choices frustrate customers and lead to confusion between products. Brand identities start to overlap, and you make customer decisions harder rather than easier.

Naming a product or product line

Naming a new product isn't simple – that's why so many brand agencies exist out there charging a fortune for the service – but you can use a number of effective methods. You can choose a word, or combination of words, that tells people about the exact character of your product – such as Salty Dog crisps, which uses the slogan 'The hand-cooked crisps that bite back' (see the nearby sidebar). This approach resembles giving a new puppy a name. You want to get a feel for its personality first and then give it a name that fits. A stand-offish poodle can be Fifi, but that name doesn't fit a playful mutt!

Potatoes with pedigree

You'd be forgiven for thinking that you can do only so much with the humble potato crisp. After all, in how many ways can you slice up and fry a potato (at least that Walkers hasn't already thought of)? Well, fortunately not everyone thinks like that – particularly the people at Chiltern Snacks, who created Salty Dog crisps. A lot of good marketing exists behind Salty Dog (although the owners would be first to admit they're no experts). The product's significant difference feeds into its name, which feeds into its packaging.

Every packet of Salty Dog carries the line 'The hand-cooked crisps that bite back', together with a cartoon of a dog on the distinctive silver-foil bags. The dog is based on the owner's real terrier puppy and the 'bite back' phrase is also based in truth. The company only uses the biggest and best potatoes, hand fries them in sunflower oil for extra crunch and gives them powerful natural flavours. So, you see, even for fairly ordinary product areas in over-supplied markets, you can succeed if you create something that's better and which tells its story in a powerful way.

You can also name your product by making up a brand-new word that has no prior meaning. This approach gives you something you can more easily protect in a court of law, but it isn't necessarily effective at communicating the character of your product. You have to invest considerable time and money in creating a meaning for the new name in consumers' minds, but when you get it right, it can be very powerful. The name 'Google' is now synonymous with searching for information online. The name itself is a mis-spelling of the word 'Googol' – the mathematical name for a '1' followed by a hundred zeros. Now, however, Google is not only the name of a search engine, it has also made it into the *Oxford English Dictionary* as a verb, 'to Google'.

Legally protecting your product's name and identity

You can gain legal protection by using, and getting legal recognition for, a unique identifier for your product, a line of products or even your entire company. A tangible product's name and/or visual symbol is a *trademark*. A business name is a *word mark* – again, offering similar protection under the law.

You establish and protect your rights to exclusive use of any unique trademark by registering it and then by using it. UK and European trademark law has seen many improvements in recent years. For starters, the definition of trademark has become very broad, giving companies better protection for all aspects of their brand than previously. Trademarks can now be words (including personal names), designs, letters, numerals or the shape of goods or their packaging. This last point is particularly important to products that come in distinctive packaging (think of a classic contoured bottle of Coke, which is now a protected trademark).

Recognising what you should trademark

Consider registering as many different aspects of your product's identity as you think are important to its commercial success (you can even register colours and smells, though companies have had mixed success with this). Don't go overboard, though. For the law to apply, you have to register the trademark (and keep it registered, as registrations usually run out after ten years) and then you have to use it – regularly.

Registering trademarks in the UK and Europe

If you want to register or search for a trademark of any kind in the UK, contact the UK Intellectual Property Office at www. ipo.gov.uk or by calling their Enquiry Unit on 0845 9 500 505.

Registering your trademark for the main foreign territories is also now relatively easy. You can cover the whole of the European Community by applying for a community trademark (CTM). For information on how to do this, contact the Office for the Harmonisation for the Internal Market, at www.oami. europa.eu. Or to cover an even wider international area, including the United States, you can have your trademark protected under the 'Madrid system'. Visit the website of the World Intellectual Property Organisation at www.wipo. int for a list of member countries. Check first, however, if the whole registering process can be done through the UK Intellectual Property Office. You may eliminate the need for an expensive army of international lawyers (unless, of course, your application is challenged).

Packaging and Labelling: Dressing Products for Success

Unplanned purchases make up the biggest category. Furthermore, specifically planned purchases are less than a third of all purchases – all the rest can be influenced at least partially by the packaging and other point-of-purchase com- munications. (The study is for packaged goods in shops, but we find that service purchases can also be strongly influenced by the brochure, sales presentation or website that packages the service.)

The packaging makes the sale in the majority of purchase decisions. Here are some ways to make sure your packaging makes the sale:

> ✔ Bump up the visibility of the packaging. Increasing the size of the brand name, the brightness or boldness of the colours and layout or the size of the package itself helps make your product more visible, as does arranging (or paying) to have shops display it more prominently. Look at the cover of this book for a good example. The *For*

Dummies series is an amazing marketing success, partly because their bold, clear cover designs mean you can easily find them in the bookshop.

✔ Choose a colour that contrasts with competitors' products. Consider easyJet's bright orange colour scheme, which stands out among the typically staid corporate liveries of the bigger airlines. Orange is a colour that shouts 'good value'.

✔ Improve the information on the packaging. In terms of clarity, less is more, so can you cut down on the number of words you use? Alternatively, ask yourself if the shopper may find any additional information useful when making a purchase decision. For example, on food products a nutritional breakdown is necessary but Walkers crisps go so far as to tell people their carbon footprint (how much energy was expended on the products) because it believes that this information is now important to its customers.

✔ Use the web to package a product in information. Many products are too technologically complicated to communicate any information of value on their actual packaging, so the websites for these businesses have become important 'packages' in their own right – think mobile phones and computers. You can use websites for more simple brands too.

Innocent makes fruit smoothies and juices – hardly complex products that need further explanation, you'd think. But like its packaging, the website contains loads of useful and entertaining information about the recipes and ingredients used in its products.

✔ Let the packaging sell the replacement, too. Make some aspect of your packaging (if only a label on the bottom) necessary for reordering, perhaps by offering a phone number or sending the user to your web page.

✔ Give your packaging or label emotional appeal. Warm colours, a friendly message, a smiling person, appealing language and a photo of children playing are all ways to make the buyer feel good when they looks at your product. Purchases are about feelings, not just logic, so give your packaging a winning personality.

✔ Increase the functionality or workability of the packaging. Can you make your packaging protect the product better? Can you make it easier to open, useful for storage or easier to recycle? Packages have functional roles, and improving functionality can help increase the product's appeal.

Use these ideas or your own to improve sales by upgrading your packaging. Whatever you do, do something. Packaging can be a significant cost in the manufacture of any product, so make sure it pays its own way by becoming a powerful marketing tool.

We can't do full justice to packaging in this book. That subject is big enough to justify a book of its own. But we can direct you to some of the leading resources out there for marketers looking to make their packaging work harder in the marketing mix:

Try looking at **The Packaging Society** (www.pi2.org.uk), the main UK trade association for packaging professionals. Or visit The Design Council website (www.designcouncil.org.uk).

Modifying an Existing Product: When and How

Always seek insights into how to improve your product. Always look for early indicators of improvements your competitors plan to make and be prepared to go one step farther in your response. And always go to your marketing oracle – the customer – for insights into how you can improve your product.

The following two sections describe tests that a product must pass to remain viable. If it doesn't pass, you need to improve or alter your product somehow.

When it's no longer special

At the point of purchase – that place or time when customers make their actual buying decisions – your product needs to have something special.

For example, if you sell sewing needles, your product may be about as good as most of the competition – but not noticeably better. But if you happen to be the company that a major retail chain uses to single-source needles for its small sewing section, then you have a distribution advantage at point of sale.

Don't assume your lack of special features means that your product isn't special. You can be special just by being there when customers need the product. You can justify keeping a product alive just by having a way of maintaining your distribution advantage. But a product at point of sale has to have at least something special about it if you expect it to generate a good return in the future – otherwise, it gets lost.

If your customers don't think your product is unique in any way, you may need to kill that product. But don't set up the noose too quickly. First, see if you can work to differentiate your product in some important way.

When it lacks champions

Champions are those customers who really love your product, who insist on buying it over others, and who tell their friends or associates to do the same. But such loyal champions are rare. Does your product have champions?

The championship test is tougher than the differentiation test. Many products lack champions. But when a product does achieve this special status – when some customers really love it – then that product is assured an unusually long and profitable life. Such high customer commitment needs to be your constant goal as you manage the life cycle of your product.

Products with champions get great word of mouth, and their sales and market shares grow because of it. Even better, champions faithfully repurchase the products they rave about. This repeat business provides your company with high-profit sales, compared with the higher costs associated with finding new customers.

How do you know if you have champions rather than regular, ordinary customers? Because when you ask them about the product, they sound excited and enthusiastic. 'I'd never drive anything but a Volvo. They're comfortable and safe, they don't break down and they last longer than other cars.' Some customers say just that when asked about their Volvos, so the company has an excellent base of repeat buyers.

Killing a Product

Unlike people and companies, products don't die on their own. Products never had a pulse anyway and product bankruptcy just doesn't exist. Consequently, the marketer needs to have the good sense to know when an old product has no more life in it and to keep it going just wastes resources that ought to go to new products instead.

When to kill a product

You need to face facts: many products are better off being put out of their misery and replaced with something fresh and innovative. 'But,' you rightly object, 'how do I know when my particular product reaches that point of no return?'

In the following sections, we discuss the warning signs that you're due to replace a product.

The market is saturated and you have a weak/falling share

Saturation means that you and your competitors are selling replacement products. You don't have many new customers around to convert. Growth slows, limited by the replacement rate for the product, plus whatever basic growth occurs in the size of the target market.

Saturation alone is no reason to give up on a product – most markets are saturated. An obviously saturated market is that for the car. You find very few adults who don't already own a car if they have the means to buy one and the need for one. So manufacturers and dealerships fight for replacement sales and first-time sales to young drivers.

Better to introduce a replacement and kill the old product than to wait it out. You have to replace the product eventually, and the sooner you do, the less your share and reputation suffer. Whatever else happens, you can't afford for customers to see you as a has-been in a saturated market!

A series of improvements fails to create momentum

Often, companies try a series of 'new and improved' versions, new packages, fancy coupon schemes, contests and point-of-purchase promotions to breathe life into products after they stop generating year-to-year sales growth. Sometimes these ploys work and help to renew growth; sometimes they don't.

Something is wrong with your product

All too often, marketers discover some flaw in a product that threatens to hurt their company's reputation or puts its customers at risk.

We don't know why some marketers keep making these mistakes but we hope that you don't. Pull the product if you find out it may cause cancer, give people electrical shocks, choke a baby or even just not work as well as you say it does. Pull the product immediately. Ask questions later.

Pulling the product may seem an incredibly tough decision but it can work in your favour if you take quick, decisive action for the good of your customers. Trust us – pulling a product takes courage but is always the best option, when the dust settles. And if you follow our advice and always invest creative energy and funds in your product development efforts, you should have something better to offer as a replacement.

How to kill or replace a product

Getting rid of old products – those that aren't faulty in any way – is the least of your troubles, because *liquidators* are happy to sell your inventory below cost to various vendors. Contact some of your distributors or your trade association for referrals.

If you want to use a more elegant strategy that avoids the negativity of customers seeing your old products offered for a tenth of their normal price, you could try staging some kind of sales promotion to move the old inventory to customers through your normal distribution channels. We much prefer this option, especially if it also introduces consumers to the new product. You can make customers feel like you're doing them a favour. But this method only works if you get started before the old product loses its appeal. So you have to aggressively replace your products. Don't wait for the market to kill your product; do the deed yourself. The following sections discuss more strategies for bowing out gracefully.

The coat-tails strategy

The *coat-tails strategy* uses the old product to introduce the new. Only your imagination limits the variety of ways in which you can put this strategy to use. You can offer a free sample coupon for the new product to buyers of the old product. You can package the two products together in a special two-for-one promotion. You can do special mailings or make personal or telephone sales calls to old customers.

The coat-tails strategy is a great promotional device for replacing an old product with a new one. But you do take a big risk with this strategy. When you make room for your new product, competing products can try to take that space instead. Why? Any customers still faithful to the old product have to reconsider their purchase patterns, and they may choose a competitor over your new option. The choice may make them wake up and realise that they don't need to buy only your brand. Similarly, retailers, distributors or other channel members may give your space to another product. So you need to hold on to your space, even as you eliminate your product. Avoid any gaps in the availability of your products.

The product line place-holding strategy

You can use *product lines* to create clear product niches and hold them for replacement products. Keep pricing consistent with product positions in your product line too – a practice called *price lining*.

For example, a bank may offer a selection of different savings options to its retail customers – a mix of straight savings accounts, easy access accounts, fixed rate bonds, mini cash ISAs and Child Trust Funds. If the bank organises these options into a coherent range of named products and lists them in a single brochure in order from lowest-risk/lowest-return to highest-risk/highest-return, then it creates a clear product line with well-defined places for these products. (The bank must be sure, however, that each product sits in a unique place on that spectrum – no overlaps, please!)

In future, when the bank wants to introduce a new product, it can substitute the new one for an old one and consumers accept that this new product fills the same spot in the product line. The bank can also extend the product line in either direction or fill gaps in it with new products.

But we bet that your bank doesn't use this strategy – few do. As a result, you're always confused when you try to get your mind around your bank's offerings, and it therefore loses some business that it should have won. The fact is that, although product lines are a very important part of any marketing strategy, marketers often neglect them.

Chapter 10

Distribution, Retail, Price and Promotions

Companies with a wide and efficient distribution network are often the most successful because it gives them access to so many potential customers.

Of course, reaching out into the world of your customers with your distribution doesn't guarantee success; it only makes success possible. The customers still have to know and like your product (which, we remind you, can be a service as well as a tangible good). And customers have to view your product as affordable, too. So distribution isn't the only important matter in marketing, but it is a big one.

In developing a marketing strategy we encourage you to treat distribution as one of the key factors, or seven Ps, of marketing. For the purposes of fitting distribution into this list of marketing Ps, it is referred to as *place* – along with *product, price, promotion, people, process* and *physical presence* – but the idea's the same. What you're doing in distribution is placing your offering when, where and how prospective customers need and want it.

Distributing Advice

This book's distribution is a simple example of how powerful the right distribution channels can be. This book receives good placement on the shelves of bookshops, especially the increasingly important major chain stores like Waterstone's and Borders, where it is placed in the marketing area of the business section, making it easy to find. *Marketing For Dummies* is also placed conveniently by topic, title and author on searchable Internet bookshops like Amazon (www. amazon.co.uk). These two main distribution channels provide broad reach into the market of people who are looking for helpful advice and information about how to market their businesses and sell their products or services. Without this broad distribution, you may never have encountered this book, regardless of how well written, packaged or priced it may be.

Keep these points in mind when considering your distribution strategies:

- ✔ If you can add distributors or expand your distribution network, your product may become available to more people and sales could rise as a result. (If not, consider the web, direct-response marketing and events as three alternatives because they bypass distributors and reach out directly to customers.

- ✔ Boost sales by improving the visibility of your product within its current distribution channel; for example, by making sure it is better displayed (a product) or better communicated (a service). Or perhaps you can find a way to shift your distribution slightly so as to give you access to more desirable or larger customers.

- ✔ Increasing the availability of products in your distribution channel can also help boost sales and profits. Can you find ways to get more inventory out there? Or can you speed up the movement of products out to customers so that they feel better able to find your product when they need it? These sorts of improvements can have a dramatic impact on sales by making finding what they want, when and where they want it, easier for more customers.

✔ We urge you to make a list of every company that has a hand of any sort in making your sales and servicing your customers and then to think about ways to strengthen your business relationship with them. Consider doing something simple, like sending them a gift at Christmas. Do something to invest in these relationships – they're very important to most businesses but too easily taken for granted.

✔ Using distributors is a low-cost way to keep expanding. Almost every business can sell through distributors if they're open minded and creative about cutting deals. If you already sell through distributors, find some more.

✔ Even if you have to give a distributor a deeper discount than you want in order to motivate them, consider doing it if you believe that your business hasn't achieved its potential until your products are readily available everywhere within your industry.

Getting Distributors on Your Side

Distributors want items that are easy to sell because customers want to buy them. Making sure your product is appealing is thus the first step in getting distributors on your side. A brilliant product and a clear way of presenting it so that its brilliance shines through is a great investment for growing any distribution system. You may still have to go out and tell distributors about it and work to support them, but if you start with a product whose unique qualities shine through, expanding your distribution is a lot easier.

When you're confident that you have something worth selling, ask yourself which distributors may be successful at selling it. Who's willing and able to distribute for you? Will wholesalers or other intermediaries be helpful? If so, who are they and how many of them can you locate? Try these sources:

✔ **Local business telephone directories or an online equivalent such as Yell** (www.yell.co.uk). These directories often reference the category of intermediary you're looking for.

✔ **Trade associations and trade shows specialising in distributors in specific industries.** If you don't already know which trade associations serve your industry, you can search the Trade Association Forum at `www.taforum.org`.

✔ **google.co.uk (or any other search engine).** Go online and search for products like yours. Once you find them, work out who's selling them. Maybe they'll sell yours, too!

✔ **Major conventions in your industry.** These are the best places to find distributors. Take along product samples and literature, put on comfortable shoes and walk around the convention hall until you find the right distributors.

✔ **Retail outlets.** Use the *Yellow Pages* or an Internet search engine to find shops operating in your local area, grouped by the types of products they sell. These shops also have their own trade associations, such as the Association of Convenience Stores, at `www.acs.org.uk`. Consult any directory of associations for extensive listings (available in the reference sections of most libraries and usually online), or consider wearing out a little shoe leather and tyre rubber to discover the leading retailers in any specific geographic market. Just visit high-traffic areas and see what shops are prominent and successful to identify the leading retailers in the area.

What do intermediaries do to earn their cut?

When deciding how to distribute your product, draw up a list of tasks you want distributors to do. For example, you may want them to find you more customers than you can find on your own. Finding customers is just one of the functions distributors may be able to perform. You're more likely to get a good match if you decide what you'd like them to do and then seek out distributors who say they want to do those things for you. Here's a starting list of functions you may want your intermediaries to perform:

✔ Finding more customers for your product than you can on your own

✔ Researching customer attitudes and desires

- 🗸 Buying and selling
- 🗸 Breaking down bulk shipments for resale
- 🗸 Setting prices
- 🗸 Managing point-of-purchase promotions
- 🗸 Advertising at the local level
- 🗸 Transporting products
- 🗸 Taking an inventory of products
- 🗸 Financing purchases
- 🗸 Separating poor-quality leads from serious customers (marketers call this *qualifying sales leads*)
- 🗸 Providing customer service and support
- 🗸 Sharing the risks of doing business
- 🗸 Combining your products with others to offer appropriate assortments

Distribution considerations

How you set up and manage your distribution channel or channels affects can have a big impact on your success. Below is a list of considerations when choosing distribution partners:

Market coverage

How well does your channel reach your target customers? If you go direct, doing everything yourself, you may be unable to cover the market as intensely as you want to. By adding even one layer of intermediaries, you suddenly have many more warm bodies or shopfronts out there. As you add more layers, the bottom of the channel grows ever larger, allowing you to achieve increasingly good market coverage.

Level of intensity

Thinking about the issue of market coverage in terms of *intensity*, defined as the extent of your geographic coverage of the market, can help you work out how many and what types of distributors to use. Conventional wisdom identifies three practical strategies:

212 Part IV: Connecting With Your Customers

✔ **Intensive distribution strategy.** Here, you attempt to put every customer within reach of your products by using as many intermediaries and layers as needed to create maximum coverage. You should use this strategy in mature markets where your competitors are trying to do the same thing, or in markets where the customer makes a convenience purchase – because intensive distribution makes your product convenient. Keep in mind that this strategy is expensive, and you may not need it in other circumstances.

✔ **Selective distribution strategy.** Here, you target the most desirable areas or members of your market. For example, the business-to-business (B2B) marketer may decide to target a geographic region where many users of her technology are based. The consumer products marketer may decide to market to areas by postcode or counties where he finds heavy users of his product.

✔ **Exclusive distribution.** Here, you cherry-pick to find the best intermediaries and customers. This strategy is appropriate when you don't have any really serious competition and you have a speciality product that you want to keep providing at the same profitable level. This method doesn't grow your market or boost share significantly, but it does maximise profit margins, which is no bad thing!

Exclusive distribution is also appropriate if you introduce an innovative new product or service. You find a limited number of early adopters – people who are quick to use your products or services in any market. Start with exclusive distribution to find those customers most interested in trying new ideas and then work up to selective distribution as competition builds and the product goes mainstream. Finally, push toward intensive distribution as the market matures and your emphasis shifts from finding first-time users to fighting over repeat business.

Speed to market

The longer the channel, the slower the product's trip from producer to customer. A relay team can never beat an individual runner in a sprint. If your customers need or want faster delivery and service, you have to prune the distribution channel until you make it fast enough to satisfy the consumers. You may even need to replace physical distributors with a website, where everything can be ordered immediately for next-day delivery.

Think about the trend toward online home-shopping in the clothing industry. Customers can obtain their choice of style and size from a large assortment and the company can deliver it within a few days or even the next day. You may think that you can shop in a department store even more quickly because you can walk out with your purchase. But the busy consumer may not have time to visit a department store for days or weeks, whereas he can take care of a late-night click of the mouse on a store's website in seconds when it suits him. Instead of spending days wandering round different shops to find what you need, you can look through a few websites in a flash. In the early days of the Internet, shops thought that people wouldn't buy clothes online because they wouldn't be able to try them on. Now every high-street shop tends to have a comprehensive website because they've realised just how many people prefer the convenience of using the mouse rather than shoe leather.

Developing merchandising strategies

Whether you retail services or goods, you need to think about your merchandising strategy. You do have one, whether you know it or not – and if you don't know it, then your strategy is based on conventions in your industry and needs a kick in the seat of the pants to make it more distinctive. *Merchandising strategy*, the selection and assortment of products offered, tends to be the most important source of competitive advantage or disadvantage for retailers.

What's your merchandising strategy? To answer this question, you need to recognise your own brilliance – what makes you especially notable – and make sure you translate that brilliance into visible, attractive aspects in both exterior and interior shop design.

The following sections describe some existing strategies, which may give you ideas for your business.

General merchandise retailing

This strategy works because it brings together a wide and deep assortment of products, thus allowing customers to easily find what they want – regardless of what the product may be. Department stores and general merchandisers fall into this category, but so too do the large out-of-town super-markets, which have expanded from groceries into non-food sales. In the UK, Tesco is leader in this area because it offers more variety (and often better prices) than nearby competitors. The warehouse store (such as CostCo and Matalan) is another example of general merchandise retailing. And, as this varied list of examples suggests, you can implement this strategy in many ways.

Limited-line retailing

This strategy emphasises depth over variety. London's Planet Organic chain of grocery stores specialises in natural and organic food products; as a result, the chain can offer far greater choice in this specialised area than the average super-market (and it picks locations with a high concentration of wealthy households). Similarly, a bakery can offer more and better varieties of baked goods because a bakery sells only those goods.

Limited-line retailing is especially common in professional and personal services. Most accounting firms, chiropractic offices and law firms offer just the one service.

Perhaps you can combine several complementary services into a less limited line than your competitors. If you can expand your line without sacrificing quality or depth of offerings, you can offer customers greater convenience – and that convenience should make you a winner.

Scrambled merchandising

Consumers have preconceived notions about what product lines and categories belong together. Looking for fresh produce in a grocery shop makes sense these days because dry goods and fresh produce have been combined by so many retailers. But 50 years ago, the idea would seem radical because specialised limited-line retailers used to sell fresh produce. When grocery shops combined these two categories, they were using a *scrambled merchandising* strategy, in which the merchant uses unconventional combinations of product lines. Today, the meat department, bakery, deli section, seafood department and many other sections combine naturally in a modern supermarket. And many supermarkets are adding other products and services, such as a coffee bar, bank, bookshop, dry cleaners, shoe repair service, hair salon, photographer, flower shop, post office and so on. In the same way, petrol stations combine with fast-food restaurants and convenience stores to offer pit stops for both car and driver. These scrambled merchandising concepts are now widely accepted.

Building price and quality strategies

Retail stores generally have a distinct place in the range of possible price and quality combinations. Some shops are obviously upscale boutiques, specialising in the finest merchandise – for the highest prices. Other shops are middle class in their positioning, and still others offer the worst junk from liquidators but sell it for so little that almost anybody can afford it. In this way, retailing still maintains the old distinctions of social class, even though the people who shop there may not.

As a retailer, this distinction means that customers can get confused about who you are unless you let them know where you stand on the class scale. Does your shop have an upper-class pedigree, or is it upper-middle, middle or lower-middle class?

After you make a decision about how to place your shop, you're ready to decide what price strategy to pursue. Don't forget that building-in upmarket appeal can be an effective strategy for attracting the mass market – because you've built in desirability. In general, the higher class the shop's image, the higher the prices that the shop can charge. But the real secret to success is to price just a step below your image. That way, customers feel like they're buying first-class products for second-class prices – which makes them very happy indeed.

If you want to get plugged into a wide variety of publications, conferences and other events of interest to retailers, get in touch with the British Retail Consortium (BRC) at `www.brc. org.uk`. The BRC is the leading retail trade association in the UK, but you can also find specialist associations covering everything from bike shops to DIY centres. And if you need to find out more about shop planning or track down experienced shop planners, try the Shop & Display Equipment Association, at www.shopdisplay.org.uk. And don't overlook the useful book, *Retail Business Kit For Dummies*, by Rick Segal (Wiley), which goes into the topic in far more depth than we can here.

Understanding the Facts of Pricing

Most companies fall prey to the myth that customers only choose a product based on its price. As a result, they set their prices lower than they need to. Or when companies need to boost sales, they do so by offering discounts or free units or the infamous BOGOF – Buy One Get One Free. If you insist on selling on the basis of price alone, your customers buy on the basis of price.

But alternatives always exist. To raise your price and still sell more, you can:

✔ **Build brand equity.** Better-known brands command a premium price.

✔ **Increase quality.** People spread the word about a good product, and that can earn the product a 5 to 10 per cent higher price than the competition.

✔ **Use prestige pricing.** Giving your product a high-class image can boost your price by 20 to 100 per cent. See later in this chapter for details on how prestige pricing works.

✔ **Create extra value through time and place advantages.** Customers consider the available product worth a lot more than one they can't get when they need it. (That's why a cup of coffee costs more at the airport – are you really going to leave the terminal, get in a taxi and go somewhere else to save a pound?)

Price is important, but it doesn't have to be customers' only consideration.

Avoiding underpricing

Lowering prices is always easier than raising prices. In general, you want to set a price a bit high in relation to the competition and see what happens. If your product sells the way you want it to, great! If not, you can take back any price increase with a subsequent price cut.

Customers may not be as price sensitive as you fear. They may tolerate an increase better than you think and they may not respond to a decrease in price as enthusiastically as you need them to in order to make that decrease profitable. Customers may even assume that price correlates with quality – in which case, they don't buy your product unless the price is high enough. Instead of assuming that you need a price cut whenever you want to boost profits, start by experimenting with a price increase. Be a contrarian. They often succeed!

Exploring the impact of pricing on customers' purchases

Price sensitivity is the degree to which purchases are affected by price level – that is, how willing are customers to pay the price you're asking? You need to estimate how price sensitive your customers are in relation to your product or service.

To check price sensitivity you need good data to look through. The following checklist is a series of *qualitative indicators* (clues we can guess from) of price sensitivity. You have to ask yourself a set of questions about your customer, product and market, ticking the box next to each question that you answer with 'yes'. Then you add up the number of ticked boxes to see which way they lean. This study isn't scientific, but is better than ignoring the problem altogether!

❑ **Does the customer view the price as reasonable?** If you're operating within an expected price range, customers aren't very price sensitive. Outside of the expected price range, they become more so.

❑ **Is the product valuable at (almost) any price?** Some products are unique and customers know that they may have a hard time finding a cheaper substitute. That fact lowers price sensitivity.

❏ **Is the product desperately needed?** Customers generally don't care how much fixing a burst pipe on a Sunday costs – certainly not their homes are filling up with water! And they're not too price sensitive about the cost of treatment by a dentist when their teeth hurt. These products meet essential needs. But if your product is a *non-essential* (something that customers want but don't have to have right now), the customer is more price sensitive.

❏ **Are substitutes unavailable?** If the customer purchases in a context where substitute products aren't readily available, price sensitivity is lower. Shopping for price requires that substitutes at different prices be available. (For example, if you're the only company offering emergency plumbing repairs on weekends in your town, your customers will pay a high price for your services.)

❏ **Is the customer unaware of substitutes?** Shopping is a complex, information-dependent behaviour. Customers can find the cheapest price available if they have the time and access to the Internet. But not everyone does. You don't have to charge the least if your customers are unable or unwilling to shop around for a lower price.

❏ **Does the customer find comparing options difficult?** Even where options exist, the consumer can have problems comparing products in some product categories. What makes one dentist better than another? Most people don't know. The technical complexity of their work, plus the fact that you can't consume dental care until after you make the purchase decision, makes comparing options hard. As a result, that difficulty makes dental care consumers less price sensitive – and dentists richer.

❏ **Does the product seem inexpensive to customers?** Customers don't worry too much about price when they feel they're getting good value. However, if customers feel the pinch in their purses when they make purchases, they pay close attention to prices. That's why you negotiate so hard when you buy a car or a house. Even products that cost far less can seem expensive if they're at the high end of a price range. For example, you're more price sensitive if you shop for a fancy, high-performance laptop than for a simple, basic desktop computer because the former probably costs 50 to 100 per cent more than the latter, making the laptop expensive by comparison.

The more boxes you ticked, the less price sensitive your customer is. If you ticked multiple boxes, you probably can raise your prices without hurting sales significantly – great news!

 You can supplement your estimate of price sensitivity (from the checklist) with actual tests. For example, if you think a 5 per cent increase in prices won't affect sales, try that increase in a test market or for a short period of time, holding the rest of your marketing constant. Were you right? If so, roll out the increase nationwide (or townwide, for you small-business people).

Following Five Easy Steps to Setting Prices

If you need to establish a price, you're facing one of the toughest decisions in business. Surveys of managers indicate they suffer from a high degree of price anxiety. So let's take you through the process logically, step by step. Price setting doesn't have to be a high-anxiety task if you do it right!

Step 1: Find out who really sets the price

This first step isn't obvious. You, as the marketer, can set a list price. But the consumer may not ultimately pay your price. You may encounter a distributor or wholesaler and a retailer, all of whom take their mark-ups. Furthermore, the manufacturer generally doesn't have the legal right to dictate the ultimate selling price. The retailer gets that job. So if you create the product yourself your list price is really just a suggestion, not an order. If the retailer doesn't like the suggested price, the product sells for another price.

So you need to start by determining who else may be setting prices along with you. Involve these parties in your decision making by asking some of them what they think about pricing your product. They may tell you that you have constraints to consider. Know what those constraints are before you start.

For example, if you're setting the price for a new range of paints, you find that the big DIY chains expect a 40–50 per cent discount off the list price. Knowing that, you can set a high enough list price to give you some profit, even at a 50 per cent discount rate. But if you don't realise that these chains expect much higher discounts than smaller DIY shops, you may be blind-sided by their requirement.

Calculating discount structures

Confused? Let's show you how to calculate prices and discounts in a complex distribution channel. Say that you discover the typical discount structure in the market where you want to introduce your product is 30/10/5. What does that mean? If you start with a £100 list price, the retailer pays at a discount of 30 per cent off the list price (0.30 × £100 = £70). The retailer, who pays £70 for the product, marks it up to (approximately) £100 and makes about £30 in gross profit.

Now, the discount structure figures tell you that other intermediaries exist – one for each discount listed. The distributor, who sells the product to the retailer, has a discount of 10 per cent off the price that she charges the retailer (that's 0.10 × £70 = £7 of gross profit for the distributor).

And this distributor must have paid £70 – £7, or £63, for the product to another intermediary (probably a manufacturer's representative or wholesaler). The marketer sells to this intermediary. And the 30/10/5 formula shows that this intermediary receives a 5 per cent discount: 0.05 × £63 = £3.15 in profit for him.

Subtracting again, you can also determine that the marketer must sell the product to this first intermediary at £63 – £3.15, or £59.85. You, as the marketer, must give away more than 40 per cent of that £100 list price to intermediaries if you use this 30/10/5 discount structure. And so you have to calculate any profit you make from a £100 list price as costs subtracted from your net of £59.85. That's all you ever see of that £100!

Marketers who operate in or through a *multilevel distribution channel* (meaning that they have distributors, wholesalers, retailers, agents or other sorts of intermediaries) need to establish the *trade discount structure*. Trade discounts (also called *functional discounts*) are what you give these intermediaries. These discounts are a form of cost to the marketer, so make sure that you know the discount structure for your product before you move on. Usually, marketers state the discount structure as a series of numbers, representing what each of the intermediaries get as a discount. But you take each discount off the price left over from the discount before it, not off the list price.

Step 2: Examine all your costs

How do you know your costs? In theory, that part's easy: your company's excellent cost accounting system captures all your costs and a man in a pinstripe suit with a calculator can simply give you the figure.

In practice, you may not have good, accurate information on the true costs of a specific product or service. Take some time to try to estimate what you're actually spending, and remember to include some value for expensive inventories if they sit around for a month or more (assume you're paying interest on the money tied up in those products to account for the loss of capital wasting away in inventory).

After you examine your costs carefully, you should have a fairly accurate idea of the least amount you can charge. That charge is, at a bare minimum, your actual costs. (Although, occasionally, you may want to give away a product for less than cost in order to introduce people to it – what's known as a *loss leader*. This approach is often used by retailers to get people into stores so they then go on to buy more products and make up for the one loss leader product.) More often, you need a price that includes the cost plus a profit margin – say, 20 or 30 per cent. So that means you have to treat your cost as 70 or 80 per cent of the price, adding in that 20 or 30 per cent margin your company requires.

Step 3: Evaluate customer perception of price

Your costs and profit requirements determine a lower limit on price. But your customers' perceptions determine an upper limit. You need to define both of these limits to know your possible price range. So you need to work out what price customers are willing to pay.

Pricing experts sometimes call the difference between the customer's desired price and a noticeably higher price the *indifference zone*. Within the indifference zone, customers are indifferent to both price increases and price decreases. However, the zone gets smaller (on a percentage basis) as the price of a product increases. How big or small is the zone of indifference in your product's case? Go back to the price sensitivity checklist. The zone is small if your customers are highly price sensitive, and large if they aren't that price sensitive. Just make some assumptions that seem reasonable for now. We know this process involves some guesswork, but still, breaking down the pricing decision into a series of smaller, educated guesses is better than plucking a number out of thin air! At worst, your errors on all those little guesses may be random, in which case they should cancel each other out.

You can also uncover customer preference by looking at the current pricing structure in your market. What are people paying for comparable products?

Setting your price at the top of the range is the simplest approach to pricing. As long as the price range is above the bottom limit (your preferred price plus the indifference zone is equal to or greater than your cost plus your required profit), you're okay.

But you can't always set your price at the top of the range. In the next step of the pricing process, we show you how to calculate what your final price should be.

Step 4: Examine secondary influences

Your two primary considerations are your costs and the customers' upper price limits. They set a price range but you also need to consider many other factors. These factors may influence your decision by forcing you to price in the middle or bottom of the price range rather than at the top, for example.

Consider competitive issues. Do you need to gain market share from a close competitor? If so, either keep price at parity and do aggressive marketing, or adjust your price to be slightly (but noticeably) below the competitor's price. Also consider likely future price trends. Are prices falling in this market? Then you need to adjust your figures down a bit to stay in synch with your market. Similarly, currency fluctuations may affect your costs and, thus, your pricing options. If you're concerned that you may take a hit from the exchange rate, better to be safe and price at the high end of the range. Finally, product line management may dictate a slightly lower or higher price. For example, you may need to price a top-of-the-range product significantly higher than others in its line just to make it clear to the customer that this product is a step above standard alternatives.

Step 5: Set your strategic objectives

You may have objectives other than revenues and profit maximisation. Many marketers price near the bottom of their price range to increase their market share.

This low-price strategy only makes sense if the customer is fairly price sensitive! If not, you're throwing away possible revenues without any real gain in market share. You should be pricing at the top of the range and using the extra revenues to invest in quality and brand-building marketing promotions in order to increase market share.

Using Discounts and Other Special Offers

Special offers are temporary inducements to make customers buy on the basis of price or price-related factors. Special offers play with the price, giving consumers (or intermediaries) a way to get the product for less – at least while the offer lasts.

You may wonder, why play with the price? If you think the price should be lower, why not just cut the price permanently? The answer is because a price cut is easy to do, but hard to undo. A special offer, on the other hand, allows you to temporarily discount the price while still maintaining the list price at its old level. When the offer ends, the list price is the same – you haven't given anything away permanently. Here are some cases in which maintaining your list price and offering a discount is a good strategy:

- ✔ When you have a short-term reason for wanting to cut the price, such as aiming to counter a competitor's special offer or responding to a new product introduction.

- ✔ When you want to experiment with the price (to find out about customer price sensitivity) without committing to a permanent price cut until you see the data.

- ✔ When you want to stimulate consumers to try your product, and you believe that, after they try it, they may like the product well enough to buy it again at full price.

- ✔ When your list price needs to stay high in order to signal quality (*prestige pricing*) or be consistent with other prices in your product line (*price lining strategy*); see the earlier section 'Understanding how customers perceive and remember prices' for details on those pricing strategies.

- ✔ When your competitors are all offering special lower prices and you think you have no choice because consumers have come to expect special offers.

What happens when competitors become too focused on making and matching each other's special offers? They flood the customers with price-based promotions. Discounts and other freebies begin to outweigh brand-building marketing messages, focusing consumer attention on price over brand and benefit considerations. Special promotions can and do increase customer sensitivity to price. They attract *price switchers*, people who aren't loyal to any brand but shop on the basis of price alone. Special promotions encourage people to become price switchers, thus reducing the size of the core customer base and increasing the number of fringe customers. So remember that special offers have the potential to erode brand equity, reduce customer loyalty and cut deeply into your profits. You can easily lose your footing on this slippery slope!

As you decide on a promotion strategy, be sure to check that the promotion is legal. Legal constraints do exist. You can't mislead consumers about what they get. And a sweepstake or contest has to be open to all, not tied to product purchase. The Institute of Sales Promotion (ISP) offers a legal checklist covering the basics of most types of promotional device. You can access it for free at www.isp.org.uk, but if you really want a guarantee that your promotion is legally watertight, you'll have to become a member to use the ISP's full legal advice service.

Designing coupons and figuring out how much to offer

Any certificate entitling the holder to a reduced price is a coupon, which gives a pretty broad definition – and that means you have a lot of room for creativity in this field. Collect a handful of recent coupons from your own and other industries to get an idea of available options and how they're utilised.

In consumer non-durables, whether toothpaste or tinned soup, research shows that you have to offer at least 50p off your list price to attract much attention. All but the most dedicated coupon clippers ignore the smaller offers. But when offers get over the 50p level, attractiveness grows rapidly – sometimes even reaching the 80 per cent level! You can find within this larger percentage of interested consumers many brand-loyal, core customers – both yours and your competitors. And you should find these core customers far more attractive than the coupon clippers who flock to smaller offers.

Forecasting redemption rates

Designing a coupon isn't the hard part – guessing the *redemption rate* (or percentage of people who use the coupon) is. And you raise the stakes when you use big offers, making them riskier to forecast.

We can tell you that, on average, customers redeem a little over 3 per cent of coupons (and the average coupon offers 25p off the list price). So you can use that figure as a good starting point for your estimate. But the range is wide – some offers are so appealing, and so easy to use, that customers redeem 50 per cent of those coupons. For others, the redemption rate can be close to zero. So how do you find out if your coupon will have a high or low redemption rate?

You can refine your redemption estimate by comparing your offer with others. Are you offering something more generous or easy to redeem than you have in the past? Than your competitors do? If so, you can expect significantly higher than average redemption rates – maybe twice as high or higher.

Coupon deals gone wild is the most common reason for marketers to lose their jobs. Back in 1992, the British arm of Hoover ran a marketing promotion offering free flights to anyone spending more than £100 on its products. So many people took up the offer that the company was overwhelmed, and estimates put the resulting cost of fulfilling so many flights at £50 million. Always check the offer against what you know of customer perception and price sensitivity to make sure that you aren't accidentally shifting the price so far that everyone and her brother want to redeem coupons.

Also, if you're distributing coupons via the Internet or e-mail, make sure you explicitly state who can use the coupon and whether it can be used once or multiple times. Christmas 2007 saw off-licence chain Threshers e-mail a 40 per cent discount coupon to their business partners; it was quickly forwarded on to friends nationwide. Unfortunately, Threshers hadn't specified that the e-mail coupon could only be used by business partners and ended up with thousands of consumers asking for a 40 per cent discount as they stocked up on Christmas cheer.

Staying Out of Trouble with the Law

You don't have to be a legal whiz to know when pricing's illegal. Whenever a customer or competitor can make a good case for unfair or deceptive pricing, you're running the risk of legal action. Make sure that you read this list correctly – these are things you should *not* do!

- ✔ **Price fixing.** Don't agree to (or even talk about) prices with other companies. The exception is a company you sell to, of course – but note that you cannot force them to resell your product at a specific price.

- ✔ **Price fixing in disguise.** Shady marketers have tried many ideas – they don't work. If your competitors want you to require the same amount of down payment, start your negotiations from the same list prices as theirs, use a standard contract for extending credit or form a joint venture to distribute all your products (at the same price) – realise that these friendly suggestions are all forms of price fixing. Just say no. And in future, refuse even to take phone calls from marketers who offer you such deals.

- ✔ **Price fixing by purchasers.** Believe it or not, you shouldn't even treat marketers unfairly. If purchasers join together in order to dictate prices from their suppliers, this practice can very well be price fixing. Have a skilled lawyer review any such plans.

- ✔ **Exchanging price information.** You can't talk to your competitors about prices. Ever. If it ever comes to light that anyone in your company gives out information about pricing and receives some in return, you're in big trouble, even if you don't feel you acted on that information. Take this warning seriously. (By the way, *price signalling* – announcing a planned price increase – is sometimes seen as an unfair exchange of price information because competitors may use such announcements to signal to others that everyone should make a price increase.)

✔ **Bid rigging.** If you're bidding for a contract, the preceding point applies. Don't share any information with anyone. Don't compare notes with another bidder. Don't agree to make an identical bid. Don't *split* by agreeing not to bid on one job if the competitor doesn't bid on another. Don't mess with the bidding process in any manner or you're guilty of *bid rigging*.

✔ **Parallel pricing.** In some cases, you could actually be charged with price fixing even if you didn't talk to competitors – just because you have similar price structures. After all, the result may be the same – to boost prices unfairly. In other cases, the law considers similar prices as natural. Here's a rule that makes good sense: don't mirror competitors' prices, unless everyone can see that you selected those prices on your own – especially if your price change involves a price increase.

Some people throw up their hands in despair because so many pricing techniques are illegal. Let us just add that trying to influence prices in certain ways is okay. You can offer volume discounts to encourage larger purchases. And, although you can't force a retailer to charge a certain price for your product, you can encourage them to by advertising the suggested retail price and by listing it as such on your product.

Also, you can always offer an effective price cut to consumers through a consumer coupon or other special offer. Retailers usually agree to honour such offers. However, if you offer a discount to your retailers, you can't force them to pass that discount on to your customers. Retailers may just put the money in the bank and continue to charge customers full price.

Part V
The Part of Tens

In this part . . .

We could give you ten good reasons to read this part but why bother – it already contains plenty of good tips.

In this part, we warn you how to avoid many of the common mistakes and causes of failures that have torpedoed other marketers and their programmes in the past. We suggest you re-read this section once a month, just to make sure that your marketing innoculations are up-to-date. It's easy to get infected by bad habits if you don't pay attention!

We bet you want to save as much money as you can on marketing. Believe me, almost every marketer shares this wish. But few accomplish it, at least not without ruining next year's revenues and profits and sending customers away angry. So please consult this part of the book to find out how to save money by being an economical marketer. Given unlimited funds, any idiot can sell something, but doing it for less is a true art form.

Chapter 11

Ten Common Marketing Mistakes to Avoid

*Y*ou don't want to reinvent the wheel (to use a popular phrase in the marketing world). Over many years, people have honed relevant and useful marketing techniques that you can benefit from. However, they've also made lots of mistakes along the way. Take a couple of minutes to find out about the all-too-common mistakes that so often derail sales and marketing efforts and then try your best to avoid them!

Don't Sell to the Wrong People

We regularly get sent a catalogue from a company specialising in maternity clothes. As we've never ordered anything from them, you'd think they'd give up. At the very least, you'd hope someone at the company would realise that none of its customers can be pregnant all of the time. What a waste of paper, time and money, not to mention the effect on the environment.

You can sort people easily by profession or gender, thus eliminating some of the more obvious mismatches. Don't waste your money on the wrong people.

Don't Give Away Money

Never use discounts and price drops unless you have clear evidence that the net result can be profitable. Sometimes, you have no choice but to slash your prices but generally, avoid competing on price. You'll find making a profit far easier when you compete on the elements that make you different and better than your rivals.

Don't Forget to Edit Before You Print

People will notice and remember if your letter, e-mail, web page, print ad, sign or poster contains a spelling error. Talk about making a bad first impression!

Don't Keep Repeating Yourself

There's nothing more irritating than getting the same communication several times in your inbox or on the doormat. Avoiding this error can be difficult. Check every list before you use it, looking for duplications that may slip by and end up causing irritation at the other end.

Don't Fall into the Wish-We-Could Trap

Every business has its core speciality. Sometimes you should expand into a new market area or try a new kind of product or service – but carry out this expansion with a well-researched and funded strategic thrust. Otherwise, to fool around in an area that you aren't expert in just invites disaster.

Don't Dole Out Impersonal Treatment

Every single one of your customers is a person and they like to be treated as such. Yet sometimes, businesses send out generic bills or mailings that have mis-spellings of customers' names. And perhaps the person who answers the phone doesn't know that the caller is an old customer. You can make these easy, casual mistakes often without even noticing that you make them. Remember to treat your customers as individuals at every point of contact.

Don't Blame the Customer

It is easy to get irritated with customers who fail to pay bills, don't behave well or fail to live up to your expecations. But remember that you represent your company and brand at all times – don't make the mistake of letting off steam and losing valuable customers forever. Make sure your customers feel respected, regardless of the situation.

Don't Avoid Upset Customers

You naturally want to avoid someone who's irritated with you – but don't. Customers can get unpleasant or abusive if they feel that they've been poorly treated. Treat the unhappy customer as your top marketing priority. And don't stop working on them until they're happy again. If you win them back, they'll be loyal and could bring you new business.

Don't Forget to Change

You can easily fall into the trap of doing the same thing with your marketing communications every year – many companies do.

Don't throw out the marketing that does work, but at least find out which aspects work best and adjust your spending accordingly. You can't test out whether a blog or mobile marketing will work for you if your entire budget is tied up in local press advertising.

Don't Stop Marketing

When things go well, you may be tempted to relax and let marketing costs slip down while you enjoy higher margin sales. Whether you notice it straight away or not, this slip undermines sales and erodes your customer base.

When things aren't going so well in an economic depression or recession, maintaining communication with customers is even more important. Study after study shows that in a downturn, those companies that keep advertising through the hard times do much better than their competitors when business picks up.

Chapter 12

Ten (or so) Ways to Save Money in Marketing

. . . .

In This Chapter

▶ Cutting costs and being creative

▶ Staying close to home

▶ Adding value to your product without adding cost

. . . .

*E*veryone wants to know how to do marketing on the cheap. But as a rule, you get what you pay for in marketing. The real money-saving techniques aren't as obvious or easy as some people try to tell you, but these techniques can really work. Usually, they involve doing real marketing, rather than substituting some cheap alternative. If you want an approach that really saves money you need to do the right things – better. This chapter gives you ideas for saving money without reducing your effectiveness or embarrassing yourself.

Planning Your Expenditure

We estimate that businesses often spend their marketing money without thinking. Companies often reprint brochures or spend money on fancy packaging without any idea of if they're making good marketing investments. Make a commitment to spend nothing on marketing without knowing why – and without considering alternatives. Make your marketing cost-effective and economical by spending time developing strategy and designing your plan.

Thinking Small in a Big Way

Grand gestures aren't necessary – you can make lots of small tweaks to your marketing budget. The following list provides ideas to help you be more focused on your target market and thus save money:

- ✔ **Targeting your audience narrowly.** Most marketing campaigns waste much of their effort on people or organisations who can never become good customers because they aren't in the target market. Look for the narrowest, most specific, way to talk to your customers and prospects. If you switch from a list with 75 per cent wasted names to a list with only 25 per cent, you can have the same impact with a mailing that costs half as much but still reaches the same number of prospects!

- ✔ **Narrowing your territory.** Think small by focusing your resources on a smaller market area. Understanding the effects of *scale* in your business is the trick to this strategy. Do some quick calculations. Can a 10 or 20 per cent share of the market in a single region, county or city cover your fixed as well as variable costs and get you significantly above your break-even point? If your fixed costs aren't too high for that market, it can. Businesses with high fixed costs – a factory, for example – usually have to think bigger when choosing a market. Consultants can think very small because they have minimal overheads. Consultants might best boost consulting sales by focusing a local marketing effort on the members of just one chamber of commerce.

- ✔ **Concentrating your resources.** Don't spread yourself too thinly. Concentrate your salespeople, your shops, your direct marketing or whatever you do in your plan into certain areas or periods of time so that you can cash in on economies of scale. *Economies of scale* means that your costs per ad or other marketing efforts go down as you do more. Take advantage of discounts from printers, mailing list houses and the media that sell ad time and space. If you can justify printing and mailing 50,000 copies of your catalogue rather than 5000 copies, your costs fall to less than half per copy.

Integrating Your Efforts

Make sure you design an overall strategy for your marketing that says what your organisation hopes to communicate through any contact with potential customers (such as adverts, PR campaigns and so on). This should allow you to cut back your budget as you are working with one goal in mind. Have one (just one) way to display your name and logo, plus one (just one) key point you want to make to sell people on your benefits. Then be consistent in all your communications.

Spending Money Wisely and Cutting Judiciously

Well-designed marketing plans are an investment in future sales. You can most obviously save money on marketing by cutting the marketing budget, but across-the-board cuts rarely work.

- **Make smarter investments.** You can save money by making smarter investments. Take a look at your results from the past year (or month, or even week if you're looking at web marketing, where you can get reports immediately) and figure out which investments are working best. Then cut out low-return investments and shift the spending into the best-performing marketing activities.

- **Cut your fixed costs.** Consider cutting your *fixed costs* (those costs that you incur regularly, like rent, regardless of what you do or don't sell). Although this advice sounds more like accounting or operations management than marketing, you can use it as an incredibly powerful strategy!

  If you're trying to work out how to introduce a new product on a shoestring budget, consider searching for a low-cost supplier who can make the product for you in small batches. Even if you end up with slightly higher total costs, you have much lower fixed costs because you don't have to order large quantities in advance or find storage for extra units. And so you can *bootstrap* (or grow your own cash flow) by making and marketing a small batch in a small market and then reinvesting your profits into a slightly bigger second batch.

✔ **Cut back where customers can't see.** From the customer's perspective, the landscaping outside the headquarters building doesn't matter (and many people inside that building feel the same way!). Most consumers couldn't care less whether you print the department's letterhead in two colours or one, or whether salespeople drive new or used cars. Put money where customers will see it, not where they won't.

Getting Publicity for Nothing

Magazines, newspapers, radio and TV stations need editorial as much as they need advertising. Getting your business on air or in print is easier than you think. All you need is a good story, or even a strong opinion, to get yourself into the pages of business-to-business (B2B) magazines, like Marketing Week, more often than your competitors. What has your company got that a local or specialist publication or TV channel might like to cover? Have you or one of your staff done something noteworthy? You can create 'good news' by doing some work in the local community, carrying out an original survey and publicising the results, or taking part in some sponsored event such as a marathon.

Giving Your Product or Service Away

You're in business to make money from sales, but sometimes making a sale involves giving would-be customers a taster of your product and service – for free. This idea works on at least a couple of levels. First, giving freebies encourages trial, which encourages purchase, which encourages repeat purchase.

Second, this idea shows your prospective customers that you believe in your own product enough to let them have some of it now and they can return for more later.

You can find ways to give away samples of your product or service no matter what business you're in. Consultants and professional advisers can provide basic documents and advice on their websites to pull customers in, food and drink manufacturers can give away samples in supermarket car parks and software and video games manufacturers can build in limited-time free usage.

Rewarding Your Customers

Give your customers a treat as a reward for their business. Send them a bottle of wine, a cake, flowers or some other treat you think they may like, along with a personal thank you note. This tip is very simple, but it does a lot to let people know that you care about their business. Customers who feel you've treated them well always send new customers your way.

Using New Channels and Media

Whenever possible, find the up-and-coming thing and hop on for the ride. Or better still, create the new thing yourself. (Can you use an exciting new event with associated publicity instead of using advertising?) Your marketing money goes much farther when you do something novel, for three reasons:

- ✔ New means unproven and advertisers are charged lower prices as a result.

- ✔ New means smaller, so you can be a big fish in a little pond.

- ✔ Your originality catches eyes and impresses customers. Be a market leader, not a follower!

Giving Solid Guarantees

If you really think that you have a good product or service, why not take the risk out of trying it? A money-back guarantee, without a lot of small print to qualify it, tends to get customer attention. And what's the cost? If they love it, the offer costs you nothing at all. If you're wrong occasionally, then you still have a pretty low cost. You can't lose on a guarantee unless you're selling a bad product – in which case, you need to upgrade it straight away because nothing is more expensive to market than a bad product!

Index

FOR **DUMMIES**®

Making Everything Easier! ™

UK editions

BUSINESS

Marketing Kit
978-0-470-74490-1

Business Plans Kit
978-0-470-74381-2

PRINCE2
978-0-470-71025-8

REFERENCE

British Politics
978-0-470-68637-9

DIY
978-0-470-97450-6

Researching Your Family History Online
978-0-470-74535-9

HOBBIES

Growing Your Own Fruit & Veg
978-0-470-69960-7

Allotment Gardening
978-0-470-68641-6

Electronics
978-0-470-68178-7

Anger Management
For Dummies
978-0-470-68216-6

Asperger's Syndrome
For Dummies
978-0-470-66087-4

Boosting Self-Esteem
For Dummies
978-0-470-74193-1

British Sign Language
For Dummies
978-0-470-69477-0

Cricket For Dummies
978-0-470-03454-5

Diabetes For Dummies,
3rd Edition
978-0-470-97711-8

Emotional Healing
For Dummies
978-0-470-74764-3

English Grammar
For Dummies
978-0-470-05752-0

Flirting For Dummies
978-0-470-74259-4

Football For Dummies
978-0-470-68837-3

Healthy Mind & Body All-in-One
For Dummies
978-0-470-74830-5

IBS For Dummies
978-0-470-51737-6

Improving Your Relationship
For Dummies
978-0-470-68472-6

Nutrition For Dummies,
2nd Edition
978-0-470-97276-2

FOR DUMMIES

A world of resources to help you grow

UK editions

SELF-HELP

978-0-470-66554-1   978-0-470-66073-7   978-0-470-66086-7

STUDENTS

978-0-470-68820-5   978-0-470-74711-7   978-0-470-74290-7

HISTORY

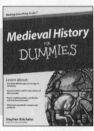

978-0-470-99468-9   978-0-470-74783-4   978-0-470-98787-2